The *Business* 2.0

B1 PRE-INTERMEDIATE Student's Book

John Allison with Paul Emmerson

MACMILLAN

The **Business** 2.0

B1 PRE-INTERMEDIATE

To the student

The objective of *The* **Business** 2.0 is to help you learn two things: how to do business in English and the language you need to do it. The new language and structures are presented in the Student's Book whilst the eWorkbook provides language practice and extension.

Here is a summary of what you will find in each.

Student's Book

The modules

The Student's Book contains 48 modules in eight units. Each unit deals with a key sector of activity in the business world. There are six different types of module:

1 About business

These modules contain information and language for the topic area of each unit. The focus is on understanding the topic and the general sense of the texts – don't worry too much about details such as new vocabulary.

2 Vocabulary

These modules build on the important words and phrases associated with the topic and provide thorough practice.

3 Grammar

These modules help you practise the grammar in a communicative and meaningful way, in business situations relating to the unit topic. Before you start, read the 'Refresh your memory' box to remind yourself of the key grammar points. Use the Grammar and practice section at the back of the book for consolidation.

4 Speaking

These modules develop understanding and speaking skills in typical business situations. In these modules, you build up a checklist of useful expressions to use in the speaking activities. The activities themselves allow you to practise these expressions and your speaking skills in realistic situations with other people.

5 Writing

These modules provide practice for the most important types of document you will need to write at work. You analyse a model text, focus on key language and use both as a basis for doing a writing output activity.

6 Case study

The case studies provide an opportunity to apply all the language, skills and ideas you have worked on in the unit. They present authentic problem-solving situations similar to those you will meet in business.

Internet research

Every module includes an Internet research task to encourage you to explore the topic in more detail. The tasks can be done before or after working on the module. Remember that to search for an exact phrase, you may get more accurate results if you put quotation marks around it.

Other features

In addition to the eight main units, the Student's Book contains the following:

Business fundamentals

This opening section introduces you to basic business principles and vocabulary. It provides a solid foundation for you to build on in the course and will help you get the most out of all components of *The* **Business** 2.0.

Reviews

These units can be used in three ways: to consolidate your work on the units, to catch up quickly if you have missed a lesson, and to revise before tests or exams.

Additional material

This section contains all the extra materials you need to do pair- or group-work activities.

Grammar and practice

This section gives a useful summary of grammar rules with clear examples, and also provides further practice of the essential grammar points in this level of the course.

Recordings

Full scripts of all the audio recordings are provided, allowing you to study the audio dialogues in detail. However, try not to rely on reading them to understand the listenings – very often you don't need to understand every word, just the main ideas.

Glossary

In each module, there is a short glossary of words you may not know. The definitions for these are in the Glossary at the back of the book. Words in red are high-frequency items, which you should try to learn and use. The others, in black, are words you just need to understand.

eWorkbook

The **Business** 2.0 eWorkbook provides everything you would find in a printed Workbook, as well as extra multimedia resources. It is mainly intended for self-study or home study and contains material to support and enhance the activities in the Student's Book.

Language practice

This section contains activities to consolidate the language presented in the Student's Book. You can practise grammar, vocabulary, listening, pronunciation, reading and writing.

Watch

This section contains a video clip and worksheet to accompany each unit in the Student's Book. The video clips are episodes of a mini-drama that illustrate the communication and people skills in each unit. The exercises allow you to practise the functional language in the video.

Tests

You can test yourself at any point in the course using the eWorkbook, by setting either the time or the number of questions. Your test scores are recorded for your reference.

Print and work

This section offers a pen-and-paper version of the activities in the Language practice section. You can also download the audio tracks required for these activities.

Grammar help

You can refer to this section for helpful grammar rules and examples.

Word lists

This section contains the keywords and definitions from the Vocabulary modules in the Student's Book.

Dictionary

Use the Dictionary Tool to link to the *Macmillan Dictionary* online http://www.macmillandictionary.com.

Writing tips

This section provides explanations and exercises on aspects of writing, such as spelling, punctuation and paragraphing.

Listen

This section contains all the audio recordings from the Student's Book and eWorkbook, together with the audioscripts. You can download all the material in this section to a mobile device for listening on the move.

We sincerely hope you will enjoy working with *The* **Business** 2.0. Good luck!

John Allison   Paul Emmerson

Contents

Business fundamentals

▶ business activities and sectors

▶ collocations relating to business activities

Business activities

Discussion

1 With a partner, match the business activities to the pictures.

> advertising   agriculture   civil engineering   construction   health care
> manufacturing   mining   oil and gas   software   transport

1 _____

2 _____

3 _____

4 _____

5 _____

6 _____

7 _____

8 _____

9 _____

10 _____

Listening

2 🔊 1:01 Put the activities in Exercise 1 into the correct sector. Then listen and check your answers.

primary sector (extracting raw materials) ☐ ☐ ☐
secondary sector (manufacturing) ☐ ☐ ☐
tertiary sector (commercial services) ☐ ☐ ☐ ☐

Collocations

3 In each set of four, match 1–8 with a–h to make collocations for talking about business activities.

1	sell to	a) a supplier	5	make	e) value
2	buy from	b) goods	6	face	f) a profit
3	make	c) services	7	develop	g) competition
4	provide	d) a customer	8	add	h) a market

4 Complete the text with the collocations from Exercise 3.

Glossary   PAGE 150

extract
mining
monopoly
profit
raw materials
supplier
USP
value

Every business needs a USP

There are many different types of business. Some (1) _____, like cars or TVs; others (2) _____, like health care or education. Many businesses work in the same way. They transform materials that they (3) _____ into something more valuable that they can (4) _____. In other words, they (5) _____ to the original materials. If they continue to find new customers, they can (6) _____. If they control their costs, they can (7) _____. But in the modern world, almost every business must (8) _____. Monopolies are very unusual. A business can sell to other companies (B2B – business to business) or to end users (B2C – business to consumer), but it always needs a USP to succeed.

Discussion

5 In small groups, list four important business activities in your country, region or city. Answer the questions for each one.

1 What is the business activity?
2 Which sector does it belong to?
3 Is it B2B or B2C?
4 What competition does it face?
5 What is the USP?
6 How does it make a profit?

▶ types of business

▶ organizational chart for a limited company

Business organization

Vocabulary

1 Read the descriptions of different types of business organization. Match them with the photos.

1 One person owns and controls the business. ☐
2 Two or more people own and manage the business. ☐
3 Several people called shareholders each own a part – or share – of the business. The shareholders are sometimes family and friends. ☐
4 This is a large company. Anyone can buy or sell its shares on the stock market. ☐
5 This is a joint venture between a local entrepreneur and a well-established business. ☐

a) a sole trader

b) a franchise

c) a public limited company (plc)

d) a partnership

e) a private limited company (Ltd)

2 With a partner, decide what type of business organization these businesses usually have. Use the information in Exercise 1 to help you.

1 doctors, lawyers and architects _____
2 independent shops, garages, hotels and restaurants _____
3 opticians, car rentals and sandwich shops _____
4 plumbers, photographers and electricians _____
5 multinationals, manufacturers and hotel chains _____

3 Look at the organizational chart for a private limited company. Answer the questions.

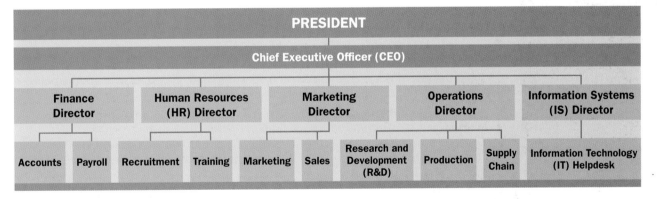

1 Write who is in charge of:
  a) money _____
  b) long-term strategy _____
  c) manufacturing _____
  d) communication _____
  e) managing the company _____
  f) employees _____
  g) data management _____

2 Write the name of the department that:
  a) invents new products _____
  b) contacts customers _____
  c) hires new staff _____
  d) pays salaries _____
  e) organizes product promotion _____
  f) helps employees develop new skills _____
  g) solves computer problems _____
  h) pays suppliers _____
  i) organizes logistics _____

Glossary   PAGE 150

entrepreneur
hire
human resources
joint venture
logistics
share
shareholder
strategy
supply chain

Listening

4 🔊 1:02–1:05 Listen to four people talking about their jobs. Answer the questions for each person.

1 Which department does he/she work in?
2 What does he/she do?
3 Does he/she like the job?

Business fundamentals

▶ profit, loss and breakeven

▶ understanding breakeven point

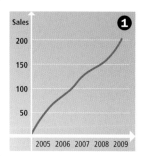

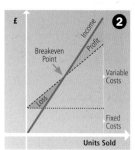

Profit and loss

Discussion

1 With a partner, match the graphs with the situations in the box.

> break even   make a loss   make a profit

2 Match these reasons with the situations in Exercise 1. Can you think of other reasons?

1 Prices are too high. The company has stock that it can't sell.
2 The company's costs are high – almost the same as its prices.
3 Customers are happy to pay high prices for beautiful products.

Reading

3 Read the first paragraph of the article. Answer the questions.

1 What does Eric sell?
2 Is this his day job?
3 How do his customers get their flash drives?

ERIC WHITE has a small business. In the evenings and at weekends he sells personalized USB flash drives on his website. Each flash drive costs Eric €12 to make and mail to his customers. He sells the flash drives for €24 each. So his **gross profit** per piece is €12.

Not bad, you say. The gross margin on each flash drive is 50%. If Eric sells a thousand per year, he can make €1,000 per month. But, wait … Eric also has to pay for his server, his website and his accountant. And don't forget his electricity, telephone and advertising bills. These are fixed costs, or **overheads**: a total of about €500 a month. If he sells 100 flash drives, or none at all, Eric still pays €500 every month.

At present, Eric sells 500 flash drives per year, so his **turnover** is €12,000. Eric's variable costs, or **cost of goods sold** (COGS), are €12 per piece: that's €6,000 for 500 pieces. So, turnover minus COGS minus fixed costs equals … €0. Sales of 500 pieces are just enough to reach **breakeven point**. Fortunately, Eric also has a day job. But if his sales are under 500, Eric will **make a loss**. On the other hand, if they are over 500, he will **make a profit** – but then he will start paying **tax**.

4 Read the rest of the article. Answer the questions and, in each case, mark the points on the graph below. Then draw a line connecting each set of points.

1 How much are Eric's fixed costs if he sells a) 0 or b) 1,000 flash drives per year?
2 How much is Eric's turnover if he sells a) 0 or b) 1,000 flash drives?
3 How much are Eric's variable costs if he sells a) 0 or b) 1,000 flash drives?
4 How much are Eric's total costs (fixed costs + variable costs) if he sells a) 0 or b) 1,000 flash drives?
5 Mark the point where the total costs line meets the turnover line. What is this called?

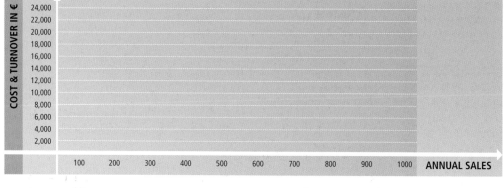

Glossary   PAGE 150

break even
cost of goods sold
day job
fixed cost
improve
margin
overheads
revenue
stock
variable cost

Vocabulary

5 With a partner, look at the words in **bold** in the text. Can you work out the meaning from the context? Use a dictionary to check.

CVs and cover letters

Reading and discussion

1 **Read the CV. Which internships can Ben apply for?**

an administrative assistant with a multinational oil company
a logistics administrator with an international cosmetics manufacturer
a technician in a civil engineering company
a trainee analyst with the London Stock Exchange

2 **Read the cover letter. Number the topics in the box in the order they are mentioned.**

☐ education ☐ next step ☐ previous experience ☐ type of work requested

BEN BROWN

DATE OF BIRTH: 3 September, 1991
NATIONALITY: British
ADDRESS: 4 Green Street, Coventry

EDUCATION

2009–2013 University of Warwick:
BSc, International Business

WORK HISTORY

September 2011–June 2012 Work placement, L'Oréal, Paris
I was responsible for conducting an online market survey.
July–August 2010 Holiday job, Car-Glazer, Prague
I worked as a technician. I repaired and replaced car windows.
November 2009–June 2011 Volunteer, University Counselling Service
I volunteered as a telephone counsellor, listening to students' problems.

POSITIONS OF RESPONSIBILITY

2012–2013 President of University Salsa Society
I managed a team of volunteers. **We organized** monthly dances and a salsa competition.

SKILLS

My skills include good spoken and written French and basic Czech.
I have a working knowledge of Microsoft™ Office.
I hold a clean driving licence.

Dear Ms Finlay,

I am a third-year student at the University of Warwick, studying International Business.
I would like to gain business experience on a one-year internship with a leading cosmetics manufacturer like Rose Inc.

I already have some experience as a trainee market analyst with L'Oréal.

I am motivated and hard-working. I am confident that I can make a valuable contribution to your organization. I will be happy to accept any position in logistics or marketing.

My CV is attached. Please feel free to contact me for more details or to arrange an interview.

Thank you for your time.

Yours sincerely,

Ben Brown

Ben Brown

Listening

3 🔊 1:06 **Listen to a conversation between Ben Brown and Ms Finlay. Which three points in work history and skills in Ben's CV are not mentioned?**

Writing and roleplay

4 **Rewrite the CV with your own details and experience. Use the expressions in bold and the CV on page 122 to help you. Then with a partner, swap CVs and roleplay a telephone interview similar to the one in Exercise 3.**

1 | Gaining experience

▶ internships in China

▶ working across cultures

(handwritten margin notes)
1. See OH
2. Put on doc. cam
3. Pair work
4. Write on BB
5. Handout

1.1 About business Internships abroad

Discussion

1 ▶ Read the statements. Do you agree or disagree with them? Tell your partner why.

1 An internship is an essential part of a university education.
No, I don't agree. I think you learn about your subject at university, but you only get real professional experience in your first job.
2 It's normal to work without pay when you are an intern.
3 Every student needs to experience life in another country.
4 It isn't difficult to adapt to a different culture.

Reading for gist

2 ▶ Read the first three paragraphs of the article opposite. Why is an internship in China a good idea?

Reading for detail

3 ▶ Read the first three paragraphs again and choose the correct answers.

1 The most important part of your CV is
a) your qualifications b) your work experience c) your references.
2 It is hard to get internships in Europe because
a) there are more and more universities b) there is competition for places
c) Chinese students want internships in Europe.
3 Shaun went to China to
a) learn the language b) acquire cross-cultural skills c) find an internship.
4 Shaun is satisfied with his internship because
a) his experience impresses employers b) he is financially more independent
c) he loves talking about Shanghai.

4 ▶ Read the last three paragraphs of the article. Answer the questions.

1 What is Julia Barton's job? *Works for placement agency*
2 What are the four essential skills for working across cultures? *Int. sensitivity, manage uncertainty, adjust comm. style, ability to build relationships*
3 In Asia, how are attitudes to time different from Europe and the USA? *Asia + more time*
4 What sort of relationships do employees have with managers and with co-workers in China? *→ Diplomatic, team spirit is NB*

Listening for gist

5 🔊 1:07–1:08 Listen to two people talking about their internships. Are they happy with them? *Lena – No   Jamie – Yes*

Listening for detail

6 🔊 1:07–1:08 Listen again. Complete the table.

Internet research

Search for the keywords *internships abroad*. What are the best offers? Compare your findings with a partner.

		Lena	Jamie
1	Where is the internship?	Hollywood, ca	Brazil
2	What type of business do they work in?	film studio	Int firm, consultants
3	Where do they live?	cheap motel	apt near beach
4	Are they paid for their work?	no	yes

Glossary   PAGE 151

acquire
crew
fierce
impress
reference
skill
team spirit

Discussion

7 ▶ In small groups, discuss the questions.

1 Would you like to do an internship? If so, where and what type of work? If not, why not?
2 Would you pay an agency to organize an internship for you? Why? Why not?

6, One-minute speech

Chinese internships impress employers

What is the most important information in your CV? Your school or university? Your degree subject? Your grades? The answer is: none of these. According to the Confederation of British Industry, 80% of employers first
5 look at the experience and skills you acquire on an internship.

Work experience is now an essential part of a university education. But competition for places in Europe and the US is fierce, so more and more students are
10 doing their internships in China. As the second biggest economy in the world, China has lots of opportunities for interns to acquire experience. It also offers the chance to learn a new language and to demonstrate the ability to live and work in a different culture.

15 'It was very difficult to find an internship in the UK,' says Shaun Duggan, a graduate in business studies, 'so I decided to go to Shanghai. It was the best decision of my life! After a year in China, I'm more independent, more confident and better at working with people who
20 are different from me. When I came back to London, I had three interviews. In each one, we talked about my experiences in China for most of the time, and all three companies offered me a job.'

So how difficult is it to live and work in China? Julia
25 Barton works for an agency that sends students to work in multinational firms in Beijing. 'There are four essential skills for working across cultures. First of all, you need intercultural sensitivity, that is to say, the ability to see things in different ways, and to
30 understand how your own cultural values are different from other people's.'

A second important skill is managing uncertainty. Barton gives the classic example of attitudes to time. 'Americans and the British always want quick decisions.
35 But Asians generally prefer to take more time rather than make the wrong decision. Multicultural teams need to be patient and live with uncertainty.' Thirdly, successful interns adjust their communication to the local style. 'Chinese organizations are hierarchical,' says
40 Duggan. 'Everyone respects the boss. You need to think carefully before you speak, and to be diplomatic.'

The fourth skill that impresses employers is the ability to build relationships between people from different cultures. Sandra Kay describes her experience
45 in Beijing. 'In China, team spirit is very important. We always had lunch together, and we often went out together after work. Now I work in an international team in Paris, and I encourage everyone to do things together. My
50 manager is impressed because the working environment is friendly and productive.'

As the second biggest economy in the world, China has lots of opportunities for interns...

1 | Gaining experience

- saying numbers and the alphabet
- telling the time
- giving dates
- exchanging personal details

Numbers

1 In small groups, practise counting.

1 Count to 30 in twos.
    2 4 6 8 ...
2 Count to 60 in threes.
    3 6 9 12 ...
3 Count to 105 in sevens.
    7 14 21 ...

May 8
← Icebreaker
↓
write on BB

2 🔊 1:09 Say these numbers. Then listen and check.

- 99 _____
- 101 _____
- 1,000 _____
- 1,500 _____
- 7,777 _____
- 88,888 _____
- 100,000 _____
- 900,999 _____
- 1,000,000 _____
- 3.5m _____
- 2.5bn _____
- 2.575 _____
- $110 _____
- €15.99 _____

Listening

3 🔊 1:10 Listen to three people playing the secret number game. What are the rules? In small groups, play the secret number game.

Pronunciation and spelling

4 🔊 1:11 Put the letters of the alphabet in the correct column. Then listen and check.

/eɪ/	/iː/	/e/	/aɪ/	/əʊ/	/uː/	/ɑː/
A, H	B, C	F	I	O	Q	R

5 Say the names of these symbols.

@   :   /   _   \   #

6 Work with a partner. Take turns to dictate:

- your full name
- your telephone number
- your postal address
- your email address
- your Twitter account name
- your favourite website URL

May 15
Icebreaker →

Time

7 Mark the time expressions A (analogue) or D (digital). Then match the times that mean the same.

1 half past two in the afternoon [A]
2 four twenty a.m. [D]
3 twenty-five to one ☐
4 (a) quarter past eight in the evening ☐
5 17.01 ☐
6 (a) quarter to two ☐
7 two thirty p.m. ☐
8 20.15 ☐

9   oh eight hundred hours ☐
10 twenty past four in the morning ☐
11 twenty-three hundred hours ☐
12 about five o'clock ☐
13 eleven o'clock at night ☐
14 eight o'clock sharp ☐
15 thirteen forty-five ☐
16 twelve thirty-five p.m. ☐

ANALOGUE

DIGITAL

8 Work with a partner. Take turns to ask what time you do the following:

get home   get up   go to bed   go to sleep   have dinner   have lunch   leave home   wake up

What time do you wake up in the morning?
I usually wake up about half past seven. But on Saturdays, I wake up after ten o'clock.

Dates

9 Say these dates.

1   9 November, 1989
2   1 January, 1999
3   11 February, 1990
4   3 August, 1492

5   21 July, 1969
6   22 January, 1901
7   11 March, 2011
8   4 July, 1776

May 15
Ice breaker

10 Complete the sentences with the dates in Exercise 9.

1   Columbus left Europe for America on _____.
2   The Great East Japan Earthquake and tsunami happened on _____.
3   The Berlin Wall fell on _____.
4   Neil Armstrong walked on the moon on _____.
5   Queen Victoria died, aged 81, on _____.
6   Nelson Mandela was released from prison on _____.
7   The USA declared independence on _____.
8   The euro was launched on _____.

Keep Score

Listening

PAIRWORK

11 🔊 1:12 Listen to two students registering for Personal Development courses. Student A: Complete Jen's details. Student B: Complete Mo's details.

May 15

	Jen	Mo
Name	*Jennifer Oxenbury*	*Mohammed Qureshi*
Date of birth	*April 15, 1994*	*Dec. 28, 1993*
Passport number	*07EI984502*	*08JGE8446669*
Room number	*A309*	*E214*
Course reference	*ASS67/GL*	*LEA43/JH*
Start date	*July 1*	*June 30*
Start time	*6:30 p.m.*	*8:45*
Instructor	*Prof. Lockhart*	*Dr. Higgs*
Cost	*$545*	*$455.*

12 With a partner, take turns to dictate the information you wrote in Exercise 11. Complete the table for both students.

WE WRITE:

'15 September, 1983'
or
'September 15, 1983'.

WE SAY:

'the fifteenth of September nineteen eighty-three'
or
'September (the) fifteenth nineteen eighty-three'.

Internet research

Search for more dates of important historical events. Hold a class history quiz in your next lesson.

Glossary   PAGE 151

analogue
badge
digital
register

---

1 | Gaining experience

1.3 Grammar   Present simple

Discussion

1 Look at the photos. What stereotypes do they suggest?

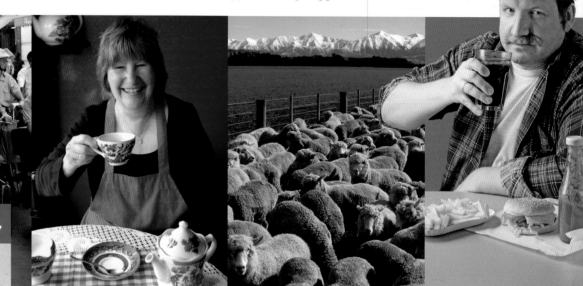

British people enjoy drinking tea.

Present simple

2 Complete the sentences about national stereotypes with the correct form of the verbs in the box.

drive   eat   live   ~~love~~   play   ride   talk   wear

1 The British ___*love*___ drinking tea.
2 Every American man _____ burgers.
3 The Chinese _____ their bicycles everywhere.
4 Every Brazilian man _____ soccer on the beach.
5 All Italians _____ with their hands.
6 More sheep _____ in New Zealand than people.
7 Germans _____ big fast cars.
8 Every Russian man _____ a fur hat.

3 Are the stereotypes in Exercise 2 true? With a partner, take turns to ask questions and give short answers. Give reasons.

A: *Do the British really love drinking tea?*
B: *Yes, they do. They have lots of tea breaks during the day.*

4 With a partner, take turns to ask and answer the questions. Use the prompts in brackets.

1 Do you put a Japanese contact's business card in your pocket?
(not in your pocket/on the table in the meeting)
No, you don't put business cards in your pocket. You put them on the table in the meeting.
2 Do British colleagues shake hands every morning?
(not every morning/just say 'good morning')
3 Do Americans wear jeans and a T-shirt to the office?
(not casual clothes/business clothes)
4 Do you disagree with a Chinese colleague in a meeting?
(not in public/only in private conversation)
5 Does a German call his boss by his first name?
(not senior colleagues/use title and surname)
6 In Indonesia, do you receive something in your left hand or point your finger?
(not left hand/not finger/use right hand/point your thumb)

Refresh your memory

Present simple
Facts:
The earth *revolves* around the sun.
Routines:
We *have* a coffee break at 11am.
Permanent situations:
The President *lives* in Washington.

▶ Grammar and practice page 124

Adverbs of frequency
always
nearly always
usually
often
sometimes
not often
rarely
never
He *always* works hard.
She is *never* late.

▶ Grammar and practice page 125

Prepositions of time
on
weekdays
dates
special days
the weekend (US)
at
night
the weekend (UK)
festivals
times
in
parts of the day
months
quarters
seasons
years

▶ Grammar and practice page 125

[handwritten: May15 : Take up homework]

[handwritten: Have them dictate to each other on the blackboard]

Internet research

Search for the keywords *national stereotypes*. Can you find facts to show they are true, or are they nonsense?

Adverbs of frequency

5 With a partner, take turns to ask and answer questions about the people in the table below.

1 Who is a good time manager? Why?
Marcus, because he always finishes on time.
2 Who is a perfectionist? Why?
3 ... a good manager?
4 ... a team player?
5 ... a leader?
6 ... a good communicator?
7 ... a good problem-solver?
8 ... a workaholic?

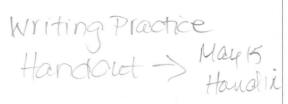

Writing Practice Handout → May 15 Handi...

	finish on time	encourage the team	make mistakes	find solutions	set a good example	go on holiday	help colleagues	share information
Marcus	always	not often	often	sometimes	rarely	often	never	not often
Francesca	never	rarely	rarely	not often	sometimes	never	not often	rarely
Tina	usually	nearly always	often	sometimes	always	not often	nearly always	usually
Miroslav	sometimes	often	sometimes	usually	usually	not often	nearly always	usually

6 Now ask and answer more questions about each person in Exercise 5.

A: *Is Marcus a good manager?*
B: *No, he isn't, because he doesn't often encourage his team.*

7 1:13–1:15 Listen to three parts of a radio programme about cultural habits in Europe. Add the countries and percentages to each chart.

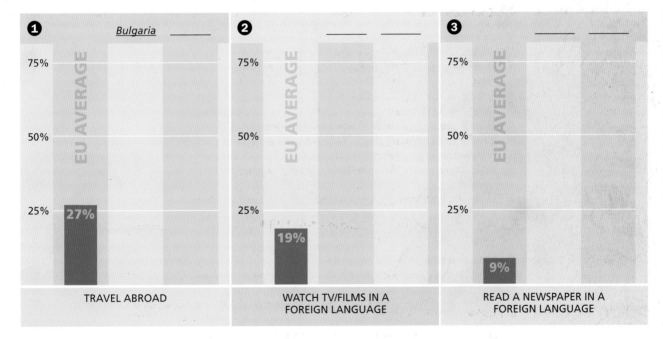

❶ Bulgaria _____

EU AVERAGE

27%

TRAVEL ABROAD

❷ _____ _____

EU AVERAGE

19%

WATCH TV/FILMS IN A FOREIGN LANGUAGE

❸ _____ _____

EU AVERAGE

9%

READ A NEWSPAPER IN A FOREIGN LANGUAGE

Glossary   PAGE 151

abroad
communicator
example
foreign
problem-solver
quarter
share
team player
workaholic

Prepositions of time

8 1:13–1:15 Listen again. Complete these phrases.

1 How _often_ do we Europeans travel abroad?
2 They travel _once_ or _twice_ a year.
3 All the time! _at_ the weekend, _on_ weekdays, _in_ the evening, ...
4 Just once _every_ six months, or once a _quarter_?

9 Look at the questionnaire on page 114. Write four more questions. Then interview your classmates.

Have 4 diff. students write one answer each on the wall away whiteboard

1 | Gaining experience

- expressions for meeting people
- expressions for making conversation
- roleplaying a conversation at a conference

Discussion

1 Complete the questions with *is*, *are* or *do*.

1 Where _are_ you staying? ☐
2 What _do_ you do? ☐
3 _Is_ your job well-paid? ☐
4 _Do_ you have children? ☐
5 _Do_ you live alone? ☐
6 _Do_ you ski? ☐
7 _Are_ you religious? ☐
8 The weather _is_ terrible, isn't it? ☐
9 What _do_ you think of the new government? ☐
10 _Is_ this your first visit to Serbia? ☐

2 Work with a partner. Are the questions in Exercise 1 appropriate to ask someone you don't know? Put a tick (✓) or a cross (✗) next to each one. Give reasons.

Listening

3 🔊 1:16–1:19 Listen to four conversations at a conference. Answer the questions for each conversation.

1 Where are the speakers? *Bus , Conf recept⁺ , Restaurant*
2 Do they know each other? *No , Yes*
3 What else do we learn about the speakers? *Greg→Sanofi   Abn→Merck   Silke GSK London in R&D   Silke→GSK*

4 🔊 1:16–1:19 With a partner, find suitable words to complete the useful expressions in the checklist. Then listen again and check your answers.

Useful expressions: Making conversation

Meeting people

Is this seat _free_ ?
Are you here for the _conferen_ ?e.
Hello. My name's Greg.
I'm _with_ (company).
Pleased/Nice to _meet_ you.
Pleased/Nice to _meet_ you, _too_ .
Alan, _great_ to see you!
Good to see you, _too_ !
Silke, _this_ is Alan Banks.

Keeping the conversation going

London? _Really_ ?
Go on.
Do tell me _more_ !
Uh-huh?
I see.
I love ..., don't you?
I think ..., don't you?

Changing the subject

Listen, _talking_ of ...
Enough about ... _let's_ talk about ...
By the _way_ , ...

Finishing a conversation

Do _excuse_ me. I really must ...
Anyway, ...
(It was) nice _talking_ to you.
See you _later_ .
It was nice meeting you.

Internet research

Search for the keywords *how to make conversation*. Make a list of tips. Compare your tips with a partner.

Glossary   PAGE 151

anyway
favour
shuttle
tip
well-paid

Making conversation

5 Cross out the **one** incorrect option in each situation.

1   Hello, my name's Felipe Conti.
    a) Pleased to meet you. b) How are you doing? c) Nice to meet you.
2   Hi, great to see you again!
    a) Pleased to meet you. b) How are you? c) Good to see you too.
3   Let me introduce you.
    a) Al, this is Khalid. b) Al, please meet Khalid. c) Al, Khalid. Khalid, Al.
4   Excuse me, I just need to talk to Gina over there.
    a) OK, it was nice meeting you. b) OK, see you later. c) Nice to meet you.
5   How are you doing?
    a) I'm good. And you? b) Working in Paris. And you? c) Not too bad. And yourself?
6   Can I help you, sir?
    a) I have a reservation for two nights. b) I'd like to check out my room.
    c) I'd like to check in, please.
7   Can I see your ticket?
    a) I booked on my computer. b) I have an online booking. c) I booked online.
8   Sorry to keep you waiting.
    a) That's all right. b) No problem. c) Please.

Ordering and speaking

6 Match the sentences and questions 1–7 with the responses a–g.

1   Is this your first visit to Greece? [c]
2   We're at the Mercure Hotel. My husband is here with me. [f]
3   I'm from Ireland, actually. But I work in London now. [a]
4   Oh, really? Lucky you! What do you do? [g]
5   I'm in the holiday business, too, actually. I'm a travel agent. [d]
6   I see. By the way, can you recommend a good restaurant in town? [b]
7   Yes, two. But they're at home with their grandparents. And you? Are you a family man? [e]

a)   Well, welcome to Greece. Where are you staying?
b)   Sure. If you like fish, the Marina is very good. I love Greek food, don't you?
c)   No, I live here. On one of the islands, actually.
d)   Uh-huh. And where are you from?
e)   Me? No! I'm single.
f)   That's nice. Do you have children?
g)   I'm a hotel manager. What about you? What sector do you work in?

7 Put the exchanges in Exercise 6 in the correct order. Then practise the conversation with a partner.

A: Is this your first visit to Greece?   *B: No, I live here. On one of the islands, actually.*

Roleplay

8 Work in groups of three. Make conversation using the chart.

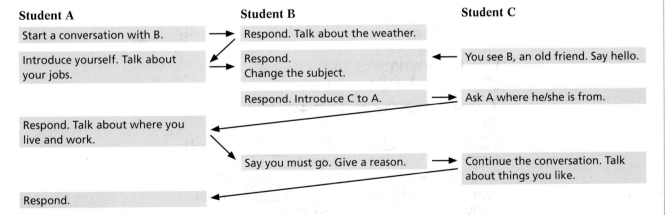

Student A	Student B	Student C
Start a conversation with B.	Respond. Talk about the weather.	
Introduce yourself. Talk about your jobs.	Respond. Change the subject.	You see B, an old friend. Say hello.
	Respond. Introduce C to A.	Ask A where he/she is from.
Respond. Talk about where you live and work.		
	Say you must go. Give a reason.	Continue the conversation. Talk about things you like.
Respond.		

eWorkbook

Now watch the video for this unit.

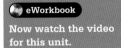

9 Work in groups. You are at an international conference. Complete the questionnaire on page 121. Use real information, or invent the details. Then stand up and socialize! Meet 'new colleagues' and make conversation.

1.4 Speaking

1.5 Writing   Informal emails

Discussion

1 In small groups, discuss the questions.

1 How many emails do you receive each day? Who are they from?
2 Do you prefer to write a letter, an email or a text message? Why?
3 In English, is it easier to write an email or make a phone call? Why?

Model

2 Read the email and underline the correct answers.

1 The reason for Gabi's email is *to thank Rita / to inform Rita / to ask Rita for help.*
2 Gabi wrote the email *a day / a week / two weeks* before the trip.
3 Gabi plans to travel by *car / train / plane.*
4 Gabi's Spanish course in Uruguay lasts *10 days / 12 days / 16 days.*

⊠ ↓ INBOX | REPLY ← | FORWARD →

Subject: Re: Spanish training in Uruguay

Hi Rita,
Thanks for your email. I'm glad to hear you passed your exams. Well done!
I'm just writing to confirm my dates and times. I leave next Friday and arrive in Montevideo at 6.30am on November 17. If you can meet me at the airport, that's great. But if not, don't worry. I can take the bus.
My course is from Monday 19 November to Friday 30 November, non-stop. But my return flight is on Tuesday 4 December at 10pm, so we can go to the beach at the weekend if the weather is good!
Is there anything I can bring you from Switzerland? Some chocolate, perhaps? Just let me know if you want anything.
See you soon,
Gabi

Analysis

3 Answer these questions about the email.

1 Rita and Gabi are probably a) sisters b) good friends c) business contacts.
2 Which of the following sentences were probably in Rita's last email to Gabi?
   a) My test scores arrived today – everything is OK!
   b) Thanks for confirming your arrival date.
   c) Let me know if you want me to pick you up when you arrive.
   d) I hope we can spend some time together while you're here.
   e) Can you bring me some Swiss chocolate, please?

Glossary   PAGE 151

instead
pick up
training

Language focus

4 Decide which hellos and goodbyes are appropriate to use in emails to:

1 people you know very well: a family member, a close friend ⊡ⓐ ⓓ ⓔ
2 people you know: a teacher, a work colleague, a manager, a customer, a supplier ⓐ ⓑ ⓒ ⓓ
3 people you *don't* know: a teacher, a work colleague, a manager, a customer, a supplier ⓑ ⓒ

Hellos

a) Hello John,/Hi John,/John,/Hi,
b) Dear Mr Jackson,/Dear Sam,/Hello Sam,

Goodbyes

c) Regards,/Best regards,/Kind regards,/Best wishes,
d) Thanks,/See you on Friday,/All the best,
e) Love,

5 Complete the email openings with the words in the box.

> about   because   to   with

1 I'm writing ___to___ confirm my dates and times.
2 I'm writing ___with___ more information about your visit.
3 I'm writing ___about___ my English course in Canterbury.
4 I'm writing ___to___ ask you a favour.
5 I'm writing ___because___ my phone is out of order.
6 I'm writing ___with___ details of the next team-building day.
7 I'm writing ___about___ your computer problem.
8 I'm writing ___to___ tell you I can't come to the seminar.

6 Match these sentences from emails with the writer.

f 1 Just let me know if you have any more problems with your product.
e 2 Just let me know when you can ship the order.
a 3 Just let us know if you'd like to come bowling with us.
c 4 Just let me know if you need any additional support while Sam's off sick.
b 5 Just let me know if you need somewhere to stay.
d 6 Just let me know when Mum wants me to pick her up.

a) a colleague
b) a close friend
c) a manager
d) a family member
e) a regular customer
f) a regular supplier

Output

7 Imagine you are Gabi's friend, Rita. Write these emails.

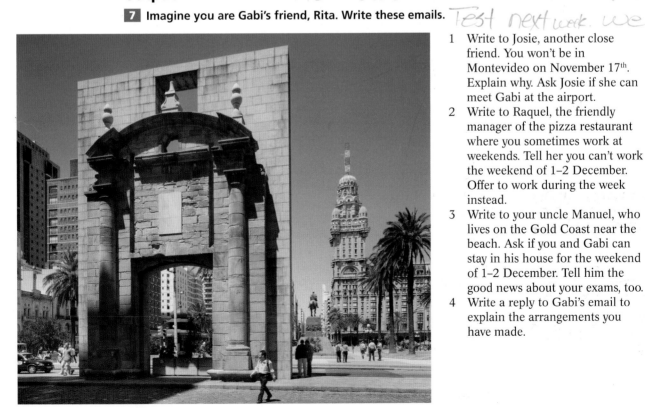

1 Write to Josie, another close friend. You won't be in Montevideo on November 17ᵗʰ. Explain why. Ask Josie if she can meet Gabi at the airport.
2 Write to Raquel, the friendly manager of the pizza restaurant where you sometimes work at weekends. Tell her you can't work the weekend of 1–2 December. Offer to work during the week instead.
3 Write to your uncle Manuel, who lives on the Gold Coast near the beach. Ask if you and Gabi can stay in his house for the weekend of 1–2 December. Tell him the good news about your exams, too.
4 Write a reply to Gabi's email to explain the arrangements you have made.

1.6 Case study   The Intern Shop

Discussion

1 How can graduate students find an internship? Think of as many different ways as possible. Put them in order from the most likely to the least likely to succeed.

Reading

2 Read the advertisement and answer the questions.

1   What services does The Intern Shop offer?
2   How long are the internships?
3   Do interns receive a salary?
4   How does The Intern Shop match candidates and internships?

INTERNET

THE**INTERN**SHOP

Today's employers want graduates with work experience and intercultural skills. But how do you get experience if you don't have a job? We can help!

The Intern Shop arranges paid and voluntary internships all over the world. After one or two years working abroad, 90% of our clients find a permanent job in less than one month.

We arrange everything: a job where you can develop your skills, a place to live, visas, language training, etc. We can even find the best travel deals and make your arrangements for you.

Just send us your CV and we will contact you to arrange a video interview.

3 Read about two internships. Which one is more attractive? Why?

INTERNET

PROJECT MANAGER, Beijing or Shanghai, China   THE**INTERN**SHOP

Working for a large electronics manufacturer, you will plan and organize projects and work schedules and manage a team of Chinese colleagues.

You have a degree in science or business, you are well-organized, you have good computer and communication skills and you enjoy working in a team. You have a TOEIC level of 750 or equivalent.

We provide free, shared accommodation, meals and language training on site, an annual return air ticket and a monthly allowance of $500.

TRAINEE WAREHOUSE SUPERVISOR, Recife, Brazil   THE**INTERN**SHOP

One of Brazil's largest providers of logistics services has an excellent opportunity for a future manager in its Recife warehouse. Working with an experienced manager, your job is to guarantee ideal stock levels and on-time deliveries to our customers (sports equipment stores).

You have a good degree, preferably in economics or business studies, and the ability to learn languages quickly. Basic Portuguese is a strong advantage.

This internship is unpaid, but the company will pay for accommodation. Paid overtime is available.

Internet research

Search for the keywords *how to find internships*. Make a list of tips. Compare with a partner.

Glossary   PAGE 151

accommodation
allowance
arrange
intercultural
overtime
TOEIC
visa
warehouse

Listening

4 🔊 1:20–1:22 The Intern Shop is interviewing three candidates for the internships in China and Brazil. Listen and complete the profiles.

1

NAME: Tai Shinawatra
DATE OF BIRTH: _Aug. 9, 1990_
NATIONALITY: _Thai_
DEGREE: Business Studies, from _Leavey school of Bus._
LANGUAGE SKILLS: Thai, English, a little Portuguese
INTERCULTURAL SKILLS: Experience of Asian and American culture
INTERESTS: Computing, electronics, rock and pop
PROFESSIONAL OBJECTIVE: _To see world & get some exp._

2

NAME: Karen O'Connor
DATE OF BIRTH: _May 5, 91_
NATIONALITY: _British_
DEGREE: Modern Languages, Bradford University
LANGUAGE SKILLS: _English, Hungarian, Japanese_
INTERCULTURAL SKILLS: Friends from all over the world at university
INTERESTS: _Travelling & Meeting people_
PROFESSIONAL OBJECTIVE: To become a manager

3

NAME: Julio Suárez
DATE OF BIRTH: December 14, 1989
NATIONALITY: _Mexican_
DEGREE: Physics, from _Univ. of West Indes @ Cave Hill_
LANGUAGE SKILLS: _Spanish English_
INTERCULTURAL SKILLS: Lives in Barbados
INTERESTS: _Computers & Software_
PROFESSIONAL OBJECTIVE: _Be a software developer._

Discussion

5 Work in small groups. Decide who is the best person for each internship.

Listening

6 🔊 1:23–1:25 Listen to the three candidates answering one final question. Does this change your decision?

Presentation

7 Present your decision to the class.

2 | Customer satisfaction

▶ keeping your customers

▶ good customer service

2.1 About business Customer service

Discussion

1 Think about your experiences of good and bad customer service. Complete the sentences. Then compare with a partner.

1 Every time I buy …
2 When I eat at …
3 If I travel by …
4 I really like it when …
5 I really don't like it if …
6 The reasons for bad service are …
7 When the service is very good, I feel …

Listening

2 🔊 1:26–1:27 Listen to two customers talking about good and bad service and answer the questions.

1 Why is the man happy to pay more?
2 What examples of good service does he give?
3 How does he feel when service is good?
4 How does the woman react to bad service?
5 What examples does she give?
6 How does she feel if service is bad?

Skim reading

3 Quickly read the article opposite. Match each picture to one paragraph in the text.

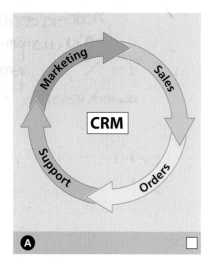

A ☐

B ☐

C ☐

Internet research

Search for the keywords *how to keep customers happy*. List the best tips. Compare with a partner.

Reading for detail

4 Read the first three paragraphs again and mark these statements *T* (true) or *F* (false).

1 It is more expensive to find new customers than to get repeat business. ☐ *T*
2 On average, 10% of a company's leads become customers. ☐ *F*
3 Companies ask customers for comments on Twitter and Facebook. ☐ *F*
4 CRM software helps companies make better long-term strategy decisions. ☐ *T*

5 Read paragraphs 4–6 again and <u>underline</u> the best options in *italics*.

The article suggests:
1 companies spend *too little / too much / enough* on customer service training.
2 contacting customers *when and how you want / when and how your boss wants / when and how they want*.
3 you don't need to share your customer's *priorities / feelings / opinions*.
4 people prefer *not* to buy from someone they *look like / dislike / like*.

Glossary PAGE 152

advocate
ally
consumer
lead
loyalty
prospect
referral
upgrade

Discussion and presentation

6 Work in small groups. Discuss and present a chart to the class.

Group A: turn to page 123.   Group B: turn to page 118.   Group C: turn to page 120.

How to keep your customers happy

① How do you keep customers happy? Today, an excellent product is not enough. Customers also want first-
5 **class support: warranties, free delivery and installation, hotlines, newsletters and upgrades. But all these services are expensive. So why do we**
10 **put so much time and money into customer support?**

Give customers what they want, when they want it.

② The simple answer is: it's less expensive than finding new customers. A typical company needs to contact a thousand leads to find just ten new
15 customers. That's a big investment in sales and marketing. So if you can keep existing customers happy and get repeat business, you actually save money.

③ How do you do it? Firstly, listen carefully
20 to what your customers tell you about your company and your product. Listen to what they tell their friends too, on social media services like Twitter and Facebook. Secondly, your marketing, sales, support, order processing
25 and accounts departments already know a lot about your customers: put all that valuable information in one place and share it! Use CRM (customer relationship management) software, for example. In this way, everybody in the
30 organization knows exactly who their customers are, what they need now and what they would like in the future.

④ But customer support is only part of the story. Every year, businesses spend millions on
35 customer service training. On every course, staff learn the ten 'golden rules' of customer service.

But there is really only one rule you need to know and it's very simple: be like your customer.

⑤ So, how can you be like your customer? Here are
40 four examples:
- Talk to customers when they want to talk. Be there to answer questions easily and quickly, in store, by phone, by email, by text message – whatever your customers like best.
45 - Give customers what they want, when they want it: the right product, in the right place, at the right time and, of course, at the right price. Make the customer's priority your priority, especially when there's a problem!
50 - Show customers that you feel like they feel, especially about problems. If they are disappointed or angry, show the same level of emotion in your determination to solve the problem.
- Talk like your customers talk: if they talk quickly or
55 in short sentences, do the same. If they talk slowly with pauses for reflection, you talk slowly too. And give them time to think.

⑥ There are many ways to be like your customer, but perhaps you're asking why? Well, we all like people
60 who are like us, so, naturally, we all prefer to buy from someone we like! Simple, isn't it?

2 | Customer satisfaction

- collocations relating to customer service
- verbs relating to telephoning

2.2 Vocabulary Contacting customers

Icebreaker

Brainstorming

1 How can a business communicate with its customers? With a partner, make a list. Then think of an advantage and a disadvantage for each.

By telephone
Advantage: direct contact with the customer   Disadvantage: cost

① *Brainstorm answers as a group*
② *Assign Telephone Adv. Dis.*

Email A D

2 Complete the text about good customer service with the collocations in the box.

> customer referral   customer satisfaction   deal with complaints   delivery date
> exchange products   repeat business   returning customers   ship products

---

INTERNET

Good customer service continues long after the customer places an order. Every contact must contribute to (1) _____ if a company wants to build a long-term relationship and get (2) _____. It is important to agree on a (3) _____ that fits the customer's schedule, and to (4) _____ on time and in perfect condition. If there are delivery problems, the company must (5) _____ politely and efficiently, and (6) _____ if necessary. Satisfied customers will come back for more. These (7) _____ are especially valuable when they make a (8) _____, that is recommend the company's products to colleagues or friends.

---

3 With a partner, take turns to give a definition and guess the collocation in Exercise 2.

A: This is when you give your supplier the name of a friend who is interested in the product.
B: A customer referral?
A: That's right.

4 Complete these posts on a customer service forum with the phrases in the box. *Do this*

> a money-back guarantee   installation problems   shipped the wrong product

	INTERNET
1	I've just received my new Internet box, but I'm having _____. Can anybody help me?
2	I ordered a new TV from a website that has _____. But the TV doesn't work. What can I do?
3	I bought a ski jacket online, but they have _____. It's too small, and it's a horrible colour. Help!

5 🌐 1:28–1:30 What can the customers in Exercise 4 do? What can the suppliers do? Choose two phrases from the box for each problem. Then listen and check. *Do this*

> apologize and exchange the product   call customer service to complain
> contact the helpline   give a refund   provide technical support   return the faulty product

Internet **research**

Search for the keywords *a dissatisfied customer is an opportunity*. List the opportunities that an unhappy customer offers. Compare with a partner.

Glossary   PAGE 152

apologize
complain
faulty
greet
refund
schedule
voicemail

Handwritten note (sticky note):

p. 24
Ex. 2

1. customer satisfaction
2. repeat business
3. delivery date
4. ship products
5. deal with complaints
6. exchange products
7. returning customers
8. customer referral

these telephone situations.

...say to your customer during the call.
...e speaking to your customer.
...customer answers.

...on't have.
...ersation.

...nswers to Exercise 6.

HOW TO TALK TO customers BY telephone

1 Prepare. Think about what you want to say before you **dial a number**. Make a checklist of the important points you want to cover with the customer.
2 Be friendly to the person who can **connect** you. They could be your next customer! If they **put you on hold**, keep smiling while you wait so that you are ready when you **get through to** the customer.
3 Greet the customer warmly. When customers **take a call**, they want to speak to a human being, not a machine.
4 If the customer is out of the office, or on voicemail, always **leave a message**. Say your name clearly (names can be difficult in another language) and give the reason you are calling. Offer to **call back** later, or invite the customer to **return your call**.
5 Speak clearly, listen carefully and don't interrupt. Use different words to show you understand your customer's needs. Be positive and avoid negative expressions like 'It isn't possible' or 'I don't know'. If you don't have the information your customer needs, promise to **get back to** them, and give a specific time.
6 Before you say goodbye and **hang up**, tell them the next step. Thank your customer and make sure they feel special!

---

8 Match the words in **bold** in the article in Exercise 7 with the definitions below.

1 put you in contact with another person ___connect___
2 press the right keys to contact someone by telephone ___dial a number___
3 agree to speak on the telephone ___take a call___
4 reach the person you want to speak to ___get through to___
5 contact someone again with more information ___get back to___
6 respond to a message from someone who wants to speak to you ___return call___
7 finish a telephone call ___hang up___
8 try again to reach the person you want to speak to ___call back___
9 record details of what your call is about ___leave a message___
10 make someone wait and listen to music ___put on hold___

Listening

9 🔊 1:31–1:36 Listen to six situations related to telephone calls. What do you do next?

2 | Customer satisfaction

2.3 Grammar Present continuous

Present continuous

1 With a partner, decide what is happening in each picture.

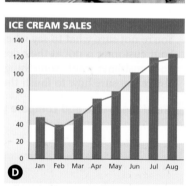

ICE CREAM SALES

Refresh your memory

Present continuous
Prices *are increasing*.
is/are + verb *+ing*
temporary activities in
progress now

► Grammar and practice
page 126

Requests
Can you ...? (informal)
Could you ...? (neutral)
Can I speak to Dan?
(informal)
Could I speak to Daniel
Black? (neutral)

► Grammar and practice
page 127

Offers of help
Shall I ...? (informal/
neutral)
Would you like me to ...?
(polite)

Invitations
Do you want to ...?
(informal/neutral)
Would you like to ...?
(polite)

► Grammar and practice
page 127

2 The pictures in Exercise 1 show temporary activities in progress. Match the pictures with the durations below.

☐ seconds ☐ minutes ☐ hours ☐ months ☐ years

3 With a partner, take turns to ask if these things are increasing or decreasing at the moment. Answer and explain why.

A: Are daytime temperatures increasing at the moment?
B: No, they aren't. They're decreasing because it's autumn, and winter is coming.

1 daytime temperatures (increase)	5 salaries (decrease)
2 inflation (fall)	6 births (go up)
3 petrol prices (go down)	7 marriages (drop)
4 unemployment (rise)	8 your English skills (improve)

Requests

4 With a partner, take turns to make requests and say no politely.

A: Can you help me with this email?
B: I'm sorry, but I'm writing an urgent report for my manager.

B: Could I use your phone, please?
A: I'm afraid I'm waiting for an important call.

1 help/with/email	sorry/write/urgent report
2 use/your phone	afraid/wait/important call
3 confirm/my order/by email	sorry/Internet/not work
4 speak to/salesperson	sorry/she/not feel/very well today
5 ask you/new software	sorry/have/a few problems with it too
6 call my customer back	afraid/go to/meeting/now
7 talk to you/at 5 o'clock	afraid/leave early/this afternoon
8 come in/early/tomorrow morning	sorry/fly/to Colombia/tomorrow

Offers of help and Invitations

5 Read the questions, then <u>underline</u> the correct options in **bold**.

1 *Do you want to leave a message?*
Would you like to leave a message?
These are **offers of help / invitations**. The caller can **say / write down** the message.

2 *Would you like me to take a message?*
Shall I take a message?
These are **offers of help / invitations**. The receiver can **say / write down** the message.

6 Complete the offers of help and invitations with suitable phrases from Exercise 5.

1 _____ call you back later?
2 _____ hold the line or leave a message?
3 _____ confirm that for you by email?
4 _____ email me your details?
5 _____ think about that before you decide?
6 _____ post it to you today?
7 _____ speak to me tomorrow about that?
8 _____ connect you to the sales manager?

7 Match these answers with the questions in Exercise 6.

a) Good idea. I'll think about it and phone you back tomorrow. ☐
b) Please. My email address is *p.peterson@lewis.ru*. ☐
c) I'm busy tomorrow. How about this afternoon? ☐
d) I'll hold, thanks. ☐
e) That's very kind of you. Could you call me on my mobile? ☐
f) Well, it isn't really a sales problem. Could you put me through to marketing? ☐
g) Yes, please. Can you send it first class? ☐
h) Yes, I'll email them right now. ☐

8 Put the lines in the conversation in the correct order.

7 Good idea. Thanks a lot.
1 I'm having problems with my laptop. It's running really slowly.
3 Oh, yes, please. Could you come over after work?
2 Do you want me to have a look at it?
6 OK. See you then. Thanks again.
5 No problem. But can you bring the installation CDs, too?
8 You're welcome.
4 I'm sorry, but I'm working late today. Do you want to bring it to my place this weekend?

PAIRS!
Have students
put in the
correct order
on whiteboard

9 With a partner, have similar conversations about the problems below. Use the flow chart.

You can't start your car.
Your Internet connection isn't working.
You're moving to a new flat.
You can't contact the TV repair service.
Your phone isn't working.
Your own ideas …

NEW PAIRS
on OH

2.3 Grammar

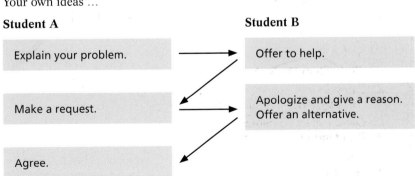

Glossary PAGE 152

decrease
drop
fall
improve
increase
rise

2 | Customer satisfaction

- ▶ expressions for telephoning
- ▶ roleplaying telephone conversations

2.4 Speaking Telephoning

Discussion

1 With a partner, mark the expressions *F* (formal) or *I* (informal). Then match the pairs of expressions that have a similar meaning.

Good morning. ☐   No problem. ☐
Hang on. ☐   Thank you very much. ☐
Hello. ☐   Thanks a lot. ☐
Hold the line, please. ☐ What can I do for you? ☐
May I help you? ☐   You're welcome. ☐

2 In your country, are telephone conversations between the people below usually formal or informal?

> assistants and managers   callers and receptionists   colleagues
> customers and customer support   customers and salespeople

Listening

3 🔘 1:37–1:38 Listen to two telephone conversations and choose the correct answers.

1 Mike and the receptionist are a) friends b) colleagues c) strangers.   F
2 Mike and Paula are a) friends b) colleagues c) strangers.   I /F
3 Sue is Paula's a) friend b) colleague c) boss.
4 Sue is a) available b) having lunch c) in a meeting.
5 Sue is Mike's a) friend b) boss c) customer.   I
6 When Sue calls back, Mike is a) not available b) having lunch c) in a meeting.

4 🔘 1:37–1:38 With a partner, find suitable words to complete the useful expressions in the checklist. Then listen and check.

Useful expressions: Telephoning

Starting	Introductions
Good morning. Can I ___help___ you?	I'm ___calling___ about …
Could I ___speak___ to (*name*), please?	I'm phoning to …
Is (*name*) there, please?	
Is that (*name*)?	
Yes, _____.	

Names	Messages
Could I ___have___ your name, please?	Can I take a message?
_____ is (*name*), from (*company*).	Could you ___ask___ her to call me back?
It's (*name*) here, _____ your call.	I'll ask her to ___get___ back to you as soon as …
	Would you like me to get her to call you back?

Connecting	Finishing
Just a moment, please.	Thanks for your help.
I'll put you ___through___	You're ___welcome___
Would you like to speak to her assistant?	Goodbye.
I'm sorry. She isn't ___available___ this morning.	Thank you for calling.

5 Work with a partner. In column 2, add reasons why your colleagues cannot take a telephone call. Make questions using columns 3 and 4.

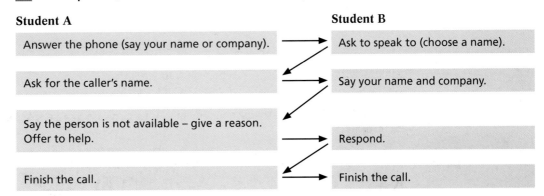

1	2	3	4
I'm afraid I'm sorry,	she isn't available at the moment. he isn't at his desk. she's in a meeting. he ... she ... he ... she ... he ...	Would you like to Can I Could you Would you like me to	call back later? help you? take a message? hold for a few minutes? speak to someone else? leave a message? tell me what it's about? get her to call you back?

6 With a partner, use the flow chart to have a telephone conversation.

Student A

Answer the phone (say your name or company).

Ask for the caller's name.

Say the person is not available – give a reason.
Offer to help.

Finish the call.

Student B

Ask to speak to (choose a name).

Say your name and company.

Respond.

Finish the call.

7 Match sentences 1–5 with responses a–e.

1   Is Sue Downing there, please? ☐
2   This is Mike Woods from Pixkel. ☐
3   I'm calling about our new product. Can we arrange a meeting? ☐
4   How about tomorrow morning? ☐
5   I'm giving a presentation until 12, but I'm free after that. ☐

a)   I'm sorry, I'm not working tomorrow. Is Friday possible?
b)   Yes, all right. When are you free?
c)   OK, let's meet at 12.30. We can have lunch in our cafeteria.
d)   Hello, Mike. What can I do for you?
e)   Yes, speaking.

Roleplay

8 With a partner, have similar conversations. Use your own names.

1   Arrange a demonstration of a new machine.
2   Arrange a meeting to discuss prices.

9 Work with a different partner. Roleplay telephone conversations between suppliers and customers. Student A: read the information below. Student B: turn to page 115.

Student A

Conversation 1: You are the supplier. Call an important customer, Ms Ashley Mertens, to invite her for lunch. You know your customer is very busy. Offer to send a taxi to pick her up from her office. You are free every day except Friday (you have a sales meeting in Brussels). Student B starts by answering the phone.

Conversation 2: You are the customer.
Part 1: You are one of Jo Parker's colleagues. Jo is away on a business trip. You receive a call from a supplier. Offer to take a message. You start by answering the phone.
Part 2: Now you are Jo Parker. Call Multiwheel back about the problems with their machines.

Internet research

Search for the keywords *cultural phone etiquette* to learn about telephoning in different countries. Compare notes with a partner.

Glossary   PAGE 152

free-to-air
hang on
hold (the line)
premium
subscription

eWorkbook
Now watch the video for this unit.

- ▶ analysing paragraph order
- ▶ starting and signing off
- ▶ writing formal emails

2.5 Writing Formal letters and emails

Discussion

1 Decide if a formal letter or a telephone call is better in these situations. Give reasons.

> apologizing for a mistake   applying for a job   cancelling a reservation
> making a complaint   negotiating a contract   placing an order

Models

2 Read the email and letter below. Answer these questions.

1 Who is writing the email?
2 Why is she writing?
3 What does she ask for?
4 Who is writing the letter?
5 Why is he writing the letter?
6 What action does he take to resolve the problem?
7 What offer does he make?

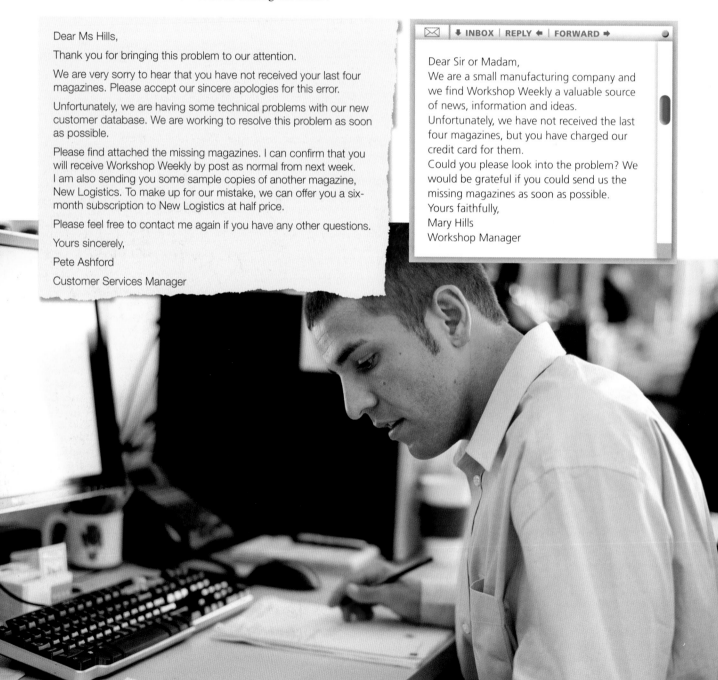

Dear Ms Hills,

Thank you for bringing this problem to our attention.

We are very sorry to hear that you have not received your last four magazines. Please accept our sincere apologies for this error.

Unfortunately, we are having some technical problems with our new customer database. We are working to resolve this problem as soon as possible.

Please find attached the missing magazines. I can confirm that you will receive Workshop Weekly by post as normal from next week. I am also sending you some sample copies of another magazine, New Logistics. To make up for our mistake, we can offer you a six-month subscription to New Logistics at half price.

Please feel free to contact me again if you have any other questions.

Yours sincerely,

Pete Ashford

Customer Services Manager

✉ ⬇ INBOX | REPLY ◀ | FORWARD ➡

Dear Sir or Madam,
We are a small manufacturing company and we find Workshop Weekly a valuable source of news, information and ideas.
Unfortunately, we have not received the last four magazines, but you have charged our credit card for them.
Could you please look into the problem? We would be grateful if you could send us the missing magazines as soon as possible.
Yours faithfully,
Mary Hills
Workshop Manager

Internet research

Search for the keywords *we apologize for* *. Find your favourite apology. Compare with a partner.

Analysis

3 Number the paragraphs in the order they appear in the letter.

☐ action ☐ apology ☐ conclusion ☐ explanation ☐ introduction

Language focus

4 Complete these rules for formal letters and emails with the words in the box.

> don't know (x 2)   faithfully   know   married   sincerely   single

1 *Dear Sir or Madam – Yours* _____
2 *Dear Miss/Mrs/Ms/Mr Smith – Yours* _____
3 Use *Dear Sir or Madam* when you _____ the name of the person you are writing to.
4 Use *Dear Miss/Mrs/Ms/Mr Smith* when you _____ the name of the person you are writing to.
5 Use *Dear Ms Smith* when you _____ if Jane Smith is married or single.
6 Use *Dear Mrs Smith* when you know that Jane Smith is _____.
7 Use *Dear Miss Smith* when you know that Jane Smith is _____.

5 Put the words in the correct order to make sentences from a business letter.

1 you / the / problem / please / into / look / Could / ?
2 you / would / We / us / grateful / if / could / be / phone / as / possible / as / soon / .
3 you / problem / our / to / this / Thank / bringing / attention / for / .
4 this / sincere / our / Please / for / error / apologies / accept / .
5 working / We / to / this / soon / as / resolve / as / problem / possible / are / .
6 up / our / mistake / make / To / for / , ...

6 With a partner, decide what is wrong with these messages. Then rewrite them.

1 Dear Sir or Madam,

Many residents at 52 Primrose Avenue are older people. We really need our lift. You have charged us for repairs but the lift is out of order again! Please fix it, Mr Henry Otis, and quickly!

Best regards,

Mark Flynn

2 My dear Mark,

Nice to hear from you, and good to know about the lift.

Sorry about that. The problem is, we can't get the parts. But we're doing our best. I think we can repair the lift next week.

There's a catalogue with this letter; to say sorry for the inconvenience. Perhaps you'd like a 50% discount on a new carpet for your lift?

Give me a call if you want to talk.

Yours faithfully,

Henry Otis

Output

7 Exchange formal emails with a partner. Student A: read the information below.
Student B: turn to page 115.

Student A

1 You are the manager of a bus company. Student B has a company that supplies fuel economy systems for your buses. These systems normally save fuel, but, at the moment, your buses are using 10% more fuel than usual. Write a formal email to Student B to complain.

2 You receive a formal email from Student B. Write a reply.

Student B: turn to page 115.

Glossary   PAGE 152

apology
database
discount
inconvenience
lift
make up for
workshop

2.5 Writing

The **Business** 2.0   **31**

- ▶ identifying problems and solutions
- ▶ writing emails
- ▶ agreeing on a plan of action in a meeting

2.6 Case study Rock tour

Discussion

1 In small groups, imagine you are a rock group on a world tour. What sort of problems can you face?

Reading

2 Read the article and answer these questions.

1. Approximately how many fans attended each U2 concert on their 2009–2011 tour?
2. Approximately how much did U2 fans pay for a ticket?
3. Why are most roadies young and single?
4. Why are there so few older groups like U2 and The Rolling Stones?
5. Would you like to be a tour manager? Why? Why not?

ON THE
ROAD AGAIN

A concert tour is a multinational business with hundreds of employees and millions of customers. U2's 2009–2011 tour, for example, sold more than 7 million tickets at over 100 venues around the world. It had gross revenues of more than $700 million. Travelling around the world playing rock music sounds glamorous and exciting, but the reality of life on the road is very different. The musicians and technicians (or 'roadies') are away from home for weeks or months at a time. They work long nights and spend most days travelling in buses from one hotel to the next. There is constant pressure and stress. Few roadies are over 35 and most are single or divorced. Most rock groups split up after only a few years on the road. But perhaps the hardest job is the tour manager's. A tour manager needs to meet every deadline and keep everybody happy – fans, artists, roadies and, of course, the record company.

3 Einstein are a rock group, currently touring the USA for Hoffmann Records. Read the letter that the record company received and answer these questions.

1. What two problems does Alice Chang mention?
2. Why isn't the letter addressed to the person who reserves the rooms?
3. What two things does she want Hoffmann Records to do?
4. What is on Einstein's schedule next week?

Dear Sir or Madam,

I am writing to complain about damage to our Illinois hotels. In Springfield and Burlington, the rock group Einstein or their roadies broke furniture, lights and glasses in bedrooms and in the hotel restaurant. In addition, numerous guests complained about loud music and shouting late at night.

I understand that your people work hard and need to relax, but this behavior is completely unacceptable. We value your company's business but, if these problems continue next week in Iowa and Kansas, we will refuse any future bookings for rock tours.

We would be grateful if you could pay the attached invoice for damages as soon as possible.

Sincerely,

Alice Chang (Ms)

Customer Relations Manager, Redding Hotels

Internet research

Search for the keywords *top concert tours*. Choose some interesting statistics. Dictate them to a partner.

Listening

4 🎵 1:39 **Listen to a voicemail message to Einstein's tour manager and answer these questions.**

1 Who is the caller?
2 What are his two problems?
3 What action does he request?

Writing

5 **Work in pairs. Write and exchange emails.**

Student A: You work for Hoffmann Records. Write an email to Einstein's tour manager (Student B). Ask them to make sure there are no more problems with Redding Hotels.
Student B: You are Einstein's tour manager. Write an email to your contact at Hoffmann Records (Student A). Ask them to try to find solutions to the problems with concert venues.

Discussion

6 **After receiving the emails in Exercise 5, the tour manager and Hoffmann Records need a telephone meeting. Student A: read the information below. Student B: look at page 115. Then phone each other to discuss your agendas.**

Student A
You work for Hoffmann Records. Read your agenda and the ideas given. Prepare what you want to say to the tour manager in the telephone meeting.

1 Reactions to your email to Einstein's tour manager about the damage to the hotels.
 (Who is responsible? If roadies, ask tour manager to fire them. Ask tour manager to write to Alice Chang to apologize.)
2 Reactions to email from tour manager about venues.
 (impossible to change venues now – it's too late)
3 Einstein only playing 75 minutes (contract = 90 minutes) and not signing autographs. Ask tour manager to solve problems.
4 New album planned for end of year. Recording in September. New songs ready?
5 Any other business

Glossary   PAGE 153

awesome
behavior
deadline
fire
gross revenues
invoice
roadie
venue

2.6 Case study

Review 1

Gaining experience

1 Match the verbs 1–10 with the phrases a–j to make expressions about internships abroad.

1	work	a)	your communication to the local style
2	acquire	b)	together after work
3	experience	c)	without pay
4	adjust	d)	skills on an internship
5	go out	e)	life in another country
6	build	f)	before you speak and be diplomatic
7	live	g)	relationships between people from different cultures
8	take	h)	with uncertainty
9	think	i)	employers with your experience
10	impress	j)	time to make a decision

2 Complete the sentences with four expressions from Exercise 1.

1 It is common for interns to _____, but the experience they gain compensates for not receiving a salary.
2 In China, team spirit is very important and people often _____ to get to know each other.
3 Multicultural teams may take more time to make decisions. You need to be patient and _____ for a while.
4 In a hierarchical organization, everyone respects the boss. Adjust your communication to the local style, _____ so that people don't think you are rude.

3 How do you say these numbers, prices, email addresses, times and dates?

> 1,400   7,650   3.75   100,000   £4.2m $820
> maria@bt.com   info@myworld.biz/news   4.30pm
> 10.40am   4 June 2014   21 March 1996

4 Use an item from the first box and one from the second box to complete the sentences. Look carefully at the whole context.

> always   nearly always   never   often   rarely   sometimes

> advertise   arrive   discuss   have   leave   let

1 Yes, it's true. I _____ at my office a few minutes late. The traffic is normally bad.
2 Before I got my new job, I played tennis with my friends every week, but now I _____ time. We only play a few games a year now, in the summer.
3 I'm a sales rep, so I know that you _____ the customer talk first and tell you their needs. It's important to listen, and then start selling.
4 We _____ our products in glossy magazines like Vogue, but it's expensive. We do this for 30 to 40% of our products.
5 I _____ the office at lunchtime, buy a sandwich and sit in the park. Occasionally, I have lunch at my desk, but I don't enjoy it.
6 I _____ my personal life at work. No-one needs to know about it, and I don't ask other people.

5 Complete the expressions for meeting people and making conversation.

1 I'm at the Marriott. Where are you _____?
2 **A:** Nice to meet you. **B:** Nice to meet you, _____.
3 Excuse me, is this seat _____?
4 I'm sorry, I _____ must go now.
5 I see that you work at Siemens. What exactly _____ you do there?
6 By the _____, did you hear the news about Japan?
7 Is this your first visit _____ Dubai?
8 Mei, _____ is Gerard from our Paris office.
9 Enough about me. _____ talk about you.
10 It was nice _____ to you.

6 Match the expressions in Exercise 5 with these uses.

a) a first line with a stranger ☐
b) introductions and greetings ☐☐
c) the early part of a conversation ☐☐☐
d) changing the subject ☐☐
e) finishing a conversation ☐☐

7 Complete these sentences from emails with a pair of words from the box.

> ask/mind   call/confirm   information/visit   let/problems
> ship/order   tell/can't

1 Following our _____ this morning, I'm writing to _____ the dates and times.
2 I'm writing with more _____ about your _____ to our offices in Zürich next week.
3 I'm writing to _____ you a favour. I hope you don't _____.
4 I'm writing to _____ you that I _____ come to the seminar this week. I'm sorry, but I have to go abroad on business.
5 Just _____ me know if you have any more _____ with your product.
6 Please let me know when you can _____ the _____.

8 Read the sentences about internships and <u>underline</u> the correct words in *italics*.

1 Today's employers want graduates with work *experience / experiences* and intercultural *tasks / skills*.
2 The Intern Shop arranges paid and *voluntary / free* internships all over the *world / worldwide*.
3 After working *abroad / in abroad* for a year, 90% of our clients find a *fixed / permanent* job in less than a month.
4 You will plan and organize work *schedules / registers* and manage a team of *colleagues / colleges*.
5 We provide free accommodation and language training *on site / on the site*, and a monthly *money / allowance* of $500.
6 One of Brazil's largest providers of *logistic / logistics* services has an excellent *option / opportunity* for a future manager in its Recife warehouse.
7 You have a good *degree / graduation*, preferably in *economy / economics* or business studies, and the ability to learn languages quickly.

Review 2

Customer satisfaction

1 Match the words in the box with the definitions 1–5.

> consumer   customer   lead   prospect   referral

1   This person is a possible future customer. The chances of this are low, but the company still contacts them. _____

2   This person is a possible future customer. The chances of this are high, and the company may already be in contact with them. _____

3   This person goes into a store and buys something. They are the end user. _____

4   This person buys something at any point in the chain. They may be a manufacturer buying from a supplier, a distributor buying from a manufacturer or the end user buying from a store. _____

5   This person becomes a new customer because an existing customer recommends them. _____

2 Read the text. Replace the definitions in **bold** with the expressions in the box.

> a faulty product   apologize   customer satisfaction
> deal with complaints properly   delivery date
> dial the number   exchange the product
> get back to them   get through   give a refund
> hang up   provide technical support   return your call
> ship a product

In business, it's important to keep a high level of (1) **pleasure that people get when they buy things from you**. How do you do this?

First, make sure that when you (2) **send a product by air, sea or road**, the customer receives it by the agreed (3) **time that the goods arrive at a place**.

Second, (4) **take the right action when the customer says there is a problem**. So, if somebody calls to complain about (5) **something that is not working or is broken**, make sure you (6) **say sorry** first and then offer to (7) **change the product for a new one** or (8) **give them their money back**. Third, make sure you have a helpline to (9) **give help with complicated things like computers** if customers have any problems.

When you speak to customers on the phone, try to make a good impression. First, think about what you want to say before you (10) **press the buttons on your phone**. Then greet the customer and be friendly. If the customer needs information that you don't have, promise to (11) **call them again later**. Before you (12) **finish talking to them**, review the main points and say what the next step is. Of course, sometimes you don't (13) **reach the person you want to speak to**, and go straight to voicemail. In this case, leave a message and say you will call back later, or invite them to (14) **phone you back**.

3 Match questions 1–5 with the contexts a–e.

1   Can I call you back later? ☐
2   Could you call me back later? ☐
3   Would you like to call back later? ☐
4   Would you like me to call you back later? ☐
5   Shall I call you back later? ☐

a)   asking if you can do something: informal
b)   asking if you can do something: informal/neutral
c)   asking if you can do something: polite
d)   asking if the other person can do something: neutral
e)   asking if the other person can do something: polite

4 Put the telephone conversation in the correct order. Then read it with a partner to check that it makes sense.

A:

☐ a)   Just a moment, please. I'll put you through. [*no answer*]

☐ b)   So, that's Pierre Bonnet from Design Solutions on 0033 12365478.

☐ c)   I'm sorry. She isn't available this morning. Can I take a message?

[1] d)   Good morning, DataSoft. How can I help you?

☐ e)   Good. I'll ask her to get back to you as soon as possible.

☐ f)   Of course. Could I have your name, please?

B:

☐ g)   Yes, please. Could you ask her to call me back? My number is 0033 – that's the code for France – 12365478.

[2] h)   Good morning. I'm calling about a project I'm working on with Magda Kowalski. I'd like to talk to her about something.

☐ i)   That's right.

☐ j)   Yes, this is Pierre Bonnet from Design Solutions.

5 Complete these sentences from emails with a pair of words from the box.

> apologies/error   behaviour/unacceptable
> complain/addition   contact/questions   grateful/possible
> problem/attention   unfortunately/technical
> working/resolve

1   Thank you for bringing this _____ to our _____.
2   Please accept our sincere _____ for this _____.
3   _____ we are having some _____ problems.
4   We are _____ to _____ this problem.
5   We would be _____ if you could phone us as soon as _____.
6   Please feel free to _____ me again if you have any other _____.
7   I am writing to _____ about damage to our hotel by the rock group *Einstein*. In _____, guests said there was shouting late at night.
8   This _____ is completely _____.

3 Product and process

3.1 About business Supply chain management

Brainstorming

1 Read the text. With a partner, discuss what 'right' means in each sentence.

> **Every company tries to deliver:**
>
> - the right product
> - in the right quantity and condition
> - with the right documentation
> - to the right place
> - at the right time
> - at the right price.

The 'right' product is exactly the product that the customer needs or wants and can't buy from another manufacturer.

Reading

2 Read the first two paragraphs of the article opposite and complete the flow chart.

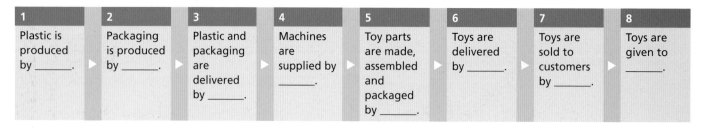

1	2	3	4	5	6	7	8
Plastic is produced by _____.	Packaging is produced by _____.	Plastic and packaging are delivered by _____.	Machines are supplied by _____.	Toy parts are made, assembled and packaged by _____.	Toys are delivered by _____.	Toys are sold to customers by _____.	Toys are given to _____.

3 Read the rest of the article. Choose the best summary.

a) Lasseter has no stock, no cash and no customers. The solution is better software and planning.
b) Lasseter has no raw materials, too many customers and too much cash. The solution is better communication and automated systems.
c) Lasseter has no raw materials, too much packaging and no cash. The solution is better communication and planning.

4 Read the text again and mark these statements *T* (true) or *F* (false).

1 Lasseter's customers are children. ☐
2 It is Jake's job to coordinate purchasing, production, packaging, shipping and cash flow. ☐
3 With the recent delivery of new boxes, Lasseter can now supply the toy shops which are out of stock. ☐
4 Polyplasto can supply the plastic pellets immediately. ☐
5 The bank manager is unhappy because Lasseter doesn't give its customers credit. ☐
6 Sharing information between partners in the supply chain only helps the manufacturer. ☐

Listening

5 🎧 1:40 Listen to a meeting at Lasseter and write down the three problems they discuss. Then match the problems with the arguments they give.

Problems	Arguments
1 _____	a) Sharing information helps suppliers, but it can give competitors an advantage.
2 _____	b) Foreign suppliers offer lower prices, but local workers could lose jobs.
3 _____	c) A single supplier is risky, but having several suppliers is more expensive.

Roleplay

6 In small groups, roleplay a meeting at Lasseter. Discuss the three points on the agenda on page 115. Take decisions.

Internet research

Search for the keywords *supply chain jobs*. With a partner, discuss which jobs you would or would not like to do.

Glossary PAGE 153

cash flow
labour
pellet
process
purchasing
put all your eggs in one basket
stock
storage

Supply chain software rescues toy factory

manufacturing
distribution
supplier
customer
raw materials
consumer

Jake Lasseter is the CEO and supply chain manager at Lasseter Ltd, a family business that manufactures plastic toys. To make and deliver toys to children, Lasseter needs the help of many different partners.

5 First of all, Jake buys pellets (small balls of plastic) from Polyplasto Inc., a multinational that produces plastics from oil. Then he buys boxes and packaging for the toys from Packobox Ltd. The plastic pellets and the packaging are delivered by Bigtruck Ltd, a logistics

10 provider.

In the factory, the pellets are used to make plastic parts for toys in special machines that Jake buys from IPM (International Plastics Machines) plc. The toy parts are assembled and packaged in Lasseter's factory.

15 After that, Smalltruck Ltd (another logistics company) ships them to toy shops. Finally, the toys are sold to customers and given to children: the end users.

A supply chain needs careful management. When the factory needs more plastic, Jake calls Polyplasto

20 to place an order. Polyplasto prepares the pellets and Bigtruck delivers them. From time to time, Jake calls the toy shops. If they need more toys, Jake asks Luke, who is head of packaging, to ship some more. Every Friday, Smalltruck delivers the toys to the toy shops.

25 Everything seems efficient, and everybody is happy. Or not ...

In fact, Lasseter is in serious trouble because the supply chain is not efficient: information is not communicated from one partner to another. It's Friday,

30 and the toy shops are out of stock. When Jake calls packaging to ask them to ship more toys, Luke is very unhappy. He has 400,000 boxes, just delivered by Bigtruck, but no storage space. And there are no toys to put in all these boxes, Luke complains. Brendan, the

35 production manager, can't make any because there is no more plastic!

Jake calls Polyplasto. They have pellets in stock, but Bigtruck can't deliver them because all their trucks are busy. A Smalltruck driver is waiting outside Lasseter's

40 factory, but there are no toys ready for delivery. Finally, the bank manager is on the phone: there's no cash to pay the salaries. This is because suppliers are paid on delivery, but customers pay weeks or months later.

Fortunately, there's a happy ending when Jake

45 installs new Supply Chain Management (SCM) software. Using automated systems, all the key business processes are integrated into a single system. Now Jake can plan all Lasseter's needs for materials, services, storage space, labour, credit and

50 cash. Soon everything is more efficient. And everyone – suppliers, manufacturer, customers and bank manager – is happy again.

Using automated systems, all the key business processes are integrated into a single system.

3 | Product and process

3.2 Vocabulary   Supply chain and product life cycle

Brainstorming

1 **With a partner, read the situation and brainstorm your ideas.**

Imagine you buy a box of golf balls in a sports shop. Before you open the box, a lot of different people handle the balls, the box and the materials used to make them. Who are they?

2 **Match the partners 1–6 with their role in the supply chain a–f.**

1 A buyer   a) sells raw materials, parts or packaging to the manufacturer.
2 A supplier   b) makes products in a factory.
3 A manufacturer   c) delivers materials or products to the manufacturer or to the customer.
4 A forwarder   d) buys and uses the product.
5 A retailer   e) purchases raw materials or parts needed to make the product.
6 A customer   f) sells products to customers in a shop or a store.

Reading and vocabulary

3 **Read the text. Number the production steps in the correct order.**

☐ assembly ☐ packaging ☐ purchasing ☐ shipment ☐ testing

How does a FACTORY WORK?

In-one Ltd manufactures golf balls in its South Wales factory. The main raw materials for making golf balls are rubber and plastic. The factory's buyers **purchase** the raw materials from specialist suppliers. The materials are delivered and **checked** for quality. They are then **stored** near the production area. **Stock** is managed carefully so that the factory can never **run out of** materials. In the workshop, robots **assemble** the rubber balls and plastic covers and paint them different colours. **Labour** is expensive, so there are more machines than workers. The golf balls are inspected and some of them are tested using special equipment. After that, the finished goods are **packaged**. They are stocked in the forwarder's **warehouse**, not on the factory site. Every year, In-one **ships** several million golf balls to retailers, where customers – some of the world's 60 million golfers – can buy them.

4 **Match the words in bold in the article with the definitions below.**

1 a large building where goods are prepared for delivery _____
2 work done by people _____
3 sends products to customers _____
4 kept ready to be used _____
5 buy from another business _____
6 materials in reserve _____
7 examined to make sure everything is correct _____
8 put different parts together _____
9 not have enough _____
10 put in boxes _____

Listening

5 1:41 **Listen to a lecture about product life cycle. Number the stages in the correct order.**

☐ design ☐ distribution ☐ extraction ☐ manufacture
☐ processing ☐ recycling ☐ repair ☐ use

6 1:41 **Complete the descriptions of the product life cycle stages. Then listen again and check.**

1 Raw materials like iron ore, trees or oil are ____________ from the ground or from the sea.
2 Raw materials are ____________ to make materials like steel, wood or plastic.
3 The product is ____________ to be easy to produce and use.
4 The product is ____________ in large quantities to reduce costs.
5 The product is ____________ to customers by ship, train, truck or plane.
6 The product is ____________ by consumers.
7 If it breaks, the product is ____________ by the manufacturer.
8 The product is ____________ at the end of its useful life.

7 1:42–1:47 **Listen to six people talking about their work. Which stage in the product life cycle is each speaker talking about?**

1 ________ 2 ________ 3 ________ 4 ________ 5 ________ 6 ________

8 **Work with a partner to complete your crossword. Take turns to give definitions for the words you have. Don't say the word itself. Write the missing words. Student A: use the crossword below. Student B: use the crossword on page 122.**

B: What's 1 across?
A: A person or a company that sells materials, parts or packaging to a manufacturer.

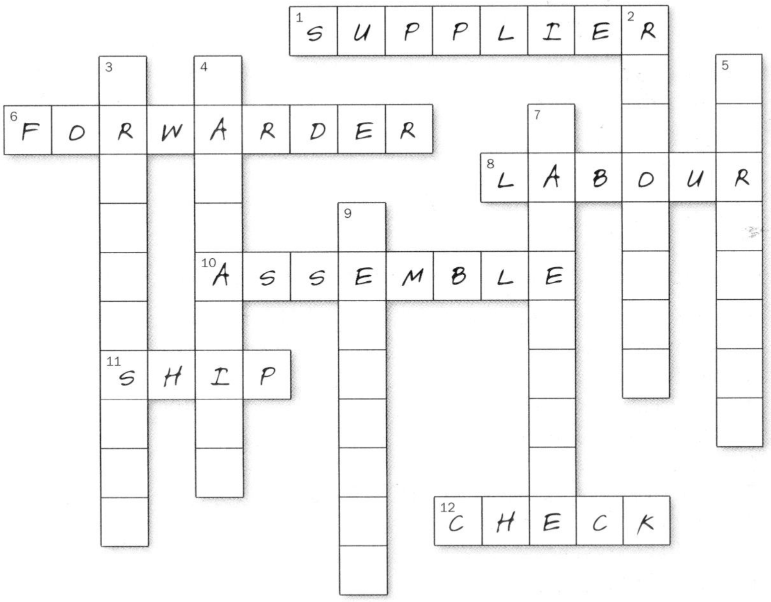
1 SUPPLIER
2
3
4
5
6 FORWARDER
7
8 LABOUR
9
10 ASSEMBLE
11 SHIP
12 CHECK

Glossary PAGE 153

ground
handle
iron
oil
ore
site
slave
steel

3 | Product and process

▶ prepositions of place

▶ prepositions of movement

▶ present simple passive

3.3 Grammar   Prepositions and present simple passive

Prepositions of place

1 Label the diagrams with the prepositions of place to say where the man in blue is.

> above   at   behind   below   between   in   in front of   next to   on   on top of   under

1 _____

2 _____

3 _____

4 _____

5 _____

6 _____

7 _____

8 _____

9 _____

10 _____

11 _____

Refresh your memory

Prepositions of place
above, at, behind, below, between, in, in front of, next to, on, on top of, under

▶ Grammar and practice
page 128

Prepositions of movement
across, down, into, out of, over, past, round, through, towards, under

▶ Grammar and practice
page 129

Present simple passive
be + past participle
often used to describe processes
Coffee *is produced* in Brazil.
Most phones *are made* in China.

▶ Grammar and practice
page 129

2 Work with a partner. Student A: look at the picture below. Student B: look at the picture on page 116. Take turns to ask and answer questions to find the differences and complete your drawings.

A: Can you see a box of tennis rackets?
B: No, I can't. Where are they?
A: They're on the rack, above the golf clubs.

Prepositions of movement

3 Complete the directions to the factory. Use the prepositions of movement in the box.

across down into out of over past round through towards under

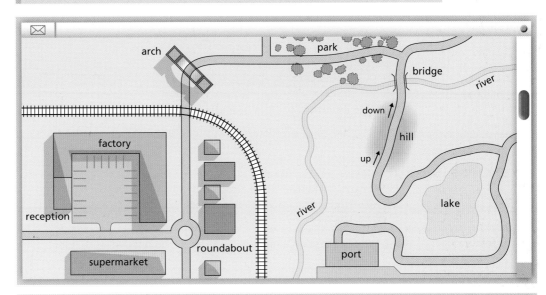

✉ ⬇ INBOX | REPLY ◀ | FORWARD ➡

📄 🖉

Hi,

Here's a map and directions to our factory. When you leave the port, turn right. The road goes (1) _____ the lake. Then, go up a small hill. When you come (2) _____ the other side, there's a river and a bridge. Go (3) _____ the bridge and turn left. Go (4) _____ the park. When you come (5) _____ the park, go straight on. Drive (6) _____ the arch. The road goes (7) _____ the arch and then (8) _____ a railway line. Be careful: it's dangerous! After that, you go (9) _____ several small buildings, then turn right at the roundabout. The factory is on the right, opposite a supermarket. Drive (10) _____ the car park. Reception is on the left. Don't worry, it's very easy to find!

4 With a partner, take turns to give directions to your home, your place of work, the airport, or the railway station.

Present simple passive

5 🔊 1:48 Listen to a visit to a cookie factory and answer these questions.

1 What is added after mixing? *choc chips*
2 Why do they use moulds? *same size, wgt*
3 How long are the cookies baked for? *11 min.*
4 Who operates the machines? *computers*
5 What happens before packaging? *cookies are cooled*
6 What is the final stage? *shipping*

6 🔊 1:48 Complete the process of how to make cookies. Use the present simple passive of the verbs in brackets. Then listen again and check.

1 First of all, the flour, butter, eggs and sugar *are mixed* in large containers. (mix)
2 Then the chocolate chips _____. (add)
3 Next, the cookie mix _____ into silicon moulds. (pour)
4 After that, the cookies _____ in the ovens for eleven minutes. (bake)
5 Everything _____ by machines. (do)
6 Excuse me, but _____ the machines _____ by people? (operate)
7 No, they aren't. They _____ by computer. (control)
8 The cookies are very hot. They _____ for fifteen minutes. (cool)
9 After that, they _____. (pack)
10 Finally, the cookies _____ to customers worldwide. (ship)

7 Work in small groups. Take turns to make virtual visits to factories that make pizzas, doughnuts, bread or cakes. Use the present simple passive to describe these processes.

- expressions for presenting a process
- presenting the ordering and returns processes

3.4 Speaking   Presenting a process

1 With a partner, use the prompts below to make questions about distribution centres.

1   How / goods / deliver to the distribution centre?
   How are the goods delivered to the distribution centre?
2   How / goods / identify?
3   Where / goods / store?
4   How / a customer's order / prepare?
5   Who / prepare / the customer's order?
6   What documents / send / with the customer's order?

2 Why is question 5 in Exercise 1 not in the passive?

3 Match the questions in Exercise 1 with the answers below.

a)   An invoice or a delivery note.
b)   Order fillers.
c)   Products are picked from the racks and packed in a box.
d)   On pallets in large trucks.
e)   On racks or in boxes on pallets.
f)   With bar codes or electronic tags.

Listening

4 🔊 1:49 Listen to a presentation about how a distribution centre works and <u>underline</u> the correct answers.

1   A distribution centre stocks *thousands / millions / billions* of products.
2   Every item is recorded on *a picking list / a packing list / a database*.
3   When you order, the store sends the distribution centre *a picking list / a packing list / a database*.
4   Goods are often shipped *48 hours / 24 hours / a few hours* after the order is placed.

5 🔊 1:49 With a partner, find suitable words to complete the useful expressions in the checklist. Then listen again and check your answers.

Useful expressions: Presenting a process

Starting

Thank you for ___inviting___ me here today.
I'm here to ___tell___ you ...
I'd like to ___start___ by ...

Sequencing

First of ___all___, ...
Next, ...
Are there any questions so ___far___?
Moving ___on___ ...
Then, ...
After ___that___, ...
Finally, ...

Finishing

I'd like to finish by ___pointing___ out ...
If you have any questions, I'll be happy to ___answer___ them.

6 Match 1–4 with a–d to make sentences about a distribution centre.

1 When you order products from an online store,
2 When the goods arrive at the distribution centre,
3 If we don't record everything in the database,
4 When you place your order,

a) they are identified with an electronic tag.
b) we don't know what we have and where everything is!
c) a picking list is sent to the distribution centre.
d) it's the distribution centre that sends your products.

7 With a partner, take turns to ask and answer questions. Invent suitable answers.

A: What happens when you press the green button?
B: When you press the green button, the machine starts.

1 when you press the green button
2 when you press the red button
3 when the picking list is received
4 when a product is not in stock
5 if two customers want the same item
6 if the electronic tags don't work
7 if the database crashes
8 if there's a truck strike

Presentation

8 Work in pairs of As and Bs to prepare a presentation. Student As: turn to page 117. Student Bs: turn to page 121.

9 Now work in A/B pairs. Student A: present your process. Student B: listen and ask questions. Then change roles.

Internet research

Search for the keywords *bad presentations* to see videos of common mistakes in presentations. List some do's and don'ts. Compare with a partner.

Glossary   PAGE 154

crash
pack
pallet
pick
picking list
strike
tag

● eWorkbook

Now watch the video for this unit.

3 | Product and process

3.5 Writing   Instructions and directions

Discussion

1 **In small groups, discuss these questions.**

1 Damaged products are usually returned to a distribution centre, not to the manufacturer. Why is that?
2 Some websites don't deliver to the customer's home. Why not?
3 What is the advantage of pickup points for a) the seller and b) the customer?

Models

2 **Read the messages to two customers and answer the questions.**

1 What are Mrs Branston's and Mr Matthews' problems?
2 What are the solutions?
3 What extra information is given to each customer?

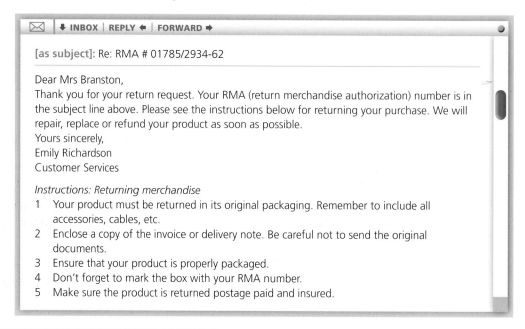

⬇ INBOX | REPLY ◀ | FORWARD ➡

[as subject]: Re: RMA # 01785/2934-62

Dear Mrs Branston,
Thank you for your return request. Your RMA (return merchandise authorization) number is in the subject line above. Please see the instructions below for returning your purchase. We will repair, replace or refund your product as soon as possible.
Yours sincerely,
Emily Richardson
Customer Services

Instructions: Returning merchandise
1 Your product must be returned in its original packaging. Remember to include all accessories, cables, etc.
2 Enclose a copy of the invoice or delivery note. Be careful not to send the original documents.
3 Ensure that your product is properly packaged.
4 Don't forget to mark the box with your RMA number.
5 Make sure the product is returned postage paid and insured.

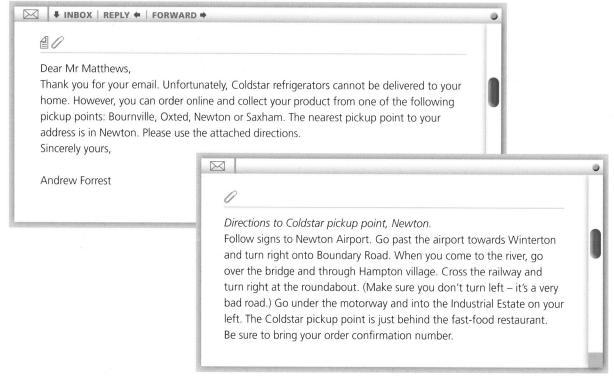

⬇ INBOX | REPLY ◀ | FORWARD ➡

Dear Mr Matthews,
Thank you for your email. Unfortunately, Coldstar refrigerators cannot be delivered to your home. However, you can order online and collect your product from one of the following pickup points: Bournville, Oxted, Newton or Saxham. The nearest pickup point to your address is in Newton. Please use the attached directions.
Sincerely yours,

Andrew Forrest

Directions to Coldstar pickup point, Newton.
Follow signs to Newton Airport. Go past the airport towards Winterton and turn right onto Boundary Road. When you come to the river, go over the bridge and through Hampton village. Cross the railway and turn right at the roundabout. (Make sure you don't turn left – it's a very bad road.) Go under the motorway and into the Industrial Estate on your left. The Coldstar pickup point is just behind the fast-food restaurant. Be sure to bring your order confirmation number.

Search for the keywords *returns policy*. Compare the returns policies of well-known retailers. Which ones are easy or difficult to understand? Compare your findings with a partner.

Internet research

Analysis

3 With a partner, complete the sentences with words from the box.

> direct 'don't forget' 'follow' indirect 'please' 'unfortunately'

1 The emails use _____ language like _____ and _____ to be polite.
2 The instructions and directions use _____ language like _____ and _____ to be clear.

Language focus

4 Match the words in the box with the places where the reader can find more information.

> above attached below enclosed the following

1 before the current paragraph _____
2 after the current paragraph _____
3 in a list after the current sentence _____
4 in a separate document with an email _____
5 in a separate document with a letter _____

5 Replace the words in **bold** with a word from Exercise 4. (One word is used twice.)

1 Please send all information to the address **at the top of the page**.
2 You will find **included in the envelope** a cheque for £25.
3 Please contact one of the after-sales service points listed **at the end of this email**.
4 Please find **in addition to this email** an Excel file with full details.
5 We cannot exchange your product for **the** reasons **listed here**: out of guarantee, …
6 As mentioned **in my introduction**, it is not our policy to give refunds.

6 Look at the example sentence below. The words in **bold** are used to emphasize instructions. Find five more expressions that are used in the same way in the instructions and directions in Exercise 2.

Remember to *include all accessories.*

7 With a partner, take turns to emphasize important instructions using the prompts in brackets.

A: I'm sending this phone back. (make sure/charger)
B: Make sure you include the charger.

1 I'm sending this phone back. (forget/postage and insurance)
2 This tablet PC is going back to the manufacturer. (ensure/RMA/on the box)
3 I don't have the original box any more. (be sure/package/properly)
4 This watch isn't waterproof. (careful/in the swimming pool)
5 I have a long flight tomorrow, but I've got my mp3 player. (remember/charge battery)
6 The RMA is only valid for 60 days. (make sure/forget to send)

Output

8 Read the email. Write a reply to Magda.

✉ | ⬇ INBOX | REPLY ← | FORWARD →

Hi,
I'm starting a new e-business! I'm selling personalized picture frames that I make for my customers' paintings and photos. They send me their picture; I frame it and send it back. Could you help me with the instructions in English for my website? I need instructions for how to place an order and pay, how to send me a painting or photo, and what to do if there's a problem.
Many thanks,
Magda

Glossary   PAGE 154

accessory
damaged
delivery note
frame
industrial estate
pickup point
policy
RMA

3.5 Writing

3 | Product and process

▶ identifying workflow problems at a factory

▶ presenting ideas for improving workflow

3.6 Case study Digidisc Ltd

Discussion

1 In small groups, answer the questions.

1 Is the room where you are working now practical and well-designed? Why? Why not?
2 What changes or improvements can you suggest?

Listening and reading

2 🔊 1:50 Digidisc Ltd is a small electronics company. It makes the Digidisc, a music player that can store your CD collection on a hard disk. Noah Evans is the site manager. He is showing Lily round the factory. It is Lily's first day. Listen and read their conversation. Match the areas on the factory plan with the words from the box.

| assembly | coffee machine | loading bay | order processing | painting | store | testing |

Noah: So, the first thing you see when you arrive in front of the building is the loading bay, on the left. This is where all the parts are delivered, and where the finished products are loaded onto trucks.

Lily: Oh, all in the same place?

Noah: Yes. But the logistics department is just behind the loading bay, and it's divided into two sections, IN on the left, and OUT on the right. OK, let's go inside. Now, as we come through the main entrance, the packaging department is straight in front of you and logistics is on your left, just round the corner.

Lily: Oh, yes, I see.

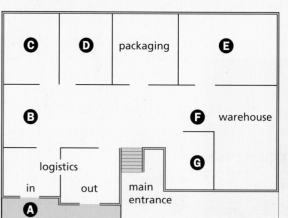

Noah: When the parts arrive from the loading bay, first they're checked in logistics and then we put them in the store, which is here on the right, between the entrance and the warehouse. Before they're assembled, some of the parts are painted. The painting department is next to packaging, on the left. After painting, the parts go to assembly, on your right, opposite the warehouse. Some of the Digidiscs are tested. The testing department is over there in the opposite corner, next to painting. After that, all the finished products are packaged and then stored in the warehouse. Any questions so far?

Lily: No, I don't think so.

Noah: OK, so there are just two more important places. The first is order processing, which is the open-plan office between logistics on one side and testing and painting on the other. That's where you're working. And, last but not least, we have the coffee machine, which is over there in front of the warehouse. Are you ready for a cup of coffee?

Lily: Oh, yes, please!

Discussion

3 With a partner, describe the workflow (how parts and products move around the factory) at Digidisc. Can you see any problems?

1 Parts to loading bay
   First of all the parts are delivered to the loading bay. This can be a problem when the finished products are ready for shipping.
2 Loading bay to logistics
3 Logistics to store
4 Store to painting
5 Painting to assembly
6 Assembly to testing and packaging
7 Packaging to warehouse
8 Warehouse to loading bay

Listening

4 🎧 1:51 Noah calls a meeting to discuss the problems. Listen and write the problems. Compare them with your ideas from Exercise 3.

Area	Problems
1 Store	
2 Order processing	
3 Packaging	
4 Warehouse	
5 Coffee machine	

Internet research

Search for the keywords *advantages and disadvantages of open-plan offices*. With a partner, roleplay a discussion between a manager and an office worker. Decide if open plan is a good idea.

Glossary PAGE 154

loading bay
open-plan
traffic
workflow

Discussion

5 With a partner, discuss how to reorganize the factory to make it more efficient. Prepare a presentation of your new organization and workflow. Use the blank site map to make your plan.

Presentation

6 Present your ideas to the class. Vote for the best solution.

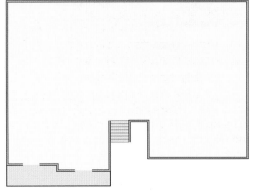

4.1 About business   Getting a job

Discussion

1 Tell a partner about a holiday job you did. What did you do? How did you find it? Did you have an interview?

Reading

2 Read the first three paragraphs of the blog opposite and answer the questions.

1 What was Lenny's dream job?
2 How did he find the job?
3 What risk did he take?

3 Read the first three paragraphs again and choose the correct answers.

1 Lenny a) had family connections b) started a company c) just got lucky.
2 Lenny contacted Julie a) by email b) by online chat c) by telephone.
3 Julie told Lenny to a) email Annie b) call Annie c) wait for a call from Annie.
4 Lenny a) wrote to Annie b) phoned Annie c) waited for Annie to phone.

4 Read the last three paragraphs of the blog and number the events in the correct order.

☐ Annie phoned Lenny twice.
☐ Lenny answered Annie's questions.
☐ Annie sent Lenny some questions.
☐ Lenny returned to Brussels.
☐ Lenny attended interviews in California.
☐ Lenny thought about the questions.
☐ Lenny got the job.
☐ Lenny attended an interview in Dublin.

5 Read the last three paragraphs again and choose the correct answers. Sometimes more than one answer is correct.

1 Lenny took his time to answer Annie's questions because a) they were very difficult b) he wanted to make a good impression c) he was passionate about his work.
2 Lenny was sure he was on the short list when he had a) an interview by phone b) an interview in Brussels c) an interview in Dublin.
3 At Google headquarters, Lenny a) played volleyball b) had interviews c) met four or five people.
4 Lenny received the job offer a) in California b) in New York c) in Brussels.

Listening

6 🌐 1:52–1:54 Listen to three people talking about how they got their jobs. Complete the table.

		Amy	Rob	Denise
1	What was he/she doing before he/she got the job?			
2	What sort of job did he/she find?			
3	How did he/she find it?			
4	Why is he/she happy?			

Discussion

7 In small groups, discuss the questions.

1 How difficult is it to get a good job in your country at the moment?
2 What are your plans for getting a job?
3 Are you prepared to work abroad?
4 What is your dream job and how will you get it?

Internet research

Search for the keywords *virtual job fair FAQs* to discover how a virtual job fair can help you find a job.

Glossary   PAGE 154

boring
creative
entry-level
exhausted
job fair
passionate
short list

HOW I GOT MY DREAM JOB

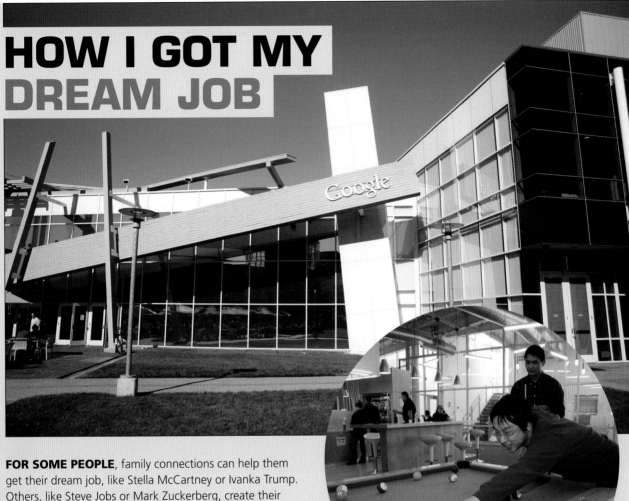

FOR SOME PEOPLE, family connections can help them get their dream job, like Stella McCartney or Ivanka Trump. Others, like Steve Jobs or Mark Zuckerberg, create their own dream. But some people just get lucky, and I guess I'm
5 one of those. My name is Lenny, I'm 28, and this is how I got my dream job with Google.

I was working in an insurance company in Brussels when I read about a virtual job fair – a website where candidates can 'meet' recruiters online. I was bored with my job, so I
10 logged in and looked around: jobs with banks, insurance companies, and then … Google! Working for an Internet company was my dream, so I opened a chat window and talked to someone called Julie from Human Resources. The opportunity that really got my attention was in New York.
15 It was exactly what I was looking for!

I think I made a good impression because Julie asked for my CV. She told me to wait for someone from New York called Annie to contact me. Well, I didn't want to wait for a call. I did some research and found Annie's full name and
20 an article she had written. I emailed her, commented on her article and said I was looking forward to talking to her. Some people say I took a risk, but I think it's important to get the employer's attention.

I was delighted when Annie replied. She sent me more
25 details about the job and some questions to answer. I took a few days to think, then wrote a very careful reply. I wanted to impress Annie and show that I was passionate about the job. She seemed satisfied. A week later, we had

two phone interviews. They went well. Annie asked me to
30 attend an interview in Dublin, so I was confident that my name was on the short list.

The final interviews were at Google headquarters in Mountain View, California. I had six interviews, some with one interviewer and others with four or five people. I also
35 played volleyball and swam in the pool. Google believe in a creative approach to work, play and life! That evening I was exhausted but happy: I was 99% sure that the job was mine.

I didn't wait long for an answer. As soon as I got back to Brussels, they offered me the job. It was difficult to leave
40 my family and friends, but the idea of living in New York was incredibly exciting. I didn't hesitate – after all, it was my dream job!

... some people just get lucky, and I guess I'm one of those.

4 | Job interviews and career

- questions about your CV
- adjectives to describe personality
- collocations relating to job-seeking

4.2 Vocabulary Job interviews

Answering questions

1 Match the questions 1–6 with the answers a–f.

1 Where were you born?
2 Where did you go to school?
3 What did you do when you left school?
4 What did you study at university?
5 Did you do an **internship**?
6 What are you doing now?

a) I worked **abroad** for a year to earn money and improve my **résumé**. ☐
b) Yes, I did a **work placement** in my third year. I was an **intern** at EDF. ☐
c) I was born in South Africa, but I **grew up** in England. ☐
d) I'm a management **trainee** with an engineering company. ☐
e) I went to **primary school** in the country and **high school** in London. ☐
f) My **degree** was in geography. I **graduated** two years ago. ☐

2 Match the words in **bold** in Exercise 1 with the definitions below.

1 changed from a baby to an adult _____
2 completed my studies _____
3 a school for children aged 5 to 11 _____
4 a course of study or university qualification _____
5 the American word for CV _____
6 a student who works in a company _____
7 someone who is learning a job or profession _____
8 a school for children aged 11 to 18 _____
9 a job that a student does to get experience (two expressions) _____ _____
10 in another country _____

Internet **research**

Search for the keywords *career personality test.* Do a test to discover what kind of career is best for you.

3 With a partner, take turns to ask and answer the questions in Exercise 1 about your own CV.

Describing personality

4 What kind of employee are you? Take the personality test to find out.

What kind of employee are you?

For each point, mark the position on the scale that best describes your personality.

			1	2	3	4	5	
The future:	optimistic	▶	1	2	3	4	5	pessimistic
My career:	ambitious	▶	1	2	3	4	5	unambitious
Working time:	flexible	▶	1	2	3	4	5	inflexible
Working with colleagues:	tolerant	▶	1	2	3	4	5	intolerant
As a manager:	demanding	▶	1	2	3	4	5	undemanding
As an employee:	loyal	▶	1	2	3	4	5	disloyal
Productivity:	hard-working	▶	1	2	3	4	5	lazy
Time management:	organized	▶	1	2	3	4	5	disorganized

5 🔊 1:55 Listen to two people talking about the test. Which points do they talk about? Which adjectives describe the woman?

6 With a partner, compare your own answers and give examples.

I'm optimistic about the future. I'm rarely pessimistic – except at exam time!

Reading and vocabulary

7 **Read the article below. Mark the statements *T* (true) or *F* (false).**

1 It isn't important if your first job is not very exciting. ☐
2 It's best to contact as many employers as possible. ☐
3 Interviewers are only interested in skills and qualifications, not in how you look. ☐
4 It's best just to answer the interviewer's questions. ☐

HOW TO FIND THE RIGHT JOB

At the beginning of your career, the most important thing is to find a job, any job where you can gain experience and develop your skills. Not many entry-level jobs are really interesting, but they *all* allow you to take the first step on your career path to promotion and management positions.

Don't just send your CV to every company in your region. Read the job ads in newspapers, magazines and online. Visit job fairs to see what sort of jobs employers are offering and what kind of people they are looking to hire. And tell everyone you know that you're looking for work – a personal recommendation can really help.

An interview is the opportunity for the company to get to know you, and for you to make a good impression. Always dress smartly when you attend an interview.

Almost every interviewer will ask about your strengths and weaknesses, so be prepared to talk about what you're good at and what you can improve. Prepare some questions, too: the employer is interviewing you, but you are also interviewing the company!

8 **In each set of five below, match the words 1–10 with a–j to make collocations. Then check your answers in the text.**

1 job	a) experience	6 attend	f) weaknesses
2 gain	b) a good impression	7 get	g) an interview
3 career	c) to hire	8 job	h) jobs
4 make	d) path	9 entry-level	i) ads
5 look	e) fairs	10 strengths and	j) to know

9 **Complete the sentences with the collocations from Exercise 8.**

1 I read all the _____ in the newspapers and visited three _____, but I didn't find a job.
2 Many companies _____ new graduates with the potential to follow a _____ to management.
3 Almost any _____ will allow you to _____ and be promoted to a better position.
4 As soon as I was asked to _____, I started to prepare for questions about my _____.
5 The first interview is to _____ the candidates; if they _____, they get a second interview.

Listening and vocabulary

10 🌐 1:56–1:60 **Listen to five people describing their job. Match the people with the jobs below.**

☐ Training Manager   ☐ Personal Assistant   ☐ Public Relations Officer
☐ Sales Representative ☐ Finance Manager

11 🌐 1:56–1:60 **Listen again and complete the sentences.**

1 I'm _____ for taking orders, presenting new products and taking _____ of customers.
2 I _____ events and I _____ with journalists.
3 I _____ a team of business analysts.
4 I _____ letters, email and phone calls and I _____ the Director's office on a day-to-day basis.
5 I _____ after the development needs of all departments. I _____ with external course providers.

Roleplay

12 **With a partner, roleplay a conversation between a student and a careers adviser.**
Student A: look at page 117. Student B: look at page 120.

Glossary   PAGE 154

coach
demanding
dress
require
smart
strength
weakness

4 | Job interviews and career

▶ past simple

▶ past continuous

Refresh your memory

Past simple
regular verbs:
infinitive + -ed
irregular verbs:
see pages 130 and 138
She *worked* hard
yesterday.
She *didn't stop* for
lunch.
Did she *finish* the job?
completed actions in
the past

▶ **Grammar and practice**
page 130

Past continuous
was/were + -ing
Sorry, I *was working*
when you called.
Were you *working* with
Holly?
No, I *wasn't working* in
the office.
activities in progress in
the past

▶ **Grammar and practice**
page 131

4.3 Grammar Past tenses

Past simple

1 🔊 1:61 **With a partner, write the pronunciation – /d/, /t/ or /ɪd/ – of the *-ed* endings of these regular past simple verbs. Then listen to Holly talking about how she found her dream job and check.**

1	looked	/ /		6	posted	/ /
2	dreamed	/ /		7	replied	/ /
3	talked	/ /		8	wanted	/ /
4	asked	/ /		9	seemed	/ /
5	emailed	/ /		10	offered	/ /

2 **Rebuild Holly's sentences with the regular verbs from Exercise 1. With a partner, practise saying them out loud.**

1 ... on his blog.
  I posted a comment on his blog.
2 They ... me the job.
3 I was delighted when Michael ...
4 ... of working for an airline.
5 Sally ... for my CV.
6 ... around a job fair.
7 I really ... to impress Michael.
8 ... to someone called Sally.
9 I ... Michael.
10 He ... satisfied.

3 **With a partner, take turns to ask and answer questions about how Holly got her dream job. Use the prompts below and the verbs in brackets.**

A: *Did she get her dream job thanks to family connections?*
B: *No, she didn't. She just got lucky.*

1 ... her dream job thanks to family connections? No ... just ... lucky. (get)
2 ... about the virtual job fair in a magazine? No ... on the Internet. (read)
3 ... it was a strange idea? No ... it was a good idea. (think)
4 ... a good impression on Sally? Yes ... a very good impression. (make)
5 ... Sally ... her to call Michael? No ... wait for Michael to contact her. (tell)
6 ... Michael's name on the website? Yes ... and ... his blog too. (find)
7 ... a risk by emailing Michael? Yes ... but ... a calculated risk to get his attention. (take)
8 ... Michael ... her an invitation to London? No ... details about the job. (send)
9 ... a quick reply? No ... a very careful reply. (write)
10 ... phone interviews ... well? Yes ... extremely well. (go)

4 **With your partner, take turns to ask and answer questions about how Sylvester Stallone got his dream job. Student A: look at page 122. Student B: look at page 119.**

Internet research

Search for a biography of a business person you admire. Give a short presentation of their career.

Past continuous

5 **Match the sentence beginnings 1–6 with the endings a–f.**

1 I was working in an insurance company
2 His phone rang early in the morning
3 She was driving and talking on her mobile
4 I first met Magda
5 Were you already working here
6 What did they eat

a) while I was working in Germany.
b) while they were waiting to be rescued?
c) when I decided to look for a new job.
d) when she had the accident.
e) while he was taking a shower.
f) when Philip left the company?

6 **With a partner, take turns to ask what you were doing when:**

- the alarm clock rang
- the bus arrived
- the telephone rang
- the lesson began
- the fire alarm rang
- the lights went out
- the boss arrived
- you met your best friend

A: *What were you doing when the alarm clock rang?*
B: *Oh, I was dreaming about a fantastic job in California.*

7 **With a partner, take turns to ask what you did while you were:**

- waiting for the plane
- staying in New York
- waiting for the exam results
- looking for a job
- waiting to be rescued from the lift
- recovering in hospital
- waiting for the interview
- sitting in the bus

A: *What did you do while you were waiting for the plane?*
B: *Oh, I texted my friends and listened to music.*

8 **Look at Mark Zuckerberg's lifeline. Complete the sentences below with the correct form of the verbs in brackets.**

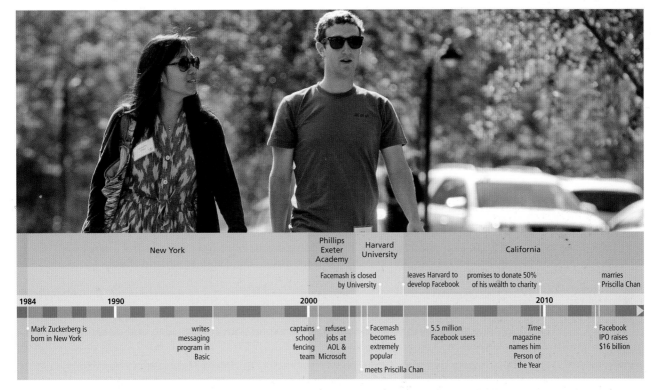

1 Zuckerberg wrote 'Zucknet', his first messaging program, when … (live)
2 Zuckerberg was captain of the fencing team while … (attend)
3 Before Zuckerberg went to Harvard, … (refuse)
4 Zuckerberg met Priscilla Chan at a party while … (study)
5 Zuckerberg's Facemash program was becoming extremely popular when … (close down)
6 Soon after Zuckerberg moved to California, 5.5 million people … (use)
7 Zuckerberg became a philanthropist like Bill Gates after *Time*™ magazine … (name)
8 Facebook became a public company one day before he… (marry)

Glossary   PAGE 155

fencing
IPO
philanthropist
raise

9 **Draw your own lifeline, real or imaginary. Present it to a partner and answer their questions.**

4 | Job interviews and career

▶ expressions for interviews

▶ roleplaying an interview

4.4 Speaking Interviews

Discussion

1 Read the statements and note your opinion in the table.

It's a good idea to ...	Yes!	Yes	Probably	No	No!
1 ... do some research on the company and the job before the interview.					
2 ... contact the interviewer on social media before the interview.					
3 ... dress smartly and arrive early.					
4 ... ask a lot of questions in the interview.					
5 ... express strong opinions in the interview.					

2 With a partner, compare your opinions on the statements in Exercise 1. Give reasons. Use these phrases.

I really do think
I think
I tend to think   *it's a good idea to ..., because ...*
I don't think
I really don't think

Listening

3 🔊 1:62 Jessica is a candidate for a job as a management trainee with Facebook. Listen to Part 1 of her interview and answer the questions.

1 Which five adjectives describe her character?

> ambitious demanding flexible hard-working loyal pessimistic tolerant

2 What opinion does Jessica disagree with?
3 What two opinions does Jessica partially agree with?

4 🔊 1:62 With a partner, find suitable words to complete the useful expressions for interviews in Part 1 of the checklist opposite. Then listen again and check.

Discussion

5 In small groups, discuss these subjects. Take turns to 'play devil's advocate' (disagree with everything the others say). Use the expressions for agreeing and disagreeing in the checklist.

1 How to find your dream job.
2 How to make a good first impression.

3 How to have a successful career.
4 How to get rich quickly.

Listening

6 🔊 1:63 Listen to Part 2 of Jessica's interview. Complete the sentences.

1 Jessica's strength is _____ her _____. She's a very _____ person.
2 Her weaknesses are that she is sometimes _____ and she's not very good at _____ _____.
3 Jessica doesn't enjoy doing things _____ _____ _____ _____.
4 She enjoys _____ _____ _____.
5 The interviewer finishes by inviting Jessica to _____ _____.

7 ♪ 1:63 With a partner, find suitable words to complete the useful expressions for interviews in Part 2 of the checklist. Then listen again and check.

Useful expressions: **Interviews**

Part 1

Discussing objectives

Why do you want to work for Facebook?
Why did you _____ for this job?
I _____ to be part of that.
I'd _____ to help the company to develop.
I _____ to gain business experience.
I _____ to be in my first management position.

Agreeing and disagreeing

I (completely) agree (with you).
I'm sorry, I _____ agree with that.
I'm afraid I don't completely agree.
I agree with you up to a _____.
Perhaps you're _____, but ...

Part 2

Discussing skills and qualities

What are your _____ and weaknesses?
I'm quite good _____ managing my work.
My friends _____ I'm never stressed.
I don't enjoy _____ things at the last minute.
Do you have any weaknesses you'd like to work on?
How _____ are your communication skills?
I really enjoy _____ with people.
I'm not _____ good at public speaking.

8 Tell your partner about your skills in these areas. Give reasons.

> computing   languages   leadership   negotiating   presenting
> problem solving   project management   time management

I'm (quite) good at languages. I speak English, Spanish and a little Chinese. *I'm not (very) good at* writing in foreign languages, though.
I enjoy speaking languages *because* I like travelling and meeting people. *I don't enjoy* writing them *because* it's more difficult for me.

Roleplay

9 With a partner, roleplay these interviews using the flow chart below. Take turns to interview and be interviewed.

1 an interview for a job with Twitter
2 an interview for a job in customer care
3 an interview for an internship in a manufacturing company
4 an interview for an internship with an international NGO (non-governmental organization)

Student A: interviewer

Explain the objective of the interview.
Ask about B's professional objectives.

Give a negative opinion.

Agree partially.
Ask about B's strengths and weaknesses.

Ask about B's communication/language/computer/management skills.

Thank B and close the interview.

Student B: interviewee

Explain your objectives.

Disagree politely.
Give a different opinion.

Describe your strengths and weaknesses.

Talk about your skills.

Internet research

Search for the keywords *questions to ask in a job interview*. List five good questions to ask. Compare with a partner.

Glossary   PAGE 155

devil's advocate
easygoing
NGO
partially

● eWorkbook
Now watch the video for this unit.

4.4 Speaking

- analysing order of information
- expressing information in a dynamic way
- writing a CV

4.5 Writing CVs

Discussion

1 What information do you include in your CV? Mark these ideas *Y* (yes), *N* (no) or *D*? (it depends).

- your age ☐
- your holiday jobs ☐
- your interests ☐
- your marital status ☐
- your pets ☐
- your photo ☐
- your professional objective ☐
- your religion ☐

Listening

2 🔊 1:64 Listen to a recruitment consultant talking about what to include in a CV. Compare what he says with your ideas from Exercise 1.

Model

3 Read the CV. <u>Underline</u> the correct answers.

1 Robin is *a woman / a man*.
2 Robin wants to become *a trainer / a volunteer / a manager*.
3 Robin studied in *Montreal / Toronto / Detroit*.
4 Robin has experience in the *restaurant / automobile / tourist* industry.
5 Robin is good at *running / singing / languages*.

ROBIN A. VANDERVELT

Date of birth: 17 April, 1992
Nationality: Canadian
Address: 134 Cedar Avenue, Montreal

CAREER OBJECTIVE

I hope to gain experience and develop my skills in a trainee management position with a large industrial company.

EDUCATION

2010–2013 B.Com, Rotman School of Management, University of Toronto

WORK HISTORY

January–June 2012 *Work placement, General Motors, Detroit, USA*
    I assisted the supply chain manager. I updated the supplier database and coordinated meetings.
July–September 2011 *Holiday job, Abbott Laboratories, Montreal*
    I worked as an administrative assistant. I dealt with all hotel and travel bookings.
June–August 2010 *Holiday job, Quebec Summer Camps*
    I designed, planned and implemented sports and outdoor activities for children aged 10 to 14.

POSITIONS OF RESPONSIBILITY

2012–2013 *Volunteer manager, University Women's Center*
    I managed a team of volunteers. We provided information and support for women students.
2011–2012 *Captain, Ontario Women's Student Basketball Team*
    I handled the team's budget, organized matches and ran events.

OTHER

Bilingual French/English, fluent Spanish, excellent computer skills
Driving licence

REFERENCES

Available on request

Internet
research

Search for the keywords *example career objectives*. Write a career objective for your CV.

Analysis

4 Number these sections in the order they appear in the CV.

- [ ] what I know about work
- [ ] who I am
- [ ] what I know about leadership
- [ ] what else I can do
- [ ] what I want to do
- [ ] what other people say about me
- [ ] what I know about my subject

5 In a CV, it is usual to put the most important information first. Robin is a student, so her education is the most important information. How is the order different for an older person with more work experience?

Language focus

6 How did Robin express this information in a dynamic way in her CV?

1 I was an intern in the supply chain department.
2 I did data entry about suppliers.
3 I checked the rooms were free.
4 I was a temporary secretary.
5 My job was booking tickets and rooms.
6 I was a sports and activities leader.
7 I helped the other volunteers.
8 I checked if we had enough money.
9 I spoke to other teams.
10 I did all the hard work at events.

7 Rewrite these sentences from CVs to give a better impression. Use the verbs in brackets.

1 I did various jobs in a production department. (assist)
   I assisted the production manager.
2 I phoned hotels and travel agencies. (deal with)
3 I opened letters and signed for deliveries. (handle)
4 I gave out brochures on the company stand at an exhibition. (run)
5 I was the receptionist for company visitors. (welcome)
6 I made sandwiches and coffee in a movie studio. (provide)
7 It was my job to imagine new procedures and make people follow them. (design, implement)
8 My job was to tell the other people what to do and show them how to do it. (manage, coach)

Output

8 Read the notes for Yann's CV. With a partner, decide which information to use and how to organize it. Then write the CV.

Glossary   PAGE 155

bartender
marital status
pet
pickup truck
regatta
sailing
stand
variable

Yann Leroux, 24 years old, born in Brest, France
Fluent English. Basic German.
Committee member, Brest sailing club, 2007–2009. Did most of the work for annual regatta.
June–August 2011 McDonald's® restaurant, South Kensington, London. Cook then supervisor.
I often go fishing – own pickup truck
January–June 2012 Work placement, Volkswagen, Wolfsburg, Germany. Various jobs in accounts department.
Driving licence
Married, one child aged 2
Helped in parents' hotel and restaurant when I was a kid.
Current address: 18, rue des Moines, Paris
Career objective: a general management position in the hotel and restaurant business
References available on request
June–September 2010 Holiday job, Club Med, Tunisia. Bartender and waiter
MA International Economics, American University of Paris
French national poker champion, 2011
Student representative at University – monthly meetings with management
Birthday – April 21st
Motor boat licence

- reading job advertisements
- completing an application form
- simulating a job interview

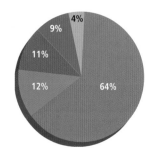

4.6 Case study   Onestop job search

Discussion

1 A *New York Times* survey asked Americans 'How did you find your job?' Try to match the answers in the box with the percentages in the pie chart.

> advertisements   Internet   networking   search firms   other

2 Turn to page 120 to see the results of the survey. What do they tell you about the best way to find a job? Is the situation the same or different in your country?

Scan reading

3 Quickly read the three jobs advertisements from onestopjobsearch.biz and answer the questions.

1 Which job involves working in front of a computer most of the time?
2 Which job involves managing people in a warehouse?
3 Which job involves visiting customers?
4 Which job does not offer training?
5 Which job offers possibilities for promotion?
6 Which job does not require a degree in business (or similar subject)?

Reading for detail

4 Read the advertisements again and find expressions that mean:

Trainee Sales Representative
1 a job in sales for graduates with no experience *an entry-level sales position*
2 good pay and job satisfaction _____
Business Analyst
3 do several tasks at the same time _____
4 finish projects on time _____
Operations Management Trainee
5 (thinking about) all steps in a process _____
6 an essential requirement _____

Writing

5 Choose one job to apply for. Complete the application form opposite.

Simulation

6 In small groups, take turns to interview each other. Candidate: Give your application form to the interviewers. Interviewers: Look at page 116.

Internet research

Search for the keywords *job interview do's and don'ts*. List some useful tips. Compare with a partner.

Glossary   PAGE 155

health care
in the field
networking
orthopaedic
rewarding

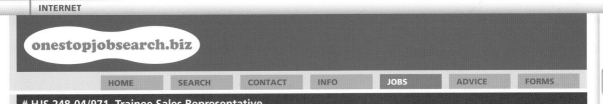

HOME   SEARCH   CONTACT   INFO   JOBS   ADVICE   FORMS

HJS 248-04/971 Trainee Sales Representative

HJS Security Solutions has an exciting opportunity for new graduates in an entry-level sales position. As a leader in our industry, we offer training with experienced professionals, an excellent salary and a rewarding career in sales.

The Sales Development Program is for candidates with a recent Bachelor's degree in business or similar. Classroom training and working in the field will help you develop your skills and become a successful Sales Representative within our company.

OH* 248-05/459 Business Analyst

The Orthopaedic Hospital is a leading specialty hospital. We have an exciting opportunity to join our team as a Business Analyst. To qualify, you must have:

- a Bachelor's degree in finance, economics, business or health care
- a working knowledge of Microsoft Excel™ and Microsoft Word™, or similar programs
- good problem-solving skills
- excellent communication skills
- the ability to manage multiple projects and meet deadlines

The successful candidate will be responsible for supporting the management team and helping the organization to achieve its goals.

UG* 248-07/564 Operations Management Trainee

UnusualGoods is an online marketplace offering high-quality goods at affordable prices. Our business is growing rapidly. We are looking to hire quick learners who enjoy solving business problems from end to end. You will begin in Distribution or Customer Service. After completing training, successful candidates will lead or manage in other parts of our business. Show us what you can do, and we will give you more responsibility. Skills and experience required:

- previous experience is not required but an interest in operations is a must
- Bachelor's degree or higher
- good communication skills

---

onestopjobsearch.biz

HOME   SEARCH   CONTACT   INFO   JOBS   ADVICE   FORMS

Application form

Vacancy number: _____/___   Position applied for: _____

Title: _____ First name: _____ Surname: _____

Email address: _____

Daytime phone number: _____

Evening phone number: _____

Work history

Employer	Position	Reason for leaving

Education

School/College/University	Qualifications/Courses of study

Any other information (e.g. skills, languages, etc.)

Signature: _____   Date: _____

Review 3

Product and process

1 Fill in the missing letters to complete these business expressions.

1 pur_ _ _ _ _ a product (= buy a product)
2 sh_ _ the goods (= send the goods)
3 manu_ _ _ _ _ _ _ a product (= make a product)
4 asse_ _ _ _ the parts (= put the parts together)
5 deli_ _ _ the goods (= take the goods to a place)
6 distr_ _ _ _ _ the goods (= supply the goods from a central place)
7 pack_ _ _ a product (= put a product in a suitable box)
8 a logi_ _ _ _ _ provider (= a transport company)
9 sell to the e_ _us_ _ (= sell to the customer in a shop)
10 integ_ _ _ _ the processes (= connect the processes so that they work better)
11 distribute to the reta_ _ _ _s (= send to the places where consumers buy things from)
12 lab_ _ _ costs (= the money paid to factory workers)

2 Match beginnings 1–6 with endings a–f to make expressions about how a factory works.

1 deliver the materials
2 run out of materials
3 purchase materials
4 package the goods
5 make or assemble the goods
6 inspect the finished goods

a) from a supplier
b) on a production line
c) if stock is not managed carefully
d) and test them using special equipment
e) to the factory, ready for use
f) and take them to an off-site distribution centre

3 Put the actions in Exercise 2 in the order they usually happen.

☐ ☐ ☐ ☐ ☐ ☐

4 Underline the correct preposition in *italics*.

1 Sales this Christmas were disappointing: 10% *above / below / next to* target.
2 Sales last quarter were good: 10% *above / on top of / in front of* target.
3 There is no direct flight *behind / between / in* London and Stuttgart.
4 When you are doing a presentation, don't stand *at / under / in front of* the screen.
5 I'll meet you *on / in / at* the bus stop – please wait for me there.
6 Visitor parking is *between / behind / next to* the office. Drive round the building and park at the back.

5 Underline the correct verb form in *italics*.

How perfume is made
Perfumes, also called fragrances, (1) *traditionally make / are traditionally made* using raw materials like leaves, spices, herbs, flowers and fruit. Alcohol and water (2) *also use / are also used* to dilute perfumes and soften the smell. First, all the ingredients (3) *bring / are brought* to a manufacturing centre. Here, the oils (4) *extract / are extracted* and any synthetic fragrances that do not occur naturally (5) *make / are made*. Extracting the oils (6) *does / is done* by specific methods, for example, by using steam. Next, scents (7) *blend / are blended* together in different quantities to create different perfumes. Cosmetics companies (8) *keep / are kept* this information secret. To create the particular strength of perfume, alcohol (9) *adds / is added*. Some of the best perfumes (10) *store / are stored* for a long time to create stronger scents. When the perfume is ready, it (11) *packages / is packaged* and shipped to distributors and retailers. As in any other industry, the Internet (12) *offers / is offered* lower prices than stores, and cosmetics companies control online sales carefully to protect their margins.

6 Match beginnings 1–8 with endings a–h to make expressions for presenting a process.

1 Thank you for
2 Well, first of
3 I'm here
4 I'd like to
5 Are there any
6 I'd like to finish
7 Moving on to
8 Finally, your order

a) all, …
b) to tell you …
c) start by explaining how …
d) inviting me …
e) the next stage, …
f) is shipped …
g) questions so far?
h) by pointing out …

7 Complete the sentences from a presentation with the expressions from Exercise 6.

1 _____ here today.
2 _____ a distribution centre works.
3 _____ what a distribution centre is.
4 _____, the distribution centre has millions of products in stock, all in one place.
5 _____ No? All right, let's continue.
6 _____ in the process: when you place your order with the store, a picking list is sent to the distribution centre.
7 _____ and an email is sent to confirm the shipment date.
8 _____ that your goods are shipped only a few hours after we receive your order.

8 Complete the instructions with the phrases in the box.

Be careful not to   Don't forget   Make sure
Remember to

Instructions: Returning merchandise

1 Your product must be returned in its original packaging. _____ include all accessories, cables, etc.
2 Enclose a copy of the invoice or delivery note. _____ send the original documents.
3 _____ to mark the box with your RMA (return merchandise authorization) number.
4 _____ the product is returned postage paid and insured.

Review 4

1 Underline the correct word or phrase in *italics*.

1 For some people, family connections can help them get their *dream job / dream work*.
2 I read on the Internet about a virtual *job market / job fair* – a website where candidates can 'meet' recruiters online.
3 I was *bored / boring* with my job, so I logged in to the website and looked around.
4 I talked to someone called Julie from *Human Resources / Personnel Resources*.
5 I think I *did / made* a good impression because Julie asked for my CV.
6 I said I was looking forward to *talk / talking* to her.
7 I think it's important to get the employer's *attention / kindness*.
8 She sent me more *details / parts* about the job and some questions to answer.
9 I wanted to *impress / impression* Annie and show that I was passionate about the job.
10 Annie asked me to *present / attend* an interview in Dublin.
11 I was confident that my name was *in / on* the short list.
12 That evening, I was *exhausted / exhausting*, but happy.
13 As soon as I got back to Brussels, they *proposed / offered* me the job.
14 The idea of *living / to live* in New York was incredibly exciting.

2 Match the pairs of words or phrases that have a similar meaning.

1	abroad	a)	ready to support someone
2	career path	b)	apprentice
3	CV	c)	difficult to please
4	degree	d)	in another country
5	demanding	e)	knowledge and skills
6	entry-level	f)	low-level
7	experience	g)	résumé
8	grew up	h)	spent your childhood
9	internship	i)	stages of your working life
10	loyal	j)	strong points
11	strengths	k)	university qualification
12	trainee	l)	work placement

3 Complete the text with words 1–12 from Exercise 2. Use each word once.

I (1) _____ in London but I went to university in Scotland. I did a (2) _____ in business administration at Heriot-Watt University. As part of my university studies, I did an (3) _____ in the US. It was a very good way to gain (4) _____. At first, I couldn't find a job in the UK, so I worked (5) _____ for a year to earn money and improve the 'work experience' section of my (6) _____. When I returned to the UK, I found an (7) _____ job as a management (8) _____. This job was difficult because my boss was very (9) _____, but this helped me to discover my real (10) _____ and weaknesses. After a few months, I left that company because things weren't going well. I know I wasn't (11) _____ but I couldn't see a (12) _____ for me if I stayed there.

4 Complete the exchanges with the correct past simple form of the words in brackets (positive, negative or question form).

1 **A:** _____ (she/get) her job thanks to family connections?
   B: No, _____ (she/just/get) lucky.
2 **A:** _____ (she/make) a good impression in her interview?
   B: Yes, _____ (she/make) a very good impression.
3 **A:** _____ (she/take) a risk by emailing the interviewer directly?
   B: Yes, _____ (she/take) a risk, but _____ (she/want) to get his attention.
4 **A:** _____ (she/do) any phone interviews?
   B: Yes, and _____ (they/go) very well.

5 Complete the sentences with the past continuous or past simple form of the verb in brackets. In each sentence, use each tense once.

1 While I _____ (check) the figures on the spreadsheet, I _____ (notice) that the sales total for June was incorrect.
2 When I _____ (join) the company, they _____ (already/expand) their activities in Central Europe.
3 The negotiations _____ (go) very well until their boss _____ (tell) them to stop talking to us.
4 The finance director suddenly _____ (resign) from the company while the auditors _____ (check) the accounts.

6 Match the beginnings and endings of the interview questions.

1	Why did you apply	a)	and weaknesses?
2	How do you feel about	b)	you would like to ask?
3	How do you see your future	c)	communication skills?
4	What are your strengths	d)	in five years' time?
5	How good are your	e)	for this job?
6	Do you have any questions	f)	working abroad?

7 Match the beginnings and endings of the replies to interview questions.

1	I'd like to help	a)	to be in a management position.
2	In five years' time, I intend	b)	the company to develop.
3	I agree with you	c)	at managing my work.
4	Well, perhaps you're	d)	up to a point, but …
5	I'm quite good	e)	things at the last minute!
6	I don't enjoy doing	f)	right, but …

8 Cover Exercises 6 and 7. Now complete these sentences with the missing prepositions.

1 Why did you apply ___ this job?
2 How do you feel ___ working abroad?
3 How do you see your future ___ five years' time?
4 I intend to be ___ a management position.
5 I agree with you ___ to a point, but …
6 I'm quite good ___ managing my work.
7 I don't enjoy doing things ___ the last minute!

5 | Marketing and selling

- the roles of sales and marketing
- smarketing

5.1 About business Sales versus marketing

Discussion

1 With a partner, decide which department usually does these tasks. Mark the activities **S** (sales) or **M** (marketing).

- brainstorm new ideas M
- get the customer's signature S
- design promotional materials M
- give product demonstrations S
- identify potential customers M
- negotiate with buyers S
- send quotations S
- provide the product that customers want M

Reading

2 Read the first three paragraphs of the article opposite and check your answers to Exercise 1.

3 Now read the whole article and choose the correct answers.

1 Sales and marketing often don't
   a) blame each other b) have separate agendas c) work together.
2 The four Ps and AIDA are the responsibility of
   a) sales b) marketing c) both sales and marketing.
3 Sales people think marketing's job is
   a) more complex than theirs b) harder than theirs c) easier than theirs.
4 Smarketing works by
   a) sharing customers b) sharing information c) sharing desks.
5 Long-term customer partnerships allow companies to
   a) satisfy more immediate needs b) describe more benefits c) anticipate more future needs.
6 Smarketing meetings involve
   a) top level staff b) low level staff c) all levels of staff.
7 Sales and marketing people are encouraged to standardize
   a) terminology b) feedback c) conferences.
8 The main result of smarketing is
   a) better language skills b) better sales c) better integration.

Listening

4 🔊 2:01 Listen to an interview with a sales representative. What three problems does Clare mention? What solutions does she suggest?

Discussion

5 In small groups, discuss the questions.

1 Do you agree with Clare's three suggestions? Why? Why not?
2 Do you know people who work in sales or marketing? Are they very different?
3 Is it a good idea to mix different departments in the same office? Why? Why not?
4 Do customers want to build long-term partnerships with sales people? Why? Why not?
5 Which job do you think is more difficult, sales or marketing? Why?

Internet research

Search for the keywords *sales versus marketing*. What do sales think about marketing? What do marketing think about sales? Make two lists and compare with a partner.

Glossary PAGE 155

agenda
awareness
benefit
blame
ceasefire
commission
feature
incompetent

SALES VERSUS MARKETING

THE WAR IS OVER!

WHY are marketing and sales always at war? The two departments often have separate offices, separate lifestyles and separate agendas. When revenues are down, sales blame marketing for not understanding
5 their customers; marketing say sales are incompetent or lazy. But aren't they supposed to work together to build relationships with customers?

According to marketing, their job is to identify, satisfy and keep customers. They do that by providing the right
10 product, at the right price, with the right promotion, in the right place (the four Ps). They create Awareness, Interest and Desire for the product. Sales, they believe, is easier: it's a simple matter of
15 obtaining Action, that is, the customer's signature.

But according to sales, their role is more complex. When marketing identify prospective customers, it's only the
20 beginning. Sales do all the hard work: they answer the prospect's enquiry, mail information, call the prospect back and arrange a sales visit. It can take eight or more contacts before the customer is ready to buy. While sales analyse the customer's needs,
25 give product demonstrations, write proposals, send quotations, meet heads of department, and negotiate with buyers, CEOs and CFOs, what are marketing doing?

Now, it seems, there is peace at last. Companies are realizing that sales need marketing, and marketing
30 need sales. The two departments are discovering that,

by working together, they can satisfy more customers and create more value for shareholders. It's called smarketing.

How does smarketing work? The key is better
35 communication. When marketing listen to what sales say about customers, they can make their advertising and promotion more effective. When sales take part in marketing strategy meetings, they learn how to sell *benefits* instead of features. Both departments can
40 build long-term partnerships, rather than satisfy customers' immediate needs.

There are regular meetings to share ideas and experience, not just between
45 sales and marketing managers, but with staff at every level. In some companies, everybody works in the same office, with every marketing person sitting next to a sales person. Sometimes the
50 shared office also includes customer service and after-sales staff. Instead of having separate conferences, sales and marketing departments now share an annual meeting. At the meeting, they exchange feedback and develop a common vocabulary.
55 So is this a temporary ceasefire, or is the war really over? Companies that introduce smarketing are seeing increased revenues and new business opportunities. After years of living separate lives, sales and marketing are learning that they can not only work together, but
60 they can also be friends!

> **Companies are realizing that sales need marketing, and marketing need sales.**

5 | Marketing and selling

5.2 Vocabulary Marketing, sales and advertising

Discussion

1 Work in small groups. Imagine you invent a pill that makes people speak perfect English for one week. How do you market this English pill? Think about *who, where, which, when, why, how, how much* and *how many*.

Marketing collocations

2 Read the marketing activities. With a partner, put the words in **bold** in the correct order.

1 **Conduct studies market** to identify trends and monitor the competition.
2 Communicate directly to **needs customer satisfy**.
3 Obtain money for marketing activities and **products help purchase customers**.
4 Use advertising campaigns to **image brand build**.
5 Decide where, when and how to **goods the deliver.**
6 Design products and services that **needs consumer meet**.
7 **Set prices competitive** and communicate them to customers.

3 Match the phrases in **bold** in Exercise 2 with the definitions below.

1 ship the product to the customer _____
2 decide how much people will pay _____
3 provide something people require _____
4 give credit or easy terms of payment _____
5 give people what they want _____
6 encourage positive feelings about your product _____
7 collect information on what people are buying and selling _____

4 Match the activities in Exercise 2 with the seven functions of marketing in the pie chart.

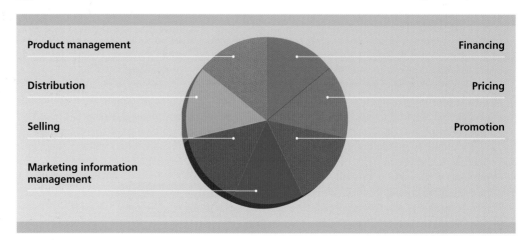

Product management   Financing

Distribution   Pricing

Selling   Promotion

Marketing information management

Sales vocabulary

5 🔊 2:02 Listen to a software salesman talking about his work. Tick (✓) the benefits he mentions.

☐ a great product
☐ a really good USP (unique selling point)
☐ friendly customers
☐ a comfortable car
☐ a private office
☐ good value for money
☐ free software
☐ commission on sales

6 🔊 2:02 With a partner, complete these expressions. Then listen again and check.

1 The selling process starts with an _____ from a _____ _____.
2 ... a few days later I call the _____ and arrange a _____ _____.
3 I usually give a _____ _____ first.
4 ... features and _____ that no similar product has.
5 Then I _____ the company's _____, ...
6 I answer questions and _____ _____ any objections they _____.
7 I write a _____ and send a _____.
8 ... our product is good _____ for _____.

Advertising collocations

7 Read the article about advertising and <u>underline</u> the correct answers.

1 Advertising campaigns are usually short for *financial / legal / strategic* reasons.
2 'Product X is best!' is not an effective message because it doesn't *give information / create desire / raise awareness*.
3 Advertisers get the best results from *TV commercials / personal recommendations / press ads*.

ADVERTISING

Why do companies advertise? Because they have a message that will help them reach new customers, build brand image and increase market share. Advertising is extremely expensive, so companies usually only run a campaign when they enter a new market or launch a new product.

Many campaigns follow the AIDA formula. First, they raise Awareness, that is, make sure that more consumers know the product and what it does. Then, advertisers try to build Interest, to persuade consumers to learn more about the product. The next step is to create Desire: to use the consumer's emotions to make them want to own the product. The final step is to take Action: to go to the store or place an order.

Companies buy space in press ads, on billboards in the street, on TV, ... in fact, anywhere they think customers will see their message. But everyone agrees the best form of advertising is word of mouth. More and more advertisers are developing strategies to obtain personal recommendations via social media.

Internet research

Search 'Images' for the keywords *product positioning map*. Draw a positioning map for the product you discussed in Exercise 10. Explain it to a partner.

Glossary PAGE 155

billboard
competitive
launch
monitor
trend
value for money
via

8 In each set of four below, match the words 1–8 with a–h to make advertising collocations. Then check your answers in the article.

1	increase	a)	a campaign	5	raise	e)	space
2	obtain	b)	a new market	6	launch	f)	awareness
3	run	c)	personal recommendations	7	buy	g)	of mouth
4	enter	d)	market share	8	word	h)	a new product

9 Match the collocations in Exercise 8 to the definitions below.

1 start selling to a different category ☐
2 publish a series of ads ☐
3 make a larger amount of total sales ☐
4 bring a new item to market ☐
5 one person tells another ☐
6 increase understanding about the product ☐
7 get approval from customers ☐
8 pay for a place to advertise ☐

Discussion

10 Think about a recent product you bought. With a partner, take turns to ask and answer the questions.

· What is your product?
· How does the company market it?
· What advertising did you see?
· What is the product's USP?
· How did the salesperson deal with your questions?
· Was the price competitive?
· Did you get a discount? Why? Why not?
· Is the product good value for money?
· Does it satisfy your need?

5 | Marketing and selling

Refresh your memory

Countable (C) nouns
a car, the car, some cars
singular and plural forms
Uncountable (U) nouns
work, the work, some work
no *a/an*, no plural form
some
We need some cars.
We need some work.
positive sentences with (C) and (U) nouns
any
Are there any cars?
There isn't any work.
questions and negatives with (C) and (U) nouns
many/much, a few/ a little
How many cars? Just a few.
How much work? Just a little.
How many and *a few* with (C) nouns
How much and *a little* with (U) nouns

▶ Grammar and practice page 132

Comparatives
This car is faster than that one.
short adjectives:
fast → faster
That model is more popular.
long adjectives:
popular → more popular
This car is easier to park.
adjectives with -*y*:
easy → easier
Superlatives
It's the fastest car on the market.
short adjectives:
fast → (the) fastest
It's the most popular car they make.
long adjectives:
popular → (the) most popular
It's the easiest car in the world to park.
adjectives with -*y*:
easy → (the) easiest

▶ Grammar and practice page 133

5.3 Grammar | Comparatives and superlatives

Discussion

1 **With a partner, imagine you are the salesman in the picture. Brainstorm some tips for selling a used car.**

2 **With a partner, complete the text with *too much*, *too many*, *a few* or *a little*. Do you think this is good advice?**

How to sell a used car

✓ Don't spend (1) _____ money on repairs, but take (2) _____ time to wash and clean the car.
✓ Take (3) _____ minutes to do (4) _____ research on the Internet to compare prices.
✓ Always ask for (5) _____ money at first. Later, you can give a discount of (6) _____ dollars.
✓ Don't give (7) _____ information. Answer the buyer's questions, but don't give (8) _____ details.
✓ Finally, take (9) _____ advice from the professionals: say you bought the car from an old lady who only drove (10) _____ miles to church on Sundays.

Countable and uncountable nouns

3 **With a partner, mark the words *C* (countable) or *U* (uncountable).**

accessory ☐   guarantee ☐   luggage ☐   repair ☐   time ☐
equipment ☐   kilometre ☐   petrol ☐   seat ☐

4 **Complete the questions about a used car. Use *How much*, *How many*, *Is there* or *Are there*.**

1 _____ is it?
2 _____ kilometres has it done?
3 _____ a guarantee?
4 _____ seats are there?
5 _____ any accessories?
6 _____ luggage can it carry?
7 _____ any repairs to do?
8 _____ petrol does it use?
9 _____ any other equipment?
10 _____ time do I have to decide?

Comparatives

5 **Complete the texts with the comparative form of the adjectives in the boxes.**

big   dangerous   expensive   green   quiet

Hybrid cars have two engines: a petrol engine and an electric engine. Consequently, they are (1) _____ to make and to buy, but more fuel efficient. They are also (2) _____ than conventional cars – for this reason, some people think they are (3) _____ for pedestrians, because they don't hear the hybrids coming. Hybrid production is more energy-intensive than for conventional cars, so are they really (4) _____, or is their carbon footprint actually (5) _____?

harmful   high   polluting   small

Well, it's true that producing hybrids, especially their batteries, is (6) _____ for the environment than manufacturing conventional vehicles. However, over a lifetime of 250,000km, a hybrid is a lot (7) _____. The difference is so big that, despite (8) _____ emissions during production, its carbon footprint is still more than 30% (9) _____ than that of a conventional car.

Superlatives

6 Complete the statements with the superlative form of the adjectives in the box.

comfortable   fast   long   luxurious   popular   slow

1 The _____ production car in the world can do over 400 kilometres per hour (kph).
2 The _____ train service in the world is from Moscow to Vladivostok.
3 The _____ colour for cars in the UK is silver.
4 The _____ bus services in the world are in New York City, with speeds as low as 3.5 miles per hour (mph).
5 The _____ economy-class airline seat in the world is on Qatar Airways.
6 The _____ cruise ship in the world is North Korea's 40-year-old Man Gyong Bong.

Listening

7 🔊 2:03 **Listen and check your answers to Exercise 6. Note down one extra piece of information for each statement.**

Discussion

8 With a partner, take turns to ask and answer the questions about your town or city. Give reasons.

1 What is the least expensive way to travel from London to your town or city?
The least expensive way is probably by bus, but it's also the slowest and the most uncomfortable. It's better to take the plane or the train, even if it is more expensive.
2 What is the most comfortable place to stay?
3 What is the best way to go sightseeing in your town or city?
4 What is the most unusual place to see?
5 What is the least interesting place to see?
6 What is the worst place to eat?
7 What is the best place to enjoy a night out?
8 What is the easiest way to meet local people?

Glossary   PAGE 156

accessory
carbon footprint
energy
harmful
hybrid
legroom
luxurious
satnav

Roleplay

9 Work with a partner to roleplay buying and selling a car. Student A: Use the information below. Student B: Look at page 117.

Student A
You want to buy a car. Your budget is €5,000. Student B has two cars for sale. Ask for information and try to negotiate a good deal.

	Toyota	Peugeot
price		
engine		
kilometres		
guarantee		
seats		
satnav		
luggage		
work needed		
petrol consumption		
other equipment		

5 | Marketing and selling

5.4 Speaking   Persuading

Brainstorming

1 In small groups, brainstorm the advantages for employees and for companies of an on-site day care centre for young children.

Listening

2 🔊 2:04 Rosie, a staff representative, is trying to persuade David, the HR manager, that their manufacturing company needs a day care centre. Listen and answer the questions.

1   According to Rosie, why is it bad for the company not to have a day care centre?   *loses 100's of hours*
2   What are David's two main objections?   *Investment & staff*   *→ service company that provides everything*
3   How does Rosie answer David's objections?   *saves $ employee pays <tax*
4   What two advantages does Rosie think the women on the board will see?   *hire & keep best young women, really good for morale.*

3 🔊 2:04 With a partner, find suitable words to complete the useful expressions for persuading in the checklist. Then listen again and check.

Useful expressions: Persuading

Explaining consequences and benefits

... which _____ (that)...
As a _____, ...
That _____ us to ...
Consequently, ...

Reacting and responding

I see your _____. But ...
I agree that ... However, ...
It's certainly _____ that ... , but ...
I know what you _____. On the other _____, ...

Reminding

Keep in _____ that ...
Don't _____ that ...

Adding information

In addition, ...
What's _____, ...

Closing

Does that make _____?
Is there anything _____ you want to ask about?
Is that all _____ with you?

Internet research

Search for the keywords *features and benefits*. List some features and benefits of a favourite thing you own.

4 With a partner, practise explaining the benefits of these features. Use the expressions in the checklist. Student A: explain the first benefit (✓). Student B: raise an objection (✗). Student A: react and respond; explain the second benefit (✓).

1 This car has heated leather front seats.
(✓ never feel cold) (✗ take a long time to get warm) (✓ so elegant)
A: This car has heated leather front seats, which means that you never feel cold in winter.
B: Yes, but they take a long time to get warm.
A: I know what you mean. On the other hand, leather seats are so elegant!
2 This is the most luxurious cruise ship in the world.
(✓ visit exotic places in comfort) (✗ very expensive) (✓ meet the best kind of people)
3 Our software is compatible with both Mac and PC.
(✓ users can choose) (✗ difficult to learn) (✓ free updates)
4 This restaurant has three stars.
(✓ delicious food) (✗ only for the rich) (✓ amazing views of the city)
5 France's TGV is the fastest train service in Europe.
(✓ Paris to Marseille in three hours) (✗ 80 minutes by plane) (✓ unlimited luggage)
6 This nightclub has three dance floors.
(✓ satisfy all musical tastes) (✗ too crowded) (✓ also two restaurants and a swimming pool)

5 With a partner, take turns to read and respond to the objections. Use the expressions in the checklist. Student A: read the objection. Student B: remind Student A about something; add information.

1 These plane tickets are really expensive! (cheaper than train; plane is faster)
A: These plane tickets are really expensive!
B: Keep in mind that they're cheaper than the train. What's more, the plane is a lot faster!
2 This car is really basic. There isn't even a radio! (not expensive; economical)
3 This hotel room is too small! (very central; comfortable)
4 This computer is so slow! (small and light; long battery life)
5 This job is extremely boring! (first step to promotion; good pay)
6 It's quicker to walk than to take this bus service! (raining outside; good way to see the city)

6 Persuade your partner about a product or service your university/company needs to buy. Use the flow chart.

Student A	Student B
Describe your product or service. Explain the benefits.	Raise an objection.
React and respond to B's objection.	Raise another objection.
React and remind B about something. Add information. Ask if B has any more questions.	Say you have no more questions.
Close.	

Roleplay

7 In small groups, take turns to persuade others to:

1 buy your car/bicycle.
2 do a six-month internship in Alaska.
3 invest in your business idea.
4 invite the whole group to dinner.
5 (your idea)

Glossary PAGE 156

acknowledge
day care
morale
objection
paperwork

eWorkbook

Now watch the video for this unit.

5 | Marketing and selling

- ▶ analysing paragraph order and content
- ▶ giving reasons and results
- ▶ writing letters or memos to 'sell' changes

5.5 Writing   'Selling' changes

Brainstorming

1 **In small groups, discuss the questions.**

1 Think of examples of recent changes in your city, university or company. Did people accept them easily? Why do some people resist change?
2 What can managers and leaders do to 'sell' changes and help people to accept them?

Models

2 **Read the letter and the memo, and answer the questions.**

1 What changes are the writers trying to 'sell'?
2 Why are the changes necessary?
3 What are the benefits of the changes?

Dear Ms Firth,

As a regular customer of Energy Choice Products, your business is important to us. We hope to continue working with you in the future.

Due to the global economic situation, raw materials and energy costs are rising. Consequently, we have no choice but to increase prices to our customers for the first time in three years.

We are proud of our products. An increase of just under 4% means that we can maintain the high standards our customers expect. We are confident you will agree that this small increase is preferable to a reduction in quality or service.

Please find attached our new price list. The new prices start on 1st January.

Thank you again for choosing Energy Choice Products. We look forward to continuing our strong business relationship for many years to come.

Yours sincerely,

Alan Strong, Sales Manager

⬇ INBOX | REPLY ← | FORWARD ➡

From: Elena Martin, site manager
To: all staff
Re: staff canteen

Thank you for your feedback on the staff canteen. Your comments are helping us to improve the quality of service.
Since the company is growing quickly, the canteen cannot now serve everybody at 1pm. As a result, waiting times are increasing. Lunch will therefore be split into two sittings, the first at 12.30pm and the second at 1.15pm.
This means that everybody can be served quickly and efficiently, and food quality will improve.
In addition, the canteen will be quieter and less crowded. I hope you agree that everybody will benefit.
The new system will be in place from 15th September. Please discuss your preferences with your manager.
I look forward to talking to you soon in a more efficient and more comfortable canteen.

Internet research

Search for the keywords *five stages of change*. Talk about a change you or a friend made. Describe the different stages.

Analysis

3 Number the descriptions in the order they appear in the models.

- ☐ a) Explain the benefits of the change
- ☐ b) Close positively
- ☐ c) Give the exact date of the change and any other details
- ☐ d) Explain the problem and the solution
- ☐ e) Make a positive connection with the reader

4 Match these extracts with the descriptions in Exercise 3.

1 As from next month we are stopping production of the B100. ☐
2 Other customers are delighted with the B150, as it is not only stronger but also lighter than the B100. ☐
3 We are delighted to offer you your first B150 at the same price as the B100, and we hope you will continue giving us your business. ☐
4 Owing to changes in international quality standards, the B100 is no longer compliant. We are therefore replacing it with a new model, the B150. ☐
5 You have ordered over 250 Model B100s from us, which means you are one of our most valued customers. ☐

Language focus

5 Find examples in Exercises 2 and 4 of phrases with *due to*, *owing to*, *since* and *as* to give reasons. Choose the correct words in **bold** to complete the rule below.

To give reasons:
Use *owing to* and *due to* with a **noun** / **verb** phrase.
Use *as*, *since* and *because* with a **noun** / **verb** phrase.

6 With a partner, complete these sentences with *owing to*, *due to*, *since*, *as* or *because*.

1 _____ an increase in the price of materials, please find attached our revised quotation.
2 _____ the price of materials increased last month, we have revised our quotation.
3 _____ safety is our first priority, we have no choice but to cancel the event.
4 Unfortunately, we cannot supply your order _____ new laws on exports.
5 We finally agreed on 30 November _____ no other date was available.
6 Future orders will be shipped from Los Angeles _____ supply chain restructuring.

7 Find examples in Exercise 2 of phrases with *consequently*, *(this) means that*, *as a result* and *therefore* to give results.

8 With a partner, complete these explanations with *consequently*, *(this) means that*, *as a result* and *therefore*.

1 International standards changed last year. (update all products)
   International standards changed last year. Consequently, we updated all our products.
2 Unfortunately, the company car park is full. (reserved spaces only for managers in future)
3 The new version is faster and less expensive. (replace old version immediately)
4 One of our receptionists is on maternity leave. (only answer calls in the morning)
5 We are outsourcing production to Asia. (all jobs transferred to our Birmingham site)
6 There is a small mechanical problem. (customers asked to return cars for inspection)

Output

9 Write letters or memos to 'sell' changes in two of these situations.

1 A letter to a customer explaining a change in your company's terms of payment.
2 A memo to your company's staff explaining a change in office hours.
3 A letter to passengers explaining your improved (but more expensive) bus service.
4 A memo to all users of your building explaining new security regulations.

Glossary   PAGE 156

compliant
feedback
owing to
proud
sitting
split

5.5 Writing

5.6 Case study Dallivan Cars

Discussion

1 With a partner, discuss how customers see these car brands. Add the brand names to the market positioning map.

Bentley BMW Ferrari General Motors Lada Skoda Tata Toyota VW

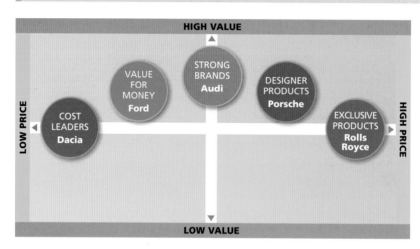

2 Dallivan Cars is a small independent car manufacturer based in Ireland. Look at the information below. What does it tell you about the company and its product?

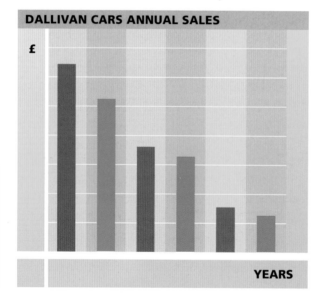

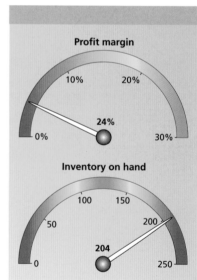

Internet research

Search 'Images' for the keywords *market positioning*. Choose an interesting image to talk about with a partner.

TELL US WHAT YOU THINK!

Model: Dallivan Compact	Performance	Reliability	Comfort	Design	Value for money
Excellent					
Good		✓			
Average	✓		✓		✓
Poor				✓	

Listening

3 ▶ 2:05 **Duncan Keefe, CEO of Dallivan Cars, is talking to Aileen Darcy, the new marketing manager. Listen to the conversation and answer the questions.**

1 The company's results are a) a big surprise b) no surprise c) good news.
2 Aileen thinks that a) her job b) the Compact c) the customer satisfaction survey is boring.
3 The Compact was developed and marketed by a) the CEO b) the new marketing manager c) the old marketing manager.
4 Aileen gives examples of a) market positioning b) market segments c) market forces.
5 The board wants Aileen to present a) a new car b) a new advertisement c) some new ideas.
6 If the new model is not a success, Dallivan Cars will a) continue with the old car b) close c) fire Aileen.

Discussion and presentation

4 **Work in groups. You are Aileen Darcy's new marketing team. Read the brief and discuss your ideas. Prepare to persuade the board of Dallivan Cars that your ideas are the best.**

DALLIVAN CARS

BRIEF

Objective: present a marketing plan for a new Dallivan car
NB The company does not have the capacity to produce large numbers of cars for a global market. We would therefore like the new model to target a small but profitable local market.

Please consider the following points:
- target market (singles/families/city car/sports model, etc.)
- market positioning
- product features and benefits
- your strategies for
  - distribution
  - selling
  - pricing
  - promotion, including your ideas for the advertising campaign

Glossary   PAGE 156

brand
inventory
segment

5 **Form new groups. Take turns to describe your group's plan and try to persuade the others that your ideas are the best. Then hold a class vote to choose the best plan.**

▶ entrepreneurs' stories

▶ buying into business

6.1 About business Entrepreneurs

Discussion and listening

1 🔊 2:06–2:08 With a partner, match the entrepreneurs with the quotations. Then listen and check your answers.

A MICHAEL DELL

B CHER WANG

C RICHARD BRANSON

1 I started a student newspaper at the age of 16. ☐
2 I studied medicine. ☐ *A*
3 I wanted to be a professional musician. ☐ *B*

2 🔊 2:06–2:08 Listen again and answer the questions.

1 How did Michael Dell find money to expand his business?
2 How much is he worth today?
3 Who was Cher Wang's father?
4 What change was the reason for HTC's success?
5 How did Richard Branson start in the music business?
6 How rich is Branson today?

Reading

3 Read the article opposite and match the headings below with the paragraphs in the text.

☐ How to find the money
☐ The advantages of buying a business
☐ Three ways to become a boss
☐ Why not buy a small business? ← *Homework for June 26*
☐ The risks of starting a business
☐ The disadvantages of being an employee
☐ How much will it cost?

4 Read the article again and mark the statements *T* (true) or *F* (false).

1 A lot of people think starting a company is cheaper than buying an established business. ☐
2 Finding a job in a big firm is the quickest way to become a top manager. ☐
3 Between 50% and 70% of new businesses are successful after five years. ☐
4 Normally, an existing business continues to make a profit after it is sold. ☐
5 The selling price of a business usually depends on how profitable it is. ☐
6 It is often easier and cheaper to borrow money from a bank than from the seller. ☐
7 In seller financing, the buyer promises to use future profits to pay for part of the business. ☐
8 It is difficult to find a small business to buy. ☐

Discussion   *Use glossary vocab*

5 In small groups, discuss the questions.

1 Why do so many new businesses not survive?
2 What are the risks of buying an existing company?
3 Is seller financing a good idea from the seller's point of view? Why? Why not?
4 Would you prefer to buy a company or start your own business/franchise? Why?

Icebreaker for June 26

Internet research

Find out more about Michael Dell, Cher Wang, Sir Richard Branson or another entrepreneur. Tell a partner their story.

Glossary   PAGE 156

borrow
failure
frustrating
funding
interest
seller financing
talent
worth

Why not buy into business?

Most new businesses are failures.
An existing business is already profitable.

1 So, you want to be your own boss? Basically, you have three options: one, find a job and get promoted; two, start your own company; or three, buy an existing business. Perhaps you think buying companies is only for millionaires? Well, let's look at some of the advantages of buying an established business and the disadvantages of the other options.

2 Your safest option is to start as an employee in a big firm. The only investment is your own time and hard work. But it can take many years to get to the top. If you really have entrepreneurial spirit, working for someone else can be an extremely frustrating experience.

3 And what about starting your own business? Being the next Richard Branson or Cher Wang is a nice idea but, in reality, most new businesses are failures. 50% don't survive the first three years. That figure rises to 70% after five years. Even a well-known franchise offers no guarantee of success.

4 On the other hand, an existing business has many advantages. First of all, it is already profitable. It already has a customer base, regular cash flow, equipment, employees, a list of suppliers, and established business processes. In a start-up, you have to build all of those from nothing. If you choose carefully, an established business has every chance of continuing to be profitable.

5 As far as price is concerned, it's a question of negotiation. The calculation is a little complex, but the starting price often equals three to five years' profits, depending on the type and size of business. The better your negotiating skills, the better the deal.

6 Finally, there are three main sources of funding. First, your own personal funds; secondly, bank loans; thirdly, seller financing. Seller financing is more and more common as it becomes more difficult to borrow money from banks. The seller agrees to wait for payment of between 50 and 75% of the agreed price, plus interest, over a period of three to five years. Both the buyer and the seller hope that, in that time, the business produces enough profit to pay the seller back.

7 The choice is yours. You can spend thirty years working your way to the top, or you can take a risk and start a business. But if you like the idea of managing a successful company right now, why not start looking for a business to buy? In every city in the world, there are hundreds of small businesses for sale, all waiting for your talent to help them grow!

6 | Entrepreneurship

- ▶ types of organization
- ▶ vocabulary relating to people in business
- ▶ collocations relating to enterprise finance

Match words and defs in pairs on whiteboard

Ice breaker

Organizations

1 Match the organizations 1–6 in **bold** with the definitions a–f below.

1 My hairdresser has her own business. She's a **sole trader**. ☐
2 My doctor works in a **partnership**. There are two other doctors and a physiotherapist. ☐
3 I often eat at a local Indian restaurant. It's a **private limited company**, owned and run by one family. ☐
4 My father invested some money in Marks & Spencer. It's a well-known **public limited company** (plc). ☐
5 There are Hertz car rental offices in over 140 countries. It's a global **franchise**. ☐
6 The YMCA is an NPO – a **non-profit organization** – that focuses on youth development. ☐

a) two or more people own and manage the business
b) one person owns and controls the business
c) a charity or cooperative usually managed by a board of directors
d) a joint venture between a local entrepreneur and a well-established business
e) a large company; anyone can buy or sell its shares on the stock market
f) several people (shareholders), often family or friends, own a part (a share) of the company

Listening

2 🔊 2:09–2:12 **Four entrepreneurs are talking about the advantages and disadvantages of their organizations. Listen and complete the table.**

	Type of organization	Advantage	Disadvantage
Speaker 1			
Speaker 2			
Speaker 3			
Speaker 4			

3 With a partner, complete these sentences with the words in brackets.

1 In a _____ operation, the _____ agrees to let the _____ use a company's name and sell its product or service on a local market. (franchisee, franchise, franchiser)
2 The _____ who controls a majority interest in the company is usually the _____. When two or more people control the company, they are usually called _____s. (partner, shareholder, owner)
3 Our _____ started the company in 1983. He is also the _____ (UK) or _____ (US). His son is a _____ in the finance department. (manager, CEO, MD (managing director), founder)
4 Bill is a _____. He doesn't work for the company, but he is on the _____, a group of people who decide company strategy. His father is the _____ (UK) or _____ (US). (board, president, director, chairman).
5 Me? I'm an ordinary _____. Our US managers call me and my colleagues _____s. In total, the company has 200 full-time _____. (staff, co-worker, employee)

4 Choose the best answer.

1 A start-up is when an entrepreneur a) buys a new car b) sets up a new business c) buys another company.
2 A merger is when two companies a) agree to become one b) share a new activity c) buy another company.
3 An acquisition is when an entrepreneur a) starts a company b) buys a company c) sells a company.
4 A takeover is when a company a) starts another company b) buys another company c) sells another company.
5 A buyout is when a company is bought by a) its own bank b) its own customers c) its own staff.
6 A joint venture is when two companies a) agree to become one b) share a new activity c) buy another company.

Internet research

Search for the keywords *entrepreneur's glossary*. List five useful words to learn. Compare with a partner.

Reading and vocabulary

5 Read the article and mark the statements *T* (true) or *F* (false).

1 Young entrepreneurs can obtain cheap finance from family or friends. ☐
2 Professional investors don't want to wait a long time to see a profit. ☐
3 If you're careful, you don't need to pay for legal assistance. ☐

BLOG

Enterprise finance

Every future entrepreneur needs finance. If you are lucky, you can borrow capital from family
or friends. If you have a strong business plan, banks will lend money, but business loans can
be expensive, so compare several offers to find the best interest rate. Venture capitalists are
sometimes prepared to invest money and know-how in start-up companies, but they will want a
quick return on investment (ROI). Finally, don't forget to budget for the corporate lawyer you need
to read and write contracts, to help you register a business and obtain all the official paperwork.

---

6 In each set of five, match the words 1–10 with a–j to make collocations. Then check your answers in the text.

1 business   d   a) capital
2 interest   c   b) capitalist
3 register   e   c) rate
4 venture   b   d) plan
5 borrow   a   e) a business

6 official   j   f) lawyer
7 business   i   g) companies
8 corporate f   h) investment
9 return on h   i) loan
10 start-up g   j) paperwork

7 Match the collocations in Exercise 7 with the definitions below.

1 government or administrative documents ☐ *official paperwork*
2 the percentage that banks charge to finance projects ☐ *interest rate*
3 money from a bank to start or help a company ☐ *business loan*
4 people or organizations who invest in new business ☐ *venture capitalist*
5 the profit on money that was used to buy something ☐ *return on investme*
6 put information about a company on an official list ☐ *register a biz*
7 receive money with a promise to pay it back ☐ *borrow capital*
8 small new businesses ☐ *start up companies*
9 a specialist in company law ☐ *corporate lawyer*
10 the written strategy for a company ☐ *biz plan*

8 Work with a partner to complete your crossword. Take turns to give definitions for the words you have. Don't say the word itself. Write the missing words. Student A: use the crossword below. Student B: use the crossword on page 121.

B: What's 2 across?
A: It's a group of people who decide company strategy.

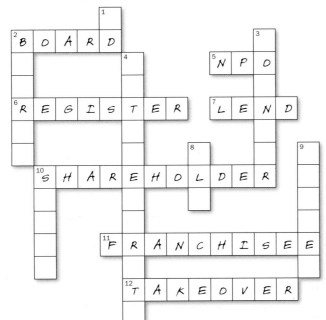

6 | Entrepreneurship

Refresh your memory

Saying something is/isn't necessary
You *have to* register your company.
= it's required (by law)
You *must* have a business plan.
= I believe it's essential
You *don't have to/don't need to* have a business plan.
= it's not required (by law)

Saying something is prohibited
You *mustn't* employ children.
You're *not allowed to* employ children.
You *can't* employ children.
= it's against the law

Giving permission
You *can* have more than one company.
You're *allowed to* have more than one company.
= it's permitted

Giving advice
You *should* ask for help.
= it's a good idea
You *shouldn't* work all night.
= it isn't a good idea

▶ Grammar and practice
pages 134–135

Verb patterns
say, tell, talk, speak, present, explain, discuss, suggest

▶ Grammar and practice
page 135

6.3 Grammar Modal verbs

Obligation and permission

1 In small groups, compare being a student with being in work. Do you have more or fewer obligations? Do you have more or less freedom? Think about money, time, exams, holidays, tax, clothes, and so on.

Students don't have much money, so they have to be very careful. Working people have more money, but less time to spend it!

2 With a partner, take turns to ask and answer a new student's questions about university rules. Use the phrases in the box.

> Can I …? Do I have to …? You can You can't You don't have to You don't need to
> You have to You must You mustn't You're (not) allowed to

A: Do I have to wear a uniform?
B: No, you don't have to wear a uniform, but you have to wear smart clothes when you visit a company.

1 wear a uniform
2 eat in the classroom
3 bring my own computer
4 attend all classes
5 pay for my course
6 record my class to listen to it again
7 take photos
8 bring a friend to class
9 do an internship
10 take exams

Advice

3 With a partner, take turns to give an American student advice about living and working in your country. Use the phrases in the box.

> Can I …? Should I …? You should You shouldn't

A: Can I help myself to a coffee at a friend's home?
B: No, you shouldn't. It isn't polite. You should wait for your friend to offer you something.

1 help myself to a coffee at a friend's home
2 shake hands with men and women I meet
3 bring something to eat or drink to a party
4 answer my phone in the bus or train
5 speak to strangers in the elevator
6 arrive early for meetings
7 ask questions in presentations
8 give my opinion in meetings
9 interrupt in discussions
10 invite colleagues home for dinner

4 In small groups, read the advice and say if you agree or disagree. Give reasons.

How to start a company … good advice?

1 You have to be a millionaire to start your own company.
   No, I don't think that's true. You don't have to be rich, because you can get money from investors.
2 You don't need to have a business degree. Anyone can run a successful business.
3 You should get advice from a corporate lawyer before hiring employees.
4 You must choose an address where customers can find you easily.
5 You don't have to advertise. Personal recommendations are cheaper and more effective.
6 You shouldn't have business partners if you can avoid it.

Verb patterns

5 Complete the sentences with the verbs in the box. There is sometimes more than one correct answer.

> discuss   explain   present   say   speak   suggest   talk   tell

1   Did Jack _____ you about his new company logo?
2   Sorry, I didn't catch that. Can you _____ more slowly, please?
3   Could you _____ the process to the group? We're not sure how it works.
4   We didn't _____ salaries with the interviewees.
5   Did the bank manager _____ contacting the Chamber of Commerce?
6   Can you _____ your business plan to the marketing department tomorrow?
7   What did you _____ to the suppliers about at the meeting?
8   Yes, Kate. Do you want to _____ something to the team?

6 Summarize the following using the verb in brackets.

1   Mark: 'Hello, Sally!' Sally: 'Oh, hello, Mark!' (say)
    Mark and Sally said hello (to each other).
2   Jackie: 'The problem is, Mum, I have to…' (explain)
    Jackie explained the problem (to her mum).
3   Fiona: 'Ask Uncle Joe to invest in your business.' (suggest)
4   Darren: 'Say – that – again – please.' George: 'I said, it's – a – very – bad – line!' (speak)
5   Bank manager: 'Let's look at the first part of your business plan.' Lara: 'OK. My idea here was to…' Bank manager: 'I see. But did you think about…?' (discuss)
6   Peter: 'Lin, it's about the new company. The thing is, …' (talk)
7   Henry: 'So, members of the board, that is our plan. I hope you like it.' (present)
8   Karen: 'Listen, John. Call me back later, OK?' (tell)

7 With a partner, take turns to ask and answer questions about conversations you had today or yesterday. Try to use as many of the verbs in Exercise 6 as possible.

*A: Did you **speak** to Jakob yesterday?*
*B: Yes, I did. We **talked** for about ten minutes at coffee time.*
*A: Did he **tell** you anything interesting?*

Listening and writing

8 🔊 2:13–2:17 Imagine you want to buy a sandwich bar franchise. Listen to five experts and report their advice using the prompts below.

1   Petra/tell/not sign/a franchise agreement alone. Suggest/ask/lawyer/explain/details.
    Petra told us not to sign a franchise agreement alone. She suggested asking a lawyer to explain the details.
2   Malcolm/explain/plan a strategy. Say/franchiser/tell/what to do.
    Malcolm explained that you don't have to plan a strategy. He said the franchiser tells you what to do.
3   Birgit/present/typical franchise fees. Say/franchisees/usually pay/$20–50,000.
4   Bernd/tell/not allowed/choose/cheapest suppliers. Explain/contract/say/have to buy/official suppliers.
5   Miguel/talk/royalty payments. Say/can choose/pay once a quarter/but/suggest/pay regularly every month. Tell/usually/pay/5–10%/sales.

Glossary   PAGE 157

elevator
fee
franchise fee
franchiser
lawyer
obligatory
royalty

6.4 Speaking   Meetings

Brainstorming

1 Work in small groups. Your group is planning to open a sandwich bar in the business district of your city. How can you make your sandwiches different from the competition? Brainstorm for five minutes. Then compare your ideas with another group.

Listening

2 🔊 2:18 Emily, Sheryl and Tim are planning to open a sandwich bar called Bread 'n' butter. Listen to the meeting and <u>underline</u> the correct answers.

1 Bread 'n' butter will be in a *residential / business / shopping* area.
2 Tim and Sheryl disagree about how to *make sandwiches / run the business / run the meeting*.
3 Sheryl suggests changing *the bread / the prices / the menu* every day.
4 Emily *completely agrees / partially agrees / completely disagrees* with Sheryl's idea.
5 Emily and Sheryl suggest inviting customers to *bring / make / design* their own sandwiches.
6 They decide to have two different *standards / sections / sandwiches*.

3 🔊 2:18 With a partner, find suitable words to complete the useful expressions for meetings in the checklist. Then listen again and check.

Useful expressions: **Meetings**

Suggestions

I suggest _____ some interesting combinations.
_____ about ham and banana?
Let's _____ everything for the moment.
What about _____ a different menu every day?
_____ not change the menu every week?
Why don't we _____ different types of bread each week?

Clarifying

Are you _____ you don't like unusual combinations?
What I _____ is, we don't have to define the recipes now.
Do you _____, some weeks you can't get apple and cheese?
What I'm saying is ...

Continuing after an interruption

As I was _____, we need a strategy.

Interrupting

I'm _____ to interrupt, Tim, but ...
_____ I interrupt?

just before test?

Suggestions

4 With a partner, take turns to ask for a suggestion, make a suggestion and give a reaction.

A: *Can you recommend a good place to eat at lunchtime?*
B: *What about buying sandwiches to eat by the river?*
A: *Good idea. It's a nice sunny day. / No, it's too cold for a picnic.*

1 … a good place to eat at lunchtime? (What about …?)
2 … a nice restaurant to take my parents for dinner? (Why don't …?)
3 … a good place to buy cakes? (I suggest …)
4 … the best place to have breakfast? (Why not …?)
5 … somewhere we can get a cup of coffee? (Let's …)
6 … a good place to celebrate passing our exams? (How about …?)

Interrupting and clarifying

5 Work in small groups. Take turns to speak for one minute about your ideas for making your hobby into a business. The rest of the group interrupts and asks for clarification as often as possible.

A: *My hobby is dancing and I'm going to talk about how to make it into a business.*
B: *I'm sorry to interrupt, but do you mean you want to be a professional dancer?*
A: *No, what I mean is, I'd like to start a dance school. As I was saying, dancing is my hobby and …*
C: *May I interrupt? Are you saying you enter dancing competitions?*

Problems and solutions

6 With a partner, brainstorm solutions to these problems. Use the flow chart below and expressions from the checklist.

1 We need to choose a corporate colour for our sandwich bar.
2 We need to decide what kind of desserts to sell.
3 We need an original idea for staff uniforms.
4 We need to find €20,000 to start the business.
5 We need to decide how to package the sandwiches.
6 We need to decide what kind of drinks to sell.
7 We need to decide our opening and closing times.
8 We need to choose the background music.

Student A   **Student B**

Explain the problem.	→	Make a suggestion.
Ask for clarification.	→	Clarify.
Disagree.	→	Make another suggestion.
Agree.		

Roleplay

7 Work in groups of three. Roleplay a meeting to decide how to promote your new sandwich bar.

Student A: chair the meeting. It is your job to follow the agenda, make sure everybody gives their opinions, and agree each point.
Student B: look at page 116.
Student C: look at page 123.

Bread 'n' butter
AGENDA

Promotional mix
1 Advertising
2 Personal selling
3 Sales promotion
4 Public relations
5 Direct marketing

6.4 Speaking

- ▶ analysing content
- ▶ putting information into minutes format
- ▶ writing an agenda and minutes

6.5 Writing   Agendas and minutes

Discussion

1 Consider these statements and mark them *A* (I agree), *D* (I disagree) or *?* (it depends). Compare your answers with a partner and give reasons for your choices.

1 A meeting without an agenda is a waste of time. ☐
2 The most important decisions should come first on the agenda. ☐
3 The person who leads the meeting should also write the minutes. ☐
4 Writing minutes is a waste of time. Nobody ever reads them. ☐

Models

2 An acquisition team is planning to buy APL Ltd, a small engineering company. Read the agenda and minutes and <u>underline</u> the correct answers.

1 Simon is probably in charge of *sales / human resources / finance*.
2 The most important decision is last because *everybody must be present / they need information from all the other items / they want to finish on time*.
3 At the meeting, *four / three / five* people were present
4 The team thinks APL will probably *accept / reject / negotiate* their offer.
5 The next meeting is *in one week / as soon as possible / in two weeks*.

ACQUISITION TEAM MEETING

Date & time: 4 October, 9–11am
Leader: Chris
Attendees: Helen, Val, Chris, Simon

TIME	ITEM	PRESENTER
9.00–9.15	1 APL *Balance sheet* – for discussion	Simon
9.15–9.30	2 APL *Sales forecast* – for information	Helen
9.30–9.45	3 APL *HR situation* – for discussion	Val
9.45–10.55	4 *Our offer* – for decision	Chris
10.55–11.00	5 AOB	Chris

MINUTES OF ACQUISITION TEAM MEETING

Date & time: 4 October, 9–11am
Present: Helen, Chris, Simon
Apologies: Val
Minutes by: Helen

ITEM	ACTION	WHO?	WHEN?
1 APL *Balance sheet*	Check inventory and report back	Simon	Next meeting
2 APL *Sales forecast*	None	-	-
3 APL *HR situation*	Check staff contracts with lawyer and report back	Val	asap
4 *Our offer*	Make first offer of €300,000 30% cash, 70% seller financing	Chris	5 October

Next meeting: 18 October, 9–11am

Analysis

3 Read the agenda again. Tick (✓) the information that is included in the agenda.

☐ the date
☐ the time
☐ the names of the people invited to the meeting
☐ the place where the meeting takes place
☐ the topics for discussion

☐ the decisions they have to make
☐ the time planned for each item
☐ the person in charge of the meeting
☐ the person in charge of minutes
☐ the person in charge of each item

4 Read the minutes again. Circle the information that is not included in the minutes.

> action to take   agreements and disagreements   apologies for absence   opinions
> the person in charge of each action   the person who wrote the minutes
> when the action should happen

Language focus

5 Read these extracts. How many words were used to write this information in the minutes?

1   Val was unable to attend the meeting because she was ill, but she sent a report on the HR situation. We discussed the contracts and decided that we need to take professional advice. Val is in charge of contacting the lawyer and informing us of his opinion as quickly as possible.

2   Simon was unhappy about our offer. However, the others agreed to make an offer of €300,000. €90,000 will be from our own funds. We will borrow the balance (€210,000) from the seller and pay it back over five years. Chris will make the offer tomorrow morning, but he thinks the seller will probably want to negotiate a better offer.

6 Rewrite the extracts as minutes. Copy and use

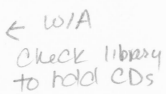

1   There was a long discussion about the cash flow   e may
need to ask the bank for more money. James is v   nnette to
investigate the situation and give a presentation

2   We had a discussion about an opportunity to bu   aid it was
very profitable. He offered to get more details an   meeting.
James felt that Oslo was too far away, but he agr

3   Heinrich asked about the situation in HR and w   explained
that she cannot do all the work herself. She said   greed for
reasons of cost. Annette suggested hiring an intern and everyone, including James, thought it was a good idea. Aiko will contact the university to see if an intern can start next week, or even this week if they can organize it.

4   James told the meeting about an offer from HBCC Bank. The interest rate they are now offering is 3.5% for a ten-year loan. James wants to write a polite letter of refusal. He said this offer is less attractive than the offer from Lawton's Bank. Everybody agreed that Lawton's offer is better. James will do this as soon as he gets back from Ukraine next week.

Output

7 🔊 2:19 Helen and Chris from the APL acquisition team are
meeting. Listen to the conversation and take notes. Then write

← w/A
check library
to hold CDs

8 🔊 2:20–2:23 The APL acquisition team are having the meeti
Exercise 7. Listen to four extracts and take notes. Then write the
template on page 118.

Internet research

Search 'Images' for the keywords *minutes template*. Choose your favourite format. Compare with a partner.

Glossary   **PAGE 157**

acquisition
AOB
apologies
chain
forecast
waste of time

▶ gathering product and market information

▶ making decisions in a meeting about starting a company

6.6 Case study Solar Mobile

Discussion

1 Work in small groups. Imagine you are starting a company that assembles and sells electronic devices. What sort of decisions do you need to make before you start doing business?

type of company –   *funding –*

Reading

2 Read the email from your friend, Tara. What does she want, and why?

✉ | **⬇ INBOX | REPLY ⬅ | FORWARD ➡**

Hi,
Hope you had a good weekend.
I went to see Henry yesterday and he showed me a gadget he made – you know, he's really good with electronics. Anyway, it's a solar battery charger. I'm really excited about it. I think this could be the business idea we're looking for!
You can buy these chargers in the shops. They use solar power to charge mobile devices like phones, tablets, mp3 players, etc. But they're expensive. Henry's version is smaller, lighter and much, much cheaper. Henry told me it's really easy to assemble from standard components. It also has a battery, so if it's not sunny, you can plug it into the wall, charge it and then use it to charge your phone when you're away from home. Everybody who has a phone needs one! I think it's a brilliant idea for a business. Can we meet to talk about it and I'll show it to you?
Best,
Tara

---

3 Read the email again and <u>underline</u> the correct answers.

1 Tara wants to meet in order to *buy / sell / demonstrate* the solar battery charger.
2 Similar devices are *already / not yet / unavailable* on the market.
3 The USP of Henry's design is *size and weight / size and price / size, weight and price.*
4 The parts for the charger are *specially designed / easy to find / difficult to connect.*
5 Tara thinks the solar battery charger is a product for *ecologists / professionals / almost everyone.*

Discussion

4 With a partner, discuss these questions.

1 What sort of people buy solar battery chargers?
2 How much are you prepared to pay for this type of product?
3 Would you like to take part in or invest in Tara's project?

Listening

5 🔊 2:24 **Tara is talking to Henry about the solar battery charger. Listen and answer the questions.**

1 How many people have a phone but no electricity?
2 How do they charge their phones?
3 What is the electricity situation in parts of rural Africa?
4 What is Tara's idea?

Discussion and roleplay

6 **You are going to take part in a meeting about starting a company called Solar Mobile. The company will assemble and sell solar battery chargers. Follow the procedure below.**

1 With a partner, read the agenda and prepare ideas for the meeting. Decide how much discussion time you need for each item.
2 Work in groups to hold the meeting. Choose someone to lead the meeting and someone to note down your decisions. Make decisions on the items on the agenda.
3 Summarize and explain your decisions to the class. Vote for the best project – but you can't vote for your own group!

AGENDA SOLAR MOBILE TEAM MEETING

Date & time: _____   Leader: _____
Present: _____

Minutes by: _____

	TIME	ITEM
1		*Type of company* – for decision sole trader? partnership? your ideas?
2		*Capital: €50,000 required* – for decision borrow from family – 0% interest? sell 40% of the company to a venture capitalist? your ideas?
3		*Business model* – for decision online sales only? sell through high street stores? your ideas?
4		*Sourcing and assembly* – for decision buy and assemble components locally? buy, assemble and ship from East Asia? your ideas?
5		*Positioning* – for decision exclusive product, high price? value for money product, low price? your ideas?
6		*Office* – for decision no office, work from home? rent office in the city centre? your ideas?
7		*Staff* – for decision hire experienced professionals? hire young graduates? your ideas?
8		*Promotion* – for discussion online only – ideas? press and radio campaign – ideas? direct marketing – ideas? your ideas?

Review 5

Marketing and selling

1 Underline the correct word in *italics*.

A useful way to think about marketing is in terms of 'the four Ps'. These are: product, (1) *packaging / price*, promotion and place. The third P – promotion – is about creating awareness, interest and (2) *desire / design*. These are the first three parts of 'AIDA'. The final part of AIDA (action) is the job of sales, not marketing: action means getting the customer's (3) *sign / signature* on the contract. But sales say their job is much more complex than that. It is the sales staff who persuade (4) *prospects / potentials* to make a purchasing decision. They have to answer (5) *requirements / enquiries*, make sales visits, analyse the customers' (6) *wanting / needs*, give product demonstrations, write proposals, send (7) *estimations / quotations*, and do all the negotiation.

In reality, of course, marketing and sales have to work together closely. Information from both departments is needed to make promotion more (8) *worth / effective*, for example, to make sure the focus is on the benefits of a product (that is, how the product can make a customer's life better) rather than just the (9) *features / factors* (that is, what the product can do).

When marketing and sales work together closely, there will be increased (10) *venues / revenues* and new business (11) *opportunities / arrivals*. Both departments are needed to build long-term (12) *partnerings / partnerships* with customers, rather than just satisfy their immediate needs.

2 Fill in the missing letters to complete these marketing collocations.

1   If you cond___ market studies, you do them in an organized way.
2   If you bu___ brand image, you develop it and make it better.
3   If you del____ the goods, you take them to a place.
4   If you m___ consumer needs, you do what is necessary to satisfy those needs.
5   If you s__ competitive prices, you decide and state what they are.
6   If you inc_____ market share, you make it grow.
7   If you en___ a new market, you start working in it.
8   If you ra___ awareness of a product, you make sure more people know about it.

3 Look at the table. Then complete the sentences below with the correct form of the adjective in brackets. Add *the*, *than*, *more/less* or *most/least*, if you need to.

Product	Value	Regular	Premium
Price	€35	€65	€80
Weight	2.2kg	2.5kg	2.8kg
Delivery time	1 week	4 weeks	3 weeks

1   Regular is _____ (cheap) Premium.
2   Of the three products, Value is _____ (cheap).
3   Regular is _____ (expensive) Value.
4   Value is _____ (expensive) Regular.
5   Of the three products, Premium is _____ (expensive).
6   Of the three products, Value is _____ (expensive).
7   Regular is _____ (heavy) Value.

8   Of the three products, Premium is _____ (heavy).
9   Value has _____ (good) delivery time of all.
10 Regular has _____ (bad) delivery time of all.
11 Let's order Premium – it looks _____ (modern) the others.
12 Premium is too complicated for our needs. Let's order Regular – it's _____ (simple). (two possible answers)

4 Match the pairs of expressions that have a similar meaning.

1   Keep in mind that …   a) and as a result …
2   which means that …   b) I know what you mean. However, …
3   What's more, …   c) Don't forget that …
4   I see your point. But … d) In addition, …

5 Complete the conversation about childcare at work with expressions 1–4 from Exercise 4.

Rosie: A lot of staff have childcare problems, (1) _____ the company loses hundreds of hours of work every year. We need a day care centre, here on site.

David: Maybe you're right. But it's a big investment. And it needs specialist staff.

Rosie: (2) _____ can we take those two issues one by one? I agree that a day care centre is a big investment. However, it can save you money. (3) _____ most of the cost is paid by the employees – the cost is taken off their salaries.

David: OK, but what about the problem of the specialist staff?

Rosie: We plan to work with a service company called Happiday. They provide the staff. (4) _____ they provide all the toys and equipment as well.

6 Complete the sentences for 'selling' changes with the pairs of words in the box.

forward/relationship   longer/replacing
materials/quotation   not only/but also
regular/important   rising/increase

1   As a _____ customer of ABC, your business is _____ to us.
2   **Due to** the economic situation, our costs are _____. **Consequently**, we have no choice but to _____ our prices.
3   **Since** the price of _____ increased last month, we have revised our _____.
4   Other customers are delighted with the new model, **as it** is _____ faster _____ lighter than the old one.
5   We look _____ to continuing our strong business _____ for many years to come.
6   **Owing to** changes in international safety laws, the G200 is no _____ compliant. **Therefore**, we are _____ it with a new model, the G250.

7 Use the six items in **bold** in Exercise 6 to complete the sentences below.

1   _____ and _____ mean the same as 'because'.
2   _____ and _____ mean the same as 'because of'.
3   _____ and _____ mean the same as 'so'.

Review 6

Entrepreneurship

1 Fill in the missing letters in this word-building exercise.

1 A million is 1,000,000. A very rich person is a million_ _ _ _ .
2 Something that helps you is an advantage. Something that causes you problems is a _ _ _advantage.
3 You invest money. You make an invest_ _ _ _ .
4 Someone who starts a new business is an entrepreneur. An entrepreneur_ _ _ person is someone who takes risks and works hard.
5 If a project doesn't succeed, it fails. It is a fail_ _ _ .
6 If you succeed, you are a succe_ _. (noun) You are success_ _ _ . (adjective)
7 If the money you gain is more than your costs, you make a profit. Your business is profit_ _ _ _ .
8 You start a new business. It is a start-_ _ .
9 A fund is an amount of money that you collect or invest. Money that you use for a specific purpose (such as a new project or new business) is called fund_ _ _ .

2 Complete the sentences with the pairs of words in the box. The words can be in any order.

> board/CEO   colleagues/co-workers   employee/employer
> franchisee/franchise   interest rate/return on investment
> money/capital   the owner/a shareholder
> venture capitalist/lawyer

1 The company you work for is your _____. You are an _____ of this company.
2 If you have shares in a company, you are _____. If you have the majority of the shares, you are _____.
3 To buy something, you need _____. Business people talk about _____ to mean money that is used to start a business or to invest.
4 Americans and Asians refer to the people they work with as their _____. The British and Europeans call them _____.
5 Do you need someone to invest in your start-up? The bank isn't interested, and neither are your family or friends. Try going to a _____. You'll need a good business plan, and make sure you speak to a _____ first.
6 McDonald's® (the company) is a _____. The person who runs the local McDonald's in your shopping centre is a _____.
7 If you want to get a bank loan, look for a good _____. If you want to get venture capital, offer the VC company a good _____.
8 A company is run day-to-day by the _____ and the senior management team. However, long-term strategy is decided by the _____, who meet once every few months (and who represent the interests of shareholders).

3 Underline the correct words in *italics* to complete the advice for a new work colleague.

1 You *should never be / shouldn't never be* late for a meeting in this company. Good time keeping is important.

2 You *mustn't be / don't have to be* the first person in the room, but I suggest getting to every meeting at least five minutes early.
3 You *must take / can take* a full hour for lunch if you want, it's no problem.
4 But you *can't bring / don't have to bring* sandwiches back to your desk – it leaves a mess.
5 You *must eat / are allowed to eat* your own food in the staff canteen. Everyone does it.
6 *You have to / You're not allowed to* use the Internet for personal reasons during work time.
7 If *you really must / you really can* check your Facebook updates, then wait until you take a break and do it in the canteen.
8 Most people take a couple of short breaks every morning, but you *shouldn't be / don't have to be* away from your desk for too long.

4 Emily and Tim are discussing ideas for a new sandwich bar. Put their conversation in the correct order. Then read it with a partner to check that it makes sense.

Emily:
☐ a) Are you saying you don't like unusual combinations of fillings?
1 b) Let's brainstorm some ideas for new sandwich fillings. How about ham and banana? Or apple and cheese? Or maybe …
☐ c) Wait a minute. Are you saying we have to make every sandwich to order? It will take too long!
☐ d) Do you mean, some weeks you can't get apple and cheese? Some customers like to eat the same thing every week.

Tim:
8 e) It's a good point. But we could have two different sections – one for standard sandwiches, and another for mix and match. And of course the prices would be different too.
☐ f) Perhaps you're right. But we do need something different. Why don't we try mix and match? You choose your bread, your fillings and your dressing.
☐ g) I'm sorry to interrupt, Emily, but I really don't think that's the best way to start the discussion.
☐ h) No, I love your ideas. What I mean is, we don't have to define the recipes right now. It's more important to decide on a strategy. For example, why not have a different menu of sandwiches every week?

5 Read the conversation in Exercise 4 aloud several times. Then cover it and complete the expressions below.

1 Let's b_____ some ideas for new sandwich fillings. H_____ a_____ ham and banana?
2 I'm s_____ to i_____, Emily.
3 W_____ I m_____ is, we don't have to define the recipes right now.
4 Perhaps you're right. W_____ d_____'t w_____ try mix and match?
5 A_____ you sa_____ we have to make every sandwich to order?
6 It's a g_____ p_____. But we could have two different sections.

7 | Business costs

7.1 About business Cutting costs

Discussion

1 Ashley is a student. Her parents give her $24,000 dollars per year to pay her school and living costs. In small groups, discuss these questions.

1 At the end of her first year, Ashley still has $2,000 left in her bank account. What can she do with the money? Think of as many options as possible.
2 Two months before the end of her second year, Ashley has no money left in her account. What can she do? Think of as many options as possible.
3 Ashley's parents own a newspaper shop. If they make a profit or a loss, how is their situation similar or different to Ashley's?

Skim reading

2 Quickly read the article opposite. Find the answer to the question *How can companies lose millions but still stay in business?*

Summarizing

3 Read the article again. Number the paragraph summaries in the order they appear in the article.

☐ a) A decrease in revenue is a problem because fixed costs do not decrease.
☐ b) Companies and families both need to plan their revenues and their costs.
☐ c) With careful management, losing money need not have serious consequences.
☐ d) Investing in better equipment can save money in the long term.
☐ e) Families and companies can use reserves or assets to survive temporary difficulties.
☐ f) Families and companies can usually reduce variable costs easily.

Reading for detail

4 Read the article again and answer the questions.

1 What examples are given of revenue for a) companies and b) families?
2 What examples are given of fixed costs for a) companies and b) families?
3 What examples are given of variable costs for a) companies and b) families?
4 What examples are given of reserves and assets? What is the difference?
5 What examples are given of investments for a) companies and b) families?

Listening

5 🔊 2:25–2:26 Listen to two people talking about cost-cutting and answer the questions for each case.

1 What was the problem?
2 What measures did the company take?
3 What were the consequences for the speaker?

Discussion

6 With a partner, discuss the questions.

1 Think about your personal budget. What are your fixed costs and your variable costs? Make two lists.
2 If your income decreases, which costs can you reduce?
3 What investments could you make to save money in the long term?
4 Think about a company you know. What are its fixed and variable costs?
5 If its revenues decrease, which costs can it reduce?
6 What investments could it make to save money in the long term?

Internet research

Search for the keywords *ways to cut costs*. Make two lists, one for personal costs and another for business costs.

Glossary   PAGE 158

account
asset
bankrupt
freeze
heating
homeless
overtime
reserves

How can companies lose millions but still stay in business?

Companies that invest in new equipment or better software can reduce long-term costs.

COMPANY FINANCES are not very different from family budgets – the numbers are just bigger. Companies and families both know approximately how much money will come in and go out. Businesses can
5 forecast sales revenues and production costs, and families can plan based on their salaries and living costs.

In both cases, the problems begin when revenue decreases. For companies, this is often due to a fall
10 in sales: perhaps products are too old, or competition is increasing. Family income can also go down if bonuses or overtime decrease, or when people are unemployed or ill. If an adult stops work, some variable costs will decrease: tax and transport for
15 example. But most payments, like the house, the children's education, energy bills and telephone bills are fixed. In business, even if sales are down 50%, there are still fixed costs like rent, administration and maintenance. When total costs are higher than
20 revenues, both companies and families have to consider what they can cut.

Fortunately, families don't usually become homeless and companies don't usually go bankrupt because of a temporary decrease in revenue.
25 Families can cut out evenings at the restaurant or cinema; they can do without a new TV or a foreign holiday. Companies can cut advertising, travel and training budgets and freeze temporary contracts.

But cutting these variable costs often takes time
30 to have an effect. In the short term, both families and companies often need to use their reserves, that is, take cash from their savings and investments. If the difficulties continue, they can borrow money using their assets, that is, by re-mortgaging their
35 home, office or factory. By using these reserves or assets, individuals and businesses can survive until their situation improves. Losses are relative: losing several million pounds is unthinkable for a family, but may only be a small percentage of a medium-sized
40 company's revenues.

Corporate and personal finance are also similar where investment is concerned. Sometimes the best way to reduce costs is to spend more money. A family that is having difficulty paying its energy
45 bills can invest in better insulation and a more modern heating system. Companies that invest in new equipment or better software can reduce long-term costs. This kind of one-time cost is often the explanation when well-managed companies appear to
50 be losing money.

In conclusion, a family or a company that has temporary financial difficulties can recover quickly if the problem is managed carefully. Most banks won't take back a car, a home or a factory when a customer
55 misses just one payment, especially if the customer has warned them in advance. But of course, families or businesses that regularly miss payments will soon have even bigger problems.

7 | Business costs

7.2 Vocabulary | Profit, loss and payment

1 **Read the information and look at the graph. Label the graph with the words in the box.**

Doug has a business that makes souvenir mugs. He spends €100,000 per year on overheads, such as administration, rent, energy, etc. In addition, each mug he makes costs €1 for materials, labour, etc. He sells the mugs for €3.50 each.

| breakeven | fixed & variable costs | loss | overheads | profit | revenues |

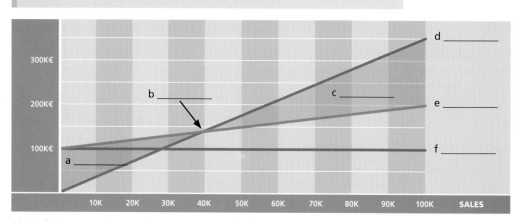

2 **Look at the graph again and answer the questions.**

1 How much money does Doug lose per year if he makes no mugs?
2 How much money does he make if he sells 100,000 mugs?
3 How many mugs does he need to make and sell in order not to lose money?

3 **Complete the text with the words and phrases in the box.**

| cost of goods sold (COGS) | gross margin | operating expenses | profit margin | turnover |

Last year, Doug sold 80,000 mugs, which means he had a (1) _____ of €280,000 (80,000 @ €3.50). His (2) _____ was €80,000, that is, €1 per mug. So his (3) _____ (before fixed costs, tax, etc.) was 71%, or €2.50 per mug. After deducting fixed costs or (4) _____ like rent and energy of €100,000, Doug declared an operating profit of €100,000. He paid €25,000 in taxes (25%), which left net income of €75,000, a healthy (5) _____ of 27%.

4 **Doug sells 80,000 mugs per year. With a partner, explain what happens to the profit margin if:**

1 Doug hires a secretary who costs the business €2,000 per month.
2 In addition, taxes increase to 33%.
3 In addition, Doug's COGS increases to €1.50 per mug.

Glossary   PAGE 158

cheque
lend
mug
souvenir
standing order

5 Read the extracts from a telephone conversation. Replace the phrases in **bold** with the words and phrases in the box.

> account   interest   invoice   outstanding balance   overdue   settle

1   Hello, Mr Jones. I'm calling about your **record of what you ordered and what you paid**.
2   There is **an amount of money which you haven't paid** of $2,000.
3   We sent you **our detailed list of money to pay** on 2 February.
4   I'm afraid it's **very late** – you were supposed to pay us three months ago.
5   The contract you signed allows us to charge you **the cost of credit** at 5%.
6   Could you please **send us payment in full for** your bill as soon as possible?

Listening

6 🔊 2:27 **A credit controller is talking about payment terms. Listen and match the expressions with the explanations.**

☐ payment in advance   ☐ cash on delivery
☐ terms and conditions   ☐ owe someone money
☐ an early payment discount   ☐ 30 days' credit
☐ settle the balance   ☐ a deposit

Roleplay

7 With a partner, roleplay a telephone conversation between an accounts department employee and a slow payer. Use the flow chart below.

Student A   **Student B**

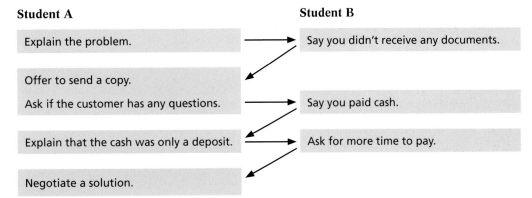

Student A	Student B
Explain the problem.	Say you didn't receive any documents.
Offer to send a copy.	
Ask if the customer has any questions.	Say you paid cash.
Explain that the cash was only a deposit.	Ask for more time to pay.
Negotiate a solution.	

Discussion

8 With a partner, compare the way you pay for the goods and services below. Say which methods of payment in the box you use, and describe the terms and conditions.

> cash   cheque   credit card   electronic transfer   PayPal   standing order

- your accommodation   - your cafeteria expenses   - your books
- your public transport   - your phone   - your music

Internet research

Search for the keywords *fixed and variable costs*. Make two lists of typical costs for companies. Compare with a partner.

Refresh your **memory**

Predictions:
will and *won't*
Prices *will increase* next year.
Customers *won't be* happy.

Instant decisions:
I'*ll have* orange juice, please.
I *won't have* anything to eat, thanks.

Promises:
I'*ll send* you the contract tomorrow.
I *won't be* late.

▶ Grammar and practice page 136

be going to
We're *going to move* to a new office soon.
plans made in advance

▶ Grammar and practice pages 136–137

first conditional
*If you pay cash, (then)
I'll give you a discount.*
if + present simple, (*then*) + *will*
probable future events

▶ Grammar and practice page 137

time expressions
We'll start the meeting *when they arrive.*
when, until, as soon as, before, after + present simple

▶ Grammar and practice page 137

Glossary   PAGE 158

bed and breakfast
contingency plan
entertainment
quote
specification
wind farm

7.3 Grammar   Future forms and first conditional

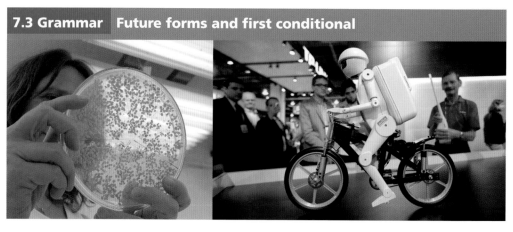

will and *won't*

1 With a partner, take turns to make predictions about the future of the items below.

A: ***We'll build*** more and more wind farms in the future. ***We won't build*** any more nuclear power stations.
B: Yes, but **I think we'll build** them at sea. **I don't think we'll build** them inland.

1 energy	3 medicine	5 environment	7 social networking
2 transport	4 entertainment	6 robots	8 languages

2 With a partner, take turns to make instant decisions and promises. Use the prompts in brackets.

A: I'm afraid your flight's cancelled.
B: Don't worry, **I'll take** the train.
A: OK, **I'll meet** you at the station.

1 I'm afraid your flight's cancelled. (train) (meet you)
2 Sorry, we didn't receive your email. (send again) (reply asap)
3 I'm afraid the hotel is full. (bed and breakfast) (list of numbers)
4 I'm sorry, we don't accept cheques. (credit card) (get the machine)
5 Our train leaves in five minutes! (not have breakfast) (buy on train)
6 This is top secret information. (not tell anyone) (destroy original message)

be going to

3 You're going on a world tour. With a partner, take turns to ask and answer questions about your plans for each place.

A: What **are you going to** do in Paris?
B: **I'm going to** visit the Eiffel Tower, and then **I'm going to** walk along the Champs-Elysées!

1 Paris	3 Berlin	5 New York	7 Cairo
2 Rome	4 Moscow	6 Rio de Janeiro	8 London

4 With a partner, take turns to talk about your plans for the future. Also make some instant decisions about the same time periods.

A: What **are you going to** do after class?
B: **I'm going to** have a cup of tea. I'm thirsty! What about you?
A: I don't know. Perhaps **I'll have** some tea with you.

1 after class/work	3 tomorrow morning	5 Friday evening	7 next holidays
2 this evening	4 tomorrow afternoon	6 Saturday	8 next year

First conditional

5 Complete the contingency plans below with your own ideas.

1 If the new product is too expensive, …
   If the new product is too expensive, we'll reduce the price.
2 We'll increase the price if …
3 We'll invest in new machines if …
4 If customers don't pay their bills, …
5 If we need more capital, …
6 We won't borrow from the bank unless …

6 With a partner, take turns to negotiate these points. Use the prompts in brackets.

A: *I'd like a discount.*
B: *OK, I'll give you a 3% discount if you pay cash.*

B: *Can you give me free delivery?*
A: *I'm sorry. I can't give you free delivery unless your order is for over €2,000.*

1 I'd like a discount. (OK/3%/if/cash)
2 Can you give me free delivery? (No/unless/order/over €2,000)
3 I'd like delivery this week. (All right/Friday/if/order today)
4 Can you deliver before Friday? (No/unless/pay for express delivery)
5 I'd like a credit period. (OK/30 days/if/regular orders)
6 Can you give me 60 days' credit? (No/unless/pay full price)
7 I'd like you to change the colour. (OK/red or blue/if/give two weeks' notice)
8 Can you add my company logo? (No/unless/order/more than 500 pieces)

Listening

7 🔊 2:28 Listen to a conversation between a buyer and a seller and answer the questions.

1 When will the seller send a quotation?
2 Why can't she quote a price now?
3 When will they start work?
4 When will the buyer receive an invoice?
5 When will the buyer need to pay?
6 When will the buyer receive the machine?

Time expressions

8 Write five questions with *When* about plans and predictions for the future. With a partner, take turns to ask your questions. Answer with *when*, *until*, *as soon as*, *before* or *after*.

A: *When are you going to leave today?*
B: *I'm going to leave **as soon as we finish** the lesson.*

B: *When do you think you'll get a job?*
A: *I won't get a job **until I pass** my exams.*

Negotiation

9 With a partner, or in groups of four, negotiate an agreement to buy a new packaging machine. Try to score as many points as possible. Student(s) A: you are the buyer. Use the information below. Student(s) B: you are the seller. Look at page 118.

Buyer
No other suppliers can make this machine, but you want:
- a discount (*score one point for each % point you get*)
- the seller to pay for delivery and installation (*one point for each*)
- delivery in one week (*two points*) or two weeks (*one point*)
- to change the machine to your corporate colour and add your logo (*one point for each*)
- no 10% deposit with the order (*one point*), but full payment after delivery (*one point*)
- a two-year guarantee (*one point*)

7 | Business costs

7.4 Speaking Negotiating

Discussion

1 With a partner, match the negotiations 1–3 with the outcomes a–c. Which is the best, and why?

1 **A:** If you can't reduce your price, we'll find another supplier.
   B: OK, you win.
2 **A:** If you can't reduce your price, we'll find another supplier.
   B: OK.
   A: OK to reduce the price?
   B: No, OK to find another supplier.
3 **A:** If you can reduce your price, we'll place regular orders.
   B: OK. I'll reduce the price, as long as you pay cash.

☐ a) lose–lose
☐ b) win–lose
☐ c) win–win

2 Why are these 'rules' good advice for negotiators?

1 Never say 'no'.   2 Never say 'yes'.   3 Always say 'if'.

Listening

Glossary	PAGE 158
concession	
downtown	
limo	
pay rise	

3 🔊 2:29 Brandon and Kayla are organizing a start-up weekend for new students. Listen to their negotiation with the travel agent. What do they get and what do they give in return?

4 🔊 2:29 With a partner, find suitable words to complete the useful expressions for negotiating in the checklist. Then listen again and check.

Useful expressions: Negotiating

Asking for a concession

Could you _____ the price _____ a little?
Can you give us a _____?

Making a counter-offer

I'm afraid we can't give you 10% _____ you can find …
That's _____, as long as everything is paid …
We agree, _____ you organize a free drink …
We will … on condition that you …

Making an offer

If you can _____ thirty participants, we can give you …
Can we _____ on 10%?
What _____ 8% for forty participants?

Accepting an offer

OK, it's a _____.
We can _____ with that.

Refusing

I'm sorry but it's _____ not _____.
I'm afraid we can't _____ that.

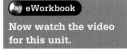

5 With a partner, take turns to make offers and counter-offers. Use the prompts below.

1 buy two/25% discount? (providing/cash)
A: *If I buy two, can you give me a 25% discount?*
B: *OK, I agree, providing you can pay cash.*
2 you pay for drinks today/I pay tomorrow. (as long as/bring my friend)
3 $150 per month rent/pay in advance. (on condition/clean kitchen/once a week)
4 confirm tomorrow/deliver this week? (afraid/unless/order today)
5 come to your house/drive me/work? (agree/but only if/pay for petrol)
6 I/salad/you/bring sandwiches? (you look after drinks)
7 I order now/30 days' credit? (afraid/regular orders)
8 I give choice of films/pay €11/person? (popcorn, ice-creams/included)

6 With a partner, take turns to roleplay short negotiations between an employee and a manager. Use the flow chart below.

1 Student A would like to leave work early today.
2 Student A wants a longer lunch break.
3 Student A wants to take holidays in September, the company's busiest time of the year.
4 Student A wants a pay rise.

Student A   **Student B**

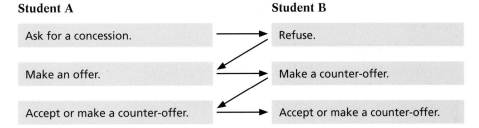

Student A	Student B
Ask for a concession.	Refuse.
Make an offer.	Make a counter-offer.
Accept or make a counter-offer.	Accept or make a counter-offer.

Roleplay

7 Work with a partner or in groups of four. Your class wants to go on a study trip to New York. Roleplay a negotiation with the travel agency. Then compare with another group. Who got the best deal? Student(s) A: use the information below. Student(s) B: use the information on page 119.

Student(s) A
You are organizing the study trip for your class. The budget is $1,300 per person. The class would like to stay as long as possible in New York. You will need plane tickets, transport between the airport and downtown, rooms and breakfast, tours and visits, etc. Negotiate with the travel agent to get the best value for money.

7.4 Speaking

7 | Business costs

7.5 Writing   Asking for payment

Roleplay

1 Business experts recommend telephoning customers to ask for payment before sending an email or letter. With a partner, read message A and roleplay the telephone conversation between Adriana Goldman and Mr Cable before Adriana sent the email.

Models

2 Read the messages and number them in order from first to last.

A ☐

Dear Mr Cable,
As discussed by telephone, our invoice number 56/4872 for $7,089 is overdue. Please find attached a copy of the invoice. Could you please send your payment as soon as possible?
Best wishes,
Adriana Goldman

D ☐

Dear Ms Goldman,
Please find enclosed a cheque for $7,089. I would like to apologize for the delay in payment. We have reorganized our accounts department, and I can assure you that all invoices will be paid on receipt in future.
I would be grateful if you could begin regular deliveries again as soon as possible.
Best regards,
Bryan Cable

B ☐

Dear Mr Cable,
Despite several requests for payment, the sum of $7,089 (our invoice number 56/4872) remains outstanding.
Please note that unless your account is paid within seven days, we will take legal action.
Yours sincerely,
Adriana Goldman

E ☐

Dear Mr Cable,
I am writing to remind you that the sum of $7,089 is still outstanding. Can you please settle this account immediately? If we do not receive payment within seven days, we will be obliged to suspend all deliveries.
Yours sincerely,
Adriana Goldman

C ☐

Dear Ms Goldman,
Unfortunately, my accountant is in hospital due to a skiing accident.
I will do my best to settle our account as soon as possible. I would appreciate your help in maintaining our regular deliveries.
Thank you for your cooperation.
Best regards, Bryan Cable

F ☐

Dear Ms Goldman,
Thank you for your reminder. My accountant will send you a cheque as soon as she returns from holiday.
Best regards,
Bryan Cable

Analysis

3 **With a partner, answer the questions.**

1 Why are messages B and D letters, not emails?
2 What happened after message F was sent?
3 What happened after message E was sent?
4 Why did Mr Cable enclose a cheque with message D?
5 Match Adriana's style in messages A, B and E with these adjectives.
☐ firm ☐ friendly ☐ threatening
6 Match Mr Cable's style in messages C, D and F with these adjectives.
☐ apologetic ☐ concerned ☐ unconcerned

Language focus

4 **Read the messages in Exercise 2 again and find two threats and three promises.**

5 **Complete the threats and promises. Use the correct form of the verbs in brackets.**

1 Unless you _____ our invoice within five days, we _____ legal action. (pay, take)
2 Our CFO _____ you a cheque as soon as he _____ from Canada. (send, return)
3 I _____ our account after the bank _____ our loan. (settle, confirm)
4 We _____ your order if we _____ your deposit within two weeks. (cancel, not receive)
5 I _____ you that we _____ all bills on time in future. (assure, pay)
6 We _____ new orders before you _____ all outstanding bills. (not accept, settle)
7 As long as you _____ the goods on time, we _____ happy to pay on receipt. (deliver, be)
8 We _____ obliged to suspend your account unless we _____ payment by the 31st. (be, receive)

6 **Put the requests in order from the most direct (1) to the most polite (5).**

I would appreciate your help in … ☐   I would be most grateful if you could … ☐
Please … ☐   Could you please …? ☐
Can you please …? ☐

Output

7 **Work with a partner or in groups of four. Write and reply to emails about a delivery problem. Student(s) A: use the information below. Student(s) B: turn to page 122.**

Student(s) A
1 You are the owner(s) of an e-business that sells photographic equipment to customers all over the world. Student B supplies the special packaging materials you need to protect your fragile equipment.
There are often mistakes in your orders from Student B: the wrong size, the wrong number, etc. Also, deliveries are often delayed. You know there are other suppliers who are better and cheaper. Write an email to Student B to complain about the service and ask for lower prices.
2 When you receive emails from Student B, write appropriate answers.

Glossary **PAGE 158**

outstanding
overdue
promise
reminder
suspend
threat

7 | Business costs

7.6 Case study   Doug's Mugs

Discussion

1 Imagine you are going to buy a company. Would you prefer to buy a profitable company for a high price, or a less profitable company for a low price? Why?

Reading

2 Read the blog and the income statement below. <u>Underline</u> the correct answers.

1 Next year will be the company's *third / fourth / fifth* year in business.
2 The company's products are designed by *Megan / Doug / temporary workers*.
3 The company's customers choose Doug's Mugs for their *low price / simple product / unique designs*.
4 The company's main problem is its *sales / cash flow / debt*.
5 This year, the company sold 40,000 mugs for *€3.00 / €3.50 / €4.00* each.
6 The production cost for each mug was *€0.80 / €1.00 / €1.20*.
7 Fixed costs are *increasing / stable / decreasing*.
8 This year, the company *made a net profit / broke even / made a net loss*.

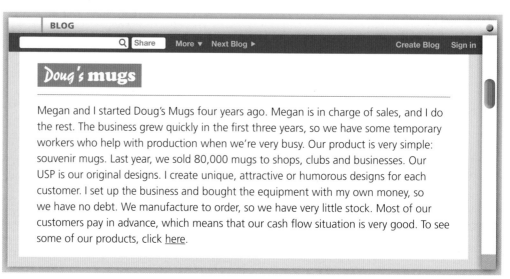

BLOG
Q Share   More ▼   Next Blog ►   Create Blog   Sign in

Doug's mugs

Megan and I started Doug's Mugs four years ago. Megan is in charge of sales, and I do the rest. The business grew quickly in the first three years, so we have some temporary workers who help with production when we're very busy. Our product is very simple: souvenir mugs. Last year, we sold 80,000 mugs to shops, clubs and businesses. Our USP is our original designs. I create unique, attractive or humorous designs for each customer. I set up the business and bought the equipment with my own money, so we have no debt. We manufacture to order, so we have very little stock. Most of our customers pay in advance, which means that our cash flow situation is very good. To see some of our products, click <u>here</u>.

INCOME STATEMENT	Last year	This year	Next year (forecast)
Sales revenue	280,000	140,000	a)
Cost of goods sold (variable costs)	80,000	40,000	b)
Gross profit/loss	200,000	100,000	c)
Selling, general & administrative expenses (overheads)	100,000	100,000	d)
Operating profit/loss	100,000	0	e)
Tax, depreciation, etc.	25,000	3,000	20,000
Net profit/loss after tax	75,000	(3,000)	f)

Listening

3 🔊 2:30 Doug is presenting the company's sales forecast for next year to his bank manager. Listen and answer the questions. Then complete a–f in the income statement.

1 Why were sales down this year?
2 Will overheads increase next year?
3 How much will customers pay per mug next year?
4 How many mugs does Doug think they can sell next year?

BLOG

Doug's mugs | Share | More ▾ | Next Blog ▶ | Create Blog | Sign in

Latest news – guess what? I've decided to emigrate to New Zealand! This spring, I met a wonderful Kiwi named Liz. Now she's back home in New Zealand, so I'm going out there and we're going to get married! I'm going to sell Doug's Mugs and find a new job in NZ. Megan will continue to work for the company, but she doesn't want to buy it. Some business students are going to help me to sell the company at a good price. I'll post more photos when I arrive in NZ.

Internet research

Search for the keywords *how to buy a business with no cash*. Compare different ways with a partner.

Reading

4 Read the latest news on Doug's blog and mark the statements *T* (true) or *F* (false).

1 Liz was born in New Zealand. ☐
2 Doug probably wasn't focusing on business this year. ☐
3 Doug and Megan are going to get married in New Zealand. ☐
4 Doug is going to continue to work for Doug's Mugs. ☐
5 Megan doesn't want to work for the company any more. ☐

Negotiation

5 Work in small groups. You are going to negotiate to sell or buy Doug's Mugs. Sellers: look at page 119. Buyers: look at page 123. Follow the procedure below.

1 Read your message and prepare your strategy for the negotiation.
2 Meet to negotiate the sale of Doug's Mugs. Use the agenda below. Write down the terms and conditions you agree, and all sign the document.
3 Compare your document with other groups. Which group got the best deal?

Glossary PAGE 159

depreciation
emigrate
Kiwi
solicitor

Doug's mugs

points for negotiation

1 Price
2 Finance
3 Stock of 10,000 mugs
4 Megan Smith's commission on sales

8 | Global trade

▶ pros and cons of franchising

▶ key issues in franchising

8.1 About business International franchising

Vocabulary

1 Read about franchising. <u>Underline</u> the correct words in the sentences below.

> Well-known brands like SUBWAY, McDonald's® and Pizza Hut have developed their business internationally by **franchising** – selling the right to use their business model to other businesses, or **franchisees**. The franchisee can use the brand and products in a specific location and for a limited time. In return, the **franchiser** receives a percentage of the **outlet's** sales revenue.

1 A person who pays for the right to open a new Pizza Hut restaurant is a *franchise / franchiser / franchisee*.
2 The new restaurant is a Pizza Hut *brand / outlet / model*.
3 The *franchisee / franchiser / restaurant* owns the Pizza Hut brand.

Discussion

2 Work with a partner. What are the advantages and disadvantages of franchising for a) the franchiser and b) the franchisee? Think about the points in the box.

> advertising   control   culture   growth   image   investment   language   profit   risk

Skim reading

3 Quickly read the article opposite. Tick (✓) the countries that offer good opportunities for international franchises.

☐ Australia   ☐ Brazil   ☐ Canada   ☐ China   ☐ France   ☐ India   ☐ Indonesia
☐ Japan   ☐ Mexico   ☐ Russia   ☐ Turkey   ☐ UK   ☐ USA

Reading for detail

4 Read the article again and answer the questions.

1 What is special about the BRICs?
2 What is changing in international franchising?
3 Why is franchising an exciting opportunity in emerging markets? Give four reasons.
4 Why isn't it enough to *'put up a Dunkin' Donuts sign and wait for customers'*?
5 Which issues do these examples illustrate?
   a) A US franchise was surprised that a local law allowed Moscow franchisees to ignore its prices.
   b) A French restaurant franchise in Argentina had no red wine left to sell to customers.
   c) Customers at a fashion boutique in Indonesia were upset by photos of models in bikinis.
   d) A franchise in Mexico did not translate its website into Spanish.
6 What justifies the extra effort of investing in Indonesia rather than in Europe?

Glossary   PAGE 159

BRIC
diversity
emerging market
GDP
outlet
penetrate
player
reward

Listening

5 🔊 2:31–2:33 Listen to three stories about international franchises. Identify the problem and the solution in each.

Discussion

6 In small groups, discuss the questions. Then present your ideas to another group.

1 Imagine you want to invest in franchises in BRIC countries. Brainstorm a list of possible franchise businesses.
2 Choose one franchise that you think will be successful in each BRIC country.
3 Agree on the changes you need to make in order to adapt the franchise to local conditions.

Internet research

Search for the keywords *top 100 franchises*. Choose a franchise to open in your city. Tell a partner why it will be a success.

FRANCHISING

a golden opportunity for developing countries

THE FUTURE IS GLOBAL

80% of the world's population lives in developing countries, like the BRICs – Brazil, Russia, India and China. Today, these emerging markets only produce
5 25% of world GDP but, by 2050, the BRICs will be in the top six economies in the world. A significant part of their future economic growth will come from franchising. Until quite recently, only a few major franchises like SUBWAY, McDonald's® and Pizza Hut
10 were truly international. Today, however, one third of America's top franchise outlets are outside the USA. Franchises from the UK, Australia, Canada, France, Spain and Germany are also beginning to go global.

WHY FRANCHISING?

15 Why is international franchising such an exciting opportunity for local entrepreneurs in emerging markets? First of all, because in countries like India, with a new middle class of 300 million people, the door is wide open. For the moment, franchisers have not
20 penetrated these new markets: in China, franchising represents only 3% of all commercial activity. Secondly, the business model is perfect for markets where local entrepreneurs have limited skills and experience: following a successful franchise's manual is the ideal
25 way to learn on-the-job. Thirdly, because franchisers can limit risk by helping new businesses avoid the mistakes that independent start-ups would make. Finally, with their franchise's marketing and financial influence, local outlets can grow more quickly than an unknown brand.

KEY ISSUES FOR INTERNATIONAL FRANCHISES

30 Of course, franchises can't just put up a Dunkin' Donuts sign and wait for customers to give them their cash. Being a top brand does not guarantee success. A number of issues require careful attention. The first
35 is language. Even if consumers speak English, it's a mistake to think they will want to shop in a foreign language. In surveys, 72% said they are more likely to buy a product in their own language; 56% said language is more important than price. Supply chain is another
40 issue, especially when the product is manufactured and sold in different hemispheres. Local legislation and the social, political and business environment can also be very different from the franchiser's domestic market. Finally, there is the issue of cultural sensitivity: local
45 entrepreneurs and global franchisers need to understand diversity in attitudes, beliefs and values.

RETURN ON INVESTMENT

The issues may be complex, but the major players have already shown that there are solutions. Economists
50 agree that future growth will come from the BRICs and other emerging markets like Mexico, Indonesia and Turkey rather than from the USA, Western Europe or Japan. It is clear that, for both franchisers and franchisees, the potential rewards are enormous, and
55 easily justify the extra effort and investment.

...one third of America's top franchise outlets are outside the USA.

8 | Global trade

8.2 Vocabulary Franchising and project management

Discussion

1 Do the quiz and circle your answers. Then look at the analysis on page 121. Compare your results with a partner.

Independent entrepreneur, franchiser or franchisee?
What's your profile?

		Yes	No	It depends
1	Do you like taking risks?	A	C	B
2	Are you a natural leader?	B	C	A
3	Are you happy to follow orders?	C	A	B
4	Are you creative?	A	C	B
5	Do you like solving problems without help?	A	C	B
6	Are you good at planning long-term strategies?	B	C	A

Collocations

2 With a partner, put the collocations in a logical order, from first to last.

- ☐ buy a franchise
- ☐ follow a manual
- ☐ open an outlet
- ☐ train staff
- ☐ follow training
- ☐ hire staff
- ☐ order stock
- ☐ find premises
- ☐ obtain a loan
- ☐ sign an agreement

Reading

3 Read the article about financing a franchise. How many kinds of payment or investment are mentioned?

> **INTERNET**
> NEWS • COMMENT • BUSINESS • **MONEY** • SPORT • TRAVEL • LIFESTYLE • ARTS
>
> SEARCH
>
> ## Financing a franchise
>
> A local entrepreneur who wants to open an international franchise needs to **raise capital** in order to **register a company** and pay the **franchise fee**. This payment covers the right to use the **brand name** and the **business model** for a specified number of years. Franchise fees often cover training too, but not the premises, equipment or furniture: franchisees have to **make** these **investments** themselves. The franchisee may also have to buy stock from the franchiser. If not, franchisees can **source suppliers** themselves. After the business is open, there is a monthly **management fee** to pay. Some franchisers charge a fixed sum; others require franchisees to pay a percentage of the sales revenue, usually between 2 and 10%.

Internet research

Search for the keywords *project management basics*. What are the key elements in project management? Compare with a partner.

4 Match the collocations in **bold** in the article above with these definitions.

1. a charge for services such as accounting, marketing, R&D, etc. _____
2. a payment for the use of a company's name and methods _____
3. a procedure for making money _____
4. the name a company chooses for its product or service _____
5. to follow the official process of creating a new business _____
6. to identify providers of products and services _____
7. to obtain money for an investment _____
8. to spend money and expect a return _____

5 Look at the chart and the examples. Then answer the questions.

1 Which project is behind schedule but on budget?
2 Which project has met the deadline and stayed within budget?
3 Which project is under budget but behind schedule?
4 Which project has missed the deadline and exceeded its budget?
5 Which project is under budget and ahead of schedule?
6 Which project has exceeded the budget but is on schedule?

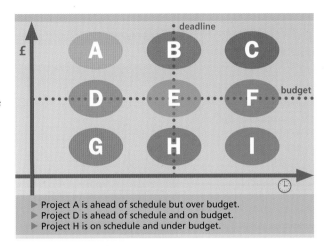

▶ Project A is ahead of schedule but over budget.
▶ Project D is ahead of schedule and on budget.
▶ Project H is on schedule and under budget.

6 Look at the table below. Write an update on each project using the words in brackets.

1 *Project J has exceeded the budget but is ahead of schedule.* (exceed)
2 *Project K* _____ (miss)
3 _____ (ahead)
4 _____ (exceed)
5 _____ (meet)
6 _____ (stay)
7 _____ (on)
8 _____ (meet)

budget = $100K deadline = 10 weeks	J	K	L	M	N	O	P	Q
cost	$120K	$100K	$80K	$130K	$90K	$100K	$110K	$100K
time	9 weeks	12 weeks	8 weeks	11 weeks	10 weeks	9 weeks	10 weeks	10 weeks

Listening

7 2:34–2:36 Listen to three project updates and complete the table.

Project	1	2	3
Objective			
Current status	half of the $200,000, a little behind schedule, on budget		
Problems		spending too much on plane tickets	
Solutions			don't know what the solution is
Completion date			

Speaking

8 Think about a real or imaginary project you are involved in. Make notes about your objective, current status, problems, solutions and completion date. With a partner, take turns to interview each other about your projects.

Glossary PAGE 159

completion
profile
recruit
status

8 | Global trade

▶ present perfect

▶ *since* and *for*

8.3 Grammar Present perfect

just

1 With a partner, take turns to ask and answer questions about the people in the photos. Use the past participles in the box.

> crashed got graduated opened signed won

A: *What have they just done?*
B: *They've just graduated.*

2 With a partner, take turns to ask and answer questions about what these people or organizations *have just* or *recently done*.

A: *What has our teacher just asked us?*
B: *She's just asked us to do this exercise.*

1 your teacher
2 your best friend
3 a TV celebrity
4 a famous sports team
5 a local business
6 a famous company
7 your president or prime minister
8 your school, university or place of work

Have you ever ...? and *never*

3 In groups of three, take turns to ask and answer questions with *Have you ever ...?* Use the prompts below. Continue each conversation as long as you can.

A: *Have you ever eaten frogs' legs?*
B: *No, I haven't. But I've eaten snails. Have you ever eaten snails?*
C: *Yes, I have. I've eaten snails three times. I ate them once in France and twice in Italy. But I've never eaten ants' eggs. Have you ever ...?*

1 eat   3 go to   5 work in   7 break
2 drink   4 see   6 drive   8 forget to

just, yet, already

4 In groups, take turns to ask and answer questions about what you *have* or *haven't done* today.

A: *Have you listened to the radio today?*
B: *Yes, I've already listened to the news. Have you listened to the radio yet?*
C: *No, not yet. But I've already watched the news on TV.*

1 radio   3 newspaper   5 tweet/blog   7 sport
2 eat   4 email   6 coffee/tea   8 work

since and for

5 Match the pairs of expressions with similar meanings.

1 since the year before last
2 for about a week
3 since the nineties
4 for as long as I can remember

a) for about twenty years
b) since I was a little kid
c) since last Wednesday
d) for about two years

How long ...?

6 With a partner, take turns to ask and answer questions with *How long ...?*

A: How long have you lived here?
B: I've lived here since September. What about you?
A: Oh, I've lived here for about three years.

1 live here
2 know your best friend
3 study English
4 be in this school/university/company
5 have your car/motorbike/bicycle
6 be awake today
7 like football/dancing/...
8 have your phone/PC/...

Listening

7 🔊 2:37 Listen to a presentation of a franchise opportunity. What kind of business is it? Where do they want to open new franchises?

8 🔊 2:37 Complete the extracts from the presentation. Then listen again and check.

1 _____ wanted to develop your people skills?
2 _____ 2004, we _____ thousands of people ...
3 We _____ in the US and the UK _____ nearly ten years.
4 We _____ franchises in five countries in Europe.
5 We _____ three new offices in South America, too.

9 With a partner, update the report on a franchise project in Mexico. Ask and answer questions to complete the report. Student A: look at the information below. Student B: look at page 120.

1 *Have they signed the franchising agreement? Have they had any problems with the agreement?*

Glossary   **PAGE 159**

frogs' legs
people skills
premises
snail

	STEP	DONE?	PROBLEMS
	PROGRESS REPORT, 1 JUNE		
1	sign franchising agreement	?	?
2	find premises	no	visit/16 buildings/since March!
3	obtain phone number	?	?
4	obtain bank loan	no	no news/six weeks
5	order stock	?	?
6	plan advertising campaign	yes, in February	but quotation was only valid for three months/price increase?
7	print flyers	?	?
8	do training	no	reserve/in March/but not pay
9	interview administrative staff	?	?
10	arrange opening event	yes	not fix/date

- expressions for handling questions
- presenting a project schedule using a Gantt chart

8.4 Speaking   Giving updates and handling questions

Discussion

1 In small groups, discuss the questions.

1 In your country, what is your attitude to time? Do you plan things carefully and do things step by step? Are your schedules flexible? Do you work on lots of projects at the same time?
2 What is your personal attitude to time? Would you like to have a different attitude to time?

2 Charlie is a franchisee. He already has four restaurants in Paris. Now he is preparing to open two outlets in Moscow. Look at the Gantt chart. Do you think Charlie has planned well? Why? Why not?

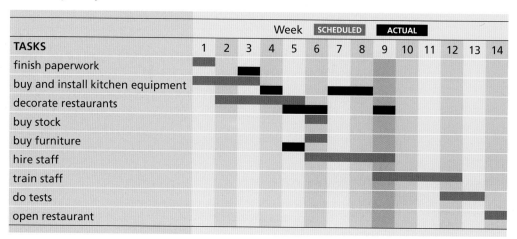

TASKS	Week SCHEDULED / ACTUAL — 1 2 3 4 5 6 7 8 9 10 11 12 13 14
finish paperwork	
buy and install kitchen equipment	
decorate restaurants	
buy stock	
buy furniture	
hire staff	
train staff	
do tests	
open restaurant	

Listening

3 🔊 2:38 Charlie is presenting a progress report to the franchisers. Listen and choose the correct answers.

1 The project is a) ahead of schedule b) on schedule c) behind schedule.
2 They bought the furniture in Week 5 to save a) time b) money c) space.
3 The restaurants will be finished in Week a) 8 b) 9 c) 10.
4 Charlie plans to use an agency to a) save money b) train staff c) go more quickly.
5 Charlie's attitude to the future schedule is a) optimistic b) reserved c) pessimistic.

4 🔊 2:39 Listen to Charlie handling questions from the franchisers and mark the statements *T* (true) or *F* (false).

1 Charlie didn't hear the first question clearly. ☐
2 Charlie has already explained that they bought the furniture in Week 5. ☐
3 At the moment they are hiring staff. ☐
4 They intend to buy stock in Week 10. ☐
5 Charlie isn't going to talk about advertising. ☐
6 The project has cost less than planned. ☐

5 🔊 2:39 With a partner, find suitable words to complete the useful expressions for handling questions in the checklist. Then listen again and check.

Useful expressions: Handling questions

Asking for clarification

Sorry, I didn't _____ that.
I'm sorry, I don't quite _____ you.

Answering questions

As I _____ earlier, …
Does that _____ your question?
_____, we've planned a very exciting campaign.

Thanking the questioner

That's a very good _____.
I'm _____ you asked me that.

Not answering questions

Can I _____ to that in a moment?
I'm afraid I can't _____ into detail right now.

Giving an update

6 With a partner, take turns to ask and answer questions about a personal project (e.g. planning a holiday, decorating a room, building a website, etc.). Use expressions from the checklist and the points below.

- why your project is on schedule, ahead of schedule or behind schedule
- when you started the project
- what you have already done
- what you haven't done yet
- any problems and consequences
- how you are going to solve any problems
- when you think you will finish

Presentation

7 With a partner, choose an example of an international business project (e.g. starting an online business, importing goods from another country, opening a franchise in your city, etc.). Follow the instructions below.

1 Brainstorm the different tasks in your project.
2 Schedule your tasks in a logical order. Fill in the Gantt chart (in red).
3 Decide which tasks you have already completed. Fill in the Gantt chart (in black).
4 Present your chart to another group and answer their questions.

	Day/Week/Month	SCHEDULED	ACTUAL
TASKS			

8 Global trade

8.5 Writing Progress reports

Punctuation

1 Match the punctuation marks in the box with their names 1–9 and functions a–i.

.   ,   :   ;   ?   !   –   ( )   '___'

1 brackets
2 colon
3 dash
4 exclamation mark
5 full stop
6 comma
7 question mark
8 quotation marks
9 semi-colon

a) indicates a question
b) indicates strong words or feelings
c) indicate a person's exact words
d) separates sentences
e) separates independent clauses
f) directs you to information that follows, e.g. a list
g) separates grammatically related parts of a sentence
h) indicates extra information or explanation
i) indicates a break in the structure of a sentence

Model

2 Helen Osman is recruiting entrepreneurs to open her franchise's gyms in Brazil. Read her progress report and answer the questions.

1 What progress has Helen made?
2 What problems has she met?
3 What does she plan to do?
4 Will she meet her objectives?

✉ ⬇ INBOX | REPLY ◀ | FORWARD ➡

To: George Mustakis
From: Helen Osman
Subject: Franchisees for Brazil
Date: 9 September

This is a progress report on our search for new franchisees for Medallist Gyms in Brazil. The project goal is to recruit ten new franchisees in Brazil's five largest cities. At the end of July, I reported that we had twenty possible candidates to interview.

During August, we interviewed all twenty candidates. Seven were unsuitable; in addition, five others have decided not to continue. We therefore have a final list of eight potential franchisees.

Consequently, we now have the problem of finding two more candidates. Moreover, we need two or three backup candidates, since there is a risk that some franchisees will not raise the $350,000 start-up capital.

As time is short, I have already started the search. We intend to hold interviews at the end of September.

Even though we have not yet found all ten candidates, we will start training the first eight on schedule. We expect to open eight gyms on 1st December, also on schedule; we hope the last two gyms will open by 1st January. However, we expect to be approximately $5,000 over budget on this project.

Analysis

3 Read the report again. Number the sections in the order they appear.

☐ problems ☐ background ☐ conclusion ☐ action plan ☐ progress

4 Which information is not included in the background section?

description of project   project budget   project objectives   status in last report

Language focus

5 <u>Underline</u> these linking words in the report. Then write them in the correct category in the table below.

as   consequently   even though   however   ~~in addition~~   moreover   since   therefore

adding information	contrasting	giving reasons	introducing consequences
in addition	*but* *although*		

6 Write these sentences in a different way. Replace the words in **bold** with the word in brackets. Change the punctuation as necessary.

1 We have sourced a supplier, **but** we have not yet agreed a price. (although)
   Although we have sourced a supplier, we have not yet agreed a price.
2 There is very little competition. We **therefore** believe the company will grow quickly. (since)
3 **As** salaries are low, our margins will be larger than in Europe. (consequently)
4 **Even though** our transport costs will increase, the product will still be profitable. (however)
5 Sometimes products are damaged during shipping **and another problem is** they are often delayed at customs. (moreover)
6 Some franchisees can't raise enough capital **and that means** we need to find backup candidates. (therefore)
7 Some candidates didn't know much about sport **and that's why** they decided not to continue. (as)
8 They made appointments **but** two people didn't come to the interview. (although)

Output

7 You work for a chain of garden centres. You are visiting suppliers in Indonesia. Use the notes below (they are not in the correct order) to write a short progress report to your boss, Martine Harris. Invent any other details you need.

plan: invited Mr Bima to visit us in Europe; make better offer than our competitor; include bonuses

objective: source two excellent suppliers (focus on quality)

completion: probably behind schedule (quality is more important than speed); a little over budget

since January: visited five suppliers; identified best two; two are unsuitable; one is already bankrupt!; have found one other possible supplier

last report, January: short list of six suppliers to visit, sustainable forests, quality products, good prices

project: import hardwood garden furniture from S. E. Asia to Europe

problem: best supplier (Mr Bima) already supplying our biggest competitor; we need him to work only for us; we will probably buy 70% of his production

8 Exchange reports with a partner. Read your partner's report and discuss what you like about the report. Explain what you think can be improved. Give reasons.

8.6 Case study   An international opportunity

Discussion

1 **With a partner, imagine you are going to buy a franchise. Decide which profiles you prefer. Give reasons.**

1   a famous brand, or a new name with a big future?
2   a focus on making money, or a focus on quality of life?
3   managing a single outlet, or building an empire?
4   high risk and high return on investment (ROI), or low risk and moderate ROI?
5   a strict manual and rules, or room for creativity?
6   a large investment and quick growth, or a small investment and slower growth?

Reading

2 **Read about three franchise opportunities. Complete the table opposite.**

INTERNET

SEARCH

HOME | NEWS | JOBS | **FRANCHISE OPPORTUNITIES** | CAREERS | CONTACT

FAIR DO'S HAIRDOS

Fair do's hairdos is a new concept in hair care: we offer quick, sensible haircuts at a reasonable price. 80% of men's and children's haircuts are simple and easy to do, so why pay more? More and more women are also happy to do without expensive extras. From our head office in Cape Town, South Africa, in just three years we have already opened over 100 franchises around the world. Although the market is very competitive, there are good opportunities for growth. Like our service, our franchise is also fair and reasonable; the investment required is less than $50,000. Our franchise fee is just $20,000 and includes two weeks' training in South Africa.

THE MOUNTIE SANDWICH SHOP

The original Mountie Sandwich Shop opened in Toronto in 1949. Since then, we have opened over 400 franchises in 23 countries. The famous Mountie Special has become an iconic sandwich, recognized around the world for its amazing flavour and value. Everybody loves the Mountie Special! You only need $80,000 to open your own Mountie Sandwich Shop; the franchise fee of $10,000 is your guarantee that a Mountie consultant will be there to help you all the way. On average, our franchisees can open a new Mountie Sandwich Shop every six months with the profits from their first outlet – don't miss this excellent opportunity for growth and return on investment!

TWEEN 'N' DREAM

Every parent wants their little girl to know she's special: since our first store for 8- to 14-year-old girls opened in 2005 in Los Angeles, Tween 'n' Dream has made millions of pre-teen girls feel like princesses, pop idols or movie stars. For short shopping trips with Mom, or birthday parties and special occasions with friends, our exciting range of clothes, accessories, perfumes, make-up, music and souvenirs make every visit a special event. Almost fifty franchisees have already chosen one of the fastest-growing businesses in the USA. If you have $120,000 to invest, contact us today. Franchise fees from only $30,000.

	Fair do's hairdos	Mountie Sandwich Shop	Tween 'n' Dream
Type of business			
Customer profile			
Franchise fee			
Investment required			
Number of franchises			
Growth potential			
Other			

Discussion

3 With a partner, discuss your opinions.

1 Which franchise offers the best opportunities for growth?
2 Which franchise has the biggest risk?
3 Which franchise is the safest investment?
4 Which franchise would you prefer to invest in?

Listening

4 2:40–2:42 Listen to three franchisees talking about their experiences of these franchises. How do they feel about their choice?

5 2:40–2:42 Listen again and answer the questions.

1 Which franchise offers the best quality of life for franchisees?
2 Which franchise offers the most room for creativity?
3 Which franchise offers the best return on investment?
4 Which franchise would you prefer to invest in now? Have you changed your opinion?

Roleplay

6 With a partner, choose one of the three franchises. Student A: you are the franchiser. Student B: you are a potential franchisee. Roleplay a meeting to decide if you can work together. Follow the instructions below.

1 Prepare for the meeting. Student A: look at page 114. Student B: look at page 118.
2 Hold the meeting. Use the agenda below.
3 Tell the class what you agreed, or why you did not agree.

Internet research

Search for the keywords *how to choose a franchise*. Make a list of do's and don'ts. Compare with a partner.

Glossary PAGE 159

Mountie
pre-teen
ROI
tween

AGENDA

1 Short presentation of the franchise, Student A
2 Questions and answers
3 Short presentation of the project, Student B
4 Questions and answers
5 Decision – to work together to open the franchise, or not

8.6 Case study

Review 7

Business costs

1 Make sentences 1–6 more business-like using the phrases in the box.

> a fall in sales   an increase in revenue
> forecast sales revenues   fixed costs
> income can go down   sales are down 50%

1 We can easily predict the amount of money coming into the company from the sales of our products.
We can easily _____.
2 Last quarter, the number of products we sold went down.
Last quarter, there was _____.
3 In the first quarter, the money we got from sales went up.
In the first quarter, there was _____.
4 The money a family gets from salaries can decrease.
Family _____.
5 We are only selling half the number of products that we did before.
Our _____.
6 We need to analyse the part of our spending which doesn't change much from month to month.
We need to analyse our _____.

2 Fill in the missing letters to complete these financial definitions.

1 The money that comes into a business from the sale of its products is called 'revenues' or 'tu____er'.
2 In finance, the word 'net' means *with things taken away*. The word 'gr___' means *with nothing taken away*.
3 To talk about profit as a percentage (%), you can use the word 'm____n'.
4 It's good to make a profit; it's bad to make a l___ .
5 The level of business activity at which a company is making neither a profit nor a loss is called the 'br_____n p___t'.
6 Another word for 'costs' is 'exp____s'.
7 Money spent regularly on rent, insurance, electricity and other things needed for a business to operate are called 'ov_____s'.
8 The various amounts that a company pays (from its profit) to the government are called 't___s'.

3 Unscramble the words in brackets to complete the profit and loss account.

	(1) _____ (Tovrunre)	1,000
minus	(2) _____ (Ctso fo odogs olsd)	- 400
equals	(3) _____ (Gossr pofrti)	= 600
minus	(4) _____ (Oatrepgni epsensxe)	- 200
equals	(5) _____ (Otperniga pitrof)	= 400
minus	(6) _____ (Txsea)	- 150
equals	(7) _____ (Nte imcoen)	= 250

4 Mark the statements about credit control *T* (true) or *F* (false).

1 An *invoice* is a request for money from a supplier to a customer. It is also called a 'bill'. ☐
2 The *outstanding balance* is the amount of money you have already paid to a supplier. ☐
3 If a payment to a supplier is *overdue*, it is late and has still not been made. ☐
4 If you *settle in full*, you agree to pay some of the money now and some later. ☐
5 If a contract says that the supplier can *charge interest* on any money still not paid, it means that they can go to court to get the money. ☐
6 In the phrase *terms and conditions,* 'terms' refers to how and when you will pay. ☐

5 Underline *will* or *be going to* to complete the grammar rules. Then use the rules to complete the sentences. Use contractions.

1 *will / be going to* is more common for general predictions.
We _____ probably have to increase our prices next year.
2 *will / be going to* is more common for predictions with strong evidence in the present.
Quick! Catch it! It _____ fall!
3 *will / be going to* is used for instant decisions (made at the moment of speaking).
I _____ have the roast chicken, please.
4 *will / be going to* is used for plans and decisions already made.
We _____ open a new production facility in Turkey next year.
5 *will / be going to* is used for promises.
I _____ confirm the details by email.

6 Complete the negotiation between Kayla and a travel agent with the words in the box.

> afraid   as long as   bring   deal   discount   guarantee
> live   unless

K: The start-up programme for new students is looking good, but could you (1) _____ the price down a little?
TA: I'm sorry, but it's just not possible.
K: What about the train tickets? Can you give us a (2) _____?
TA: OK. If you can (3) _____ 50 participants, we can give you 5% on the train tickets.
K: I'm (4) _____ we can't accept that. We're students, remember. Can we agree on 10%?
TA: I'm afraid we can't give you 10% (5) _____ you can find 50 participants.
K: I don't think we'll find that many. What about 8% for 40 participants?
TA: That's acceptable, (6) _____ everything is paid two weeks before the trip.
K: OK, it's a (7) _____, providing that you organize a free drink when we arrive at the hotel.
TA: All right. We can (8) _____ with that.

Review 8

Global trade

1 Read the sentences about international franchising. Correct the mistake in each two-word collocation in *italics*.

1 Countries such as Brazil, Russia, India and China are called *develop countries*.
2 Today, *emerging marketings* like the BRICs only produce 25% of world GDP, but, by 2050, this figure will be much higher.
3 A significant part of the BRICs' future *economic growing* will come from franchising.
4 One third of America's top *franchise outputs* are outside the USA.
5 The franchise business model is perfect for markets where *local entrepreneurials* have limited skills and experience.
6 Franchisers can limit risk by helping new businesses avoid the mistakes of an *independent stop-up*.

2 Complete the sentences about franchising with the pairs of verbs in the box.

> buy/source   hire/train   open/find   raise/register
> sign/obtain

1 A franchisee needs to _____ capital in order to _____ the company and pay the franchise fee.
2 After you _____ the agreement, the next step is to _____ a loan from the bank.
3 Before you can _____ your outlet, you have to _____ suitable premises.
4 After finding premises, you need to _____ staff and _____ them.
5 Most franchisees _____ stock from the franchiser, otherwise they have to _____ suppliers themselves.

3 Complete the sentences with the phrases in the box.

> ahead of schedule   behind schedule
> exceeded the budget   met the deadline
> missed the deadline   on budget   on schedule
> under budget

1 The project is going very slowly. It is _____.
2 The project is going very quickly. It is _____.
3 The project is following the time plan closely. It is _____.
4 The project finished late. It _____.
5 The project finished on time. It _____.
6 The project is following the spending plan closely. It is _____.
7 The project is costing less than we thought. It is _____.
8 The project is finished and it cost more than planned. We _____.

4 It is common to ask a question in the present perfect and reply in the past simple about a specific time. Use this pattern to complete the sentences.

1 **A:** How many customers _____ (you/serve) today?
   B: Well, this morning, we _____ (have) over 200 people in the shop.

2 **A:** _____ (you/ever/visit) Germany?
   B: Yes, I _____ (be) in Frankfurt earlier this year for a trade show.
3 **A:** _____ (you/finish) yet?
   B: Yes, of course. I _____ (finish) ages ago.
4 **A:** Your face looks familiar. _____ (we/meet) somewhere before?
   B: Yes, I think we _____ (meet) at the Pharma Expo last year.

5 Underline the correct time expression in *italics*. Use the verb form in **bold** to help you.

1 a) *Last year / This year* we **made** a profit of €4 million.
   b) *Last year / This year* we've **made** a bigger profit – close to €6 million.
2 a) *A few months ago / So far this month* we've **had** 15,000 hits on our website.
   b) *A few months ago / So far this year* we only **had** an average of 8,000 hits per month.
3 a) I've **worked** on this project *since it started / in the early stages*, and I'm sure it's going to be a success.
   b) I **worked** on that project *since it started / in the early stages*, but I don't work on it now.

6 Match the beginnings and endings of the expressions for handling questions.

1 Actually, we've   a) good question.
2 Can I come to that   b) follow you.
3 I'm sorry, I don't   c) earlier, ... (*+ more information*)
4 I'm afraid I can't go   d) planned ... (*+ more information*)
5 As I mentioned   e) in a moment?
6 I'm glad you asked   f) didn't catch that.
7 Sorry, I   g) me that.
8 That's a very   h) into detail right now.

7 Match the expressions in Exercise 6 with these uses.

a) asking for clarification   ☐ ☐
b) thanking the questioner   ☐ ☐
c) answering the question   ☐ ☐
d) not answering the question ☐ ☐

8 Match linking words 1–4 with two other words that have the same meaning.

1 and   since   although
2 but   consequently   moreover
3 so   however   as
4 because   in addition   therefore

9 Complete each sentence with a word from column 3 in Exercise 8.

1 The project is going well. It's on budget and, _____, it's ahead of schedule.
2 The project is on budget, ahead of schedule and the quality of work is high. _____, I want to congratulate all members of the team.
3 _____ there have been so many problems with our subcontractors, the project is now behind schedule.
4 _____ there have been a lot of problems with our subcontractors, I'm pleased to say that the project is still on schedule.

Additional material

1.3 Grammar **Present simple**
Questionnaire (page 15, Exercise 9)

Write four more questions in the questionnaire. Then interview your classmates.

A: *How often do you travel abroad?*
B: *I don't travel very often. Maybe once every two years.*
A: *And when do you travel?*
B: *Usually in the summer. Or I sometimes go abroad at Christmas.*

	How often do you ...?						When do you ...?
	never	not often	sometimes	often	always	once a week/year once every ...	in ... on ... at ...
1 travel abroad?							
2 watch TV in English?							
3 read a newspaper in English?							
4 play video games in English?							
5							
6							
7							
8							

8.6 Case study **An international opportunity**
Roleplay (page 111, Exercise 6)

Student A
Prepare for the meeting with Student B. You will need to:
1 Give a short presentation of the franchise. Invent any extra information you need.
2 Answer Student B's questions.
3 Listen to Student B's presentation of his/her project.
4 Interview Student B to decide if he/she is a good candidate to be a franchisee. Ask questions to get additional information. You are looking for someone with:
   • the motivation to make money
   • some experience in this type of business
   • excellent local knowledge
   • good basic business skills
   • new ideas to develop the business
   • enough money to invest in the business and pay the franchise fee
5 Decide if you want to work together to open the franchise, or not.

2.4 Speaking **Telephoning**
Telephone conversations (page 29, Exercise 9)

Student B

Conversation 1: You are the customer. You are Ms Ashley Mertens' personal assistant. You receive a call from a supplier. Ms Mertens is travelling a lot this week: Monday: Prague, Tuesday: Berlin, Wednesday: Rome, Thursday: Kiev, Friday: Brussels. You start by answering the phone.

Conversation 2: You are the supplier. You work for Multiwheel. You are returning a call from Jo Parker, one of your regular customers who is having problems with your machines. Arrange a date to visit. Student A starts by answering the phone.

3.1 About business **Supply chain management**
Agenda (page 36, Exercise 6)

In small groups, roleplay a meeting at Lasseter. Discuss the three points on the agenda. Take decisions.

LASSETER LTD

AGENDA

1 Packaging costs: For decision: continue working with Packobox, or buy cheaper packaging and boxes from foreign suppliers in China or India?

2 Raw materials: For decision: continue buying 100% from Polyplasto, or reduce to 70% and buy 30% from a second supplier?

3 Deliveries: For decision: share more information to help our supplier, or avoid the risk of giving information to competitors?

2.5 Writing **Formal letters and emails**
Formal emails (page 31, Exercise 7)

Student B

1 You are the manager of a company that manufactures fuel economy systems for trucks and buses. Student A has a bus company and is one of your customers. Most of your employees come to work by bus, but, at the moment, the buses are running late – 15 minutes on average. Your employees are arriving late and you are losing production time. Write a formal email to Student A to complain.

2 You receive a formal email from Student A. Write a reply.

2.6 Case study **Rock tour**
Discussion (page 33, Exercise 6)

Student B

You are Einstein's tour manager. Read your agenda and the ideas given. Prepare what you want to say to Hoffmann Records in the telephone meeting.

---

1 Reactions to email from Hoffmann Records about the damage to the hotels.
(problems caused by two sound technicians – difficult to replace them)

2 Reactions to your email about venues.
(Ask Hoffmann to write a letter to Scott Nelson with free tickets, and to contact venues to ask about removing some seats.)

3 Too many concerts on tour (55) so group and roadies very tired. Ask Hoffmann to cancel some dates.
(contract = 50 concerts)

4 Band want to travel by plane – too long by bus. No time to write new songs.

5 Any other business

3.3 Grammar **Prepositions and present simple passive**
Prepositions of place (page 40, Exercise 2)

Student B: look at the picture. Take turns to ask and answer questions to find the differences and complete your drawings.

B: *Can you see a box of footballs?*
A: *No, I can't. Where are they?*
B: *They're on the rack, below the sports shirts.*

6.4 Speaking **Meetings**
Roleplay (page 81, Exercise 7)

Student B
Suggest, develop and defend the ideas in the notes.

Bread 'n' butter
AGENDA

Promotional mix

1 Advertising advertise in local newspapers and on local radio (expensive but effective); attractive posters for offices and shops

2 Personal selling call staff representatives in large companies to offer special prices to their staff

3 Sales promotion discounts, vouchers, BOGOF (buy one, get one free)

4 Public relations contact TV, radio, newspapers, magazines, etc.

5 Direct marketing send mailshots by mail and email

4.6 Case study **Onestop job search**
Simulation (page 58, Exercise 6)

Interviewers
Thank the candidate for coming. Explain the reason for the interview.
Ask the candidate about:
* their professional objectives
* how they heard about the job
* why they applied for this job
* their education
* their work experience
* their character and personality
* their strengths and weaknesses
* their skills

At the end of the interview, thank the candidate. Explain the next step.

3.4 Speaking **Presenting a process**
Presentation (page 43, Exercises 8 and 9)

Student As
Work together to prepare a presentation about the process of ordering goods. Use the flow chart below and the useful expressions on page 42 to help you.

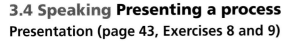

ORDERING PROCESS

customer visits online store and places items in basket

▼

customer goes to checkout

▼

password requested

▼

total calculated: customer confirms order

▼

credit card details requested and entered

▼

credit checked with bank

▼

order validated

▼

confirmation email sent to customer

▼

order details sent to distribution centre

4.2 Vocabulary **Job interviews**
Roleplay (page 51, Exercise 12)

Student A
You are a student. Answer the careers adviser's questions about:
* your CV: place of birth, school, university, internships, experience, current situation
* your personality
* your strengths and weaknesses
* your professional ambitions

Ask the adviser about:
* suitable jobs and careers for you
* more details about a job that interests you
* how to get this kind of job

5.3 Grammar **Comparatives and superlatives**
Roleplay (page 67, Exercise 9)

Student B
You sell used cars. If you sell a car for more than €5,000, you get 10% commission. For sales under €5,000, you only get 2% commission. Today, you have two cars for sale. Answer Student A's questions and try to sell the Toyota.

	Toyota	Peugeot
price	€5,999	€4,449
engine	hybrid	petrol
kilometres	110,000	90,000
guarantee	6 months	no
seats	5	4
satnav	yes	no
luggage	4 large suitcases	2 large suitcases
work needed	no	needs new tyres
petrol consumption	5.5 litres per 100km	7 litres per 100km
other equipment	air conditioning	hands-free phone

6.5 Writing Agendas and minutes
Minutes template (page 83, Exercises 6 and 8)

Minutes of: _____ Date & time: _____
Present: _____
Apologies: _____
Minutes by: _____

ITEM	ACTION	WHO?	WHEN?
1			
2			
3			
4			

Next meeting: _____

8.6 Case study An international opportunity
Roleplay (page 111, Exercise 6)

Student B
Prepare for the meeting with Student A. You will need to:
1 Listen to Student A's presentation of the franchise.
2 Interview Student A to decide if you want to invest in his/her franchise. Ask questions to get additional information.
   - ask if the franchise fee is negotiable
   - ask if the franchiser can help with finance
   - ask how many franchises have not succeeded, and why
3 Give a short presentation of your project. Explain:
   - how you will finance your project
   - where you want to open your first outlet
   - your plans for finding customers
   - why you will be a good franchisee
4 Answer Student A's questions. Invent any extra information you need.
5 Decide if you want to work together to open the franchise, or not.

7.3 Grammar Future forms and first conditional
Negotiation (page 93, Exercise 9)

Seller
You must sell a machine today, but you want:
- no discount (*score 5 points – lose one point for each % point given*)
- the buyer to pay for delivery and installation (*one point for each*)
- delivery in three weeks (*two points*) or two weeks (*one point*)
- no colour change and no logo (*one point for each*)
- 10% deposit with the order (*one point*) and full payment before shipment (*one point*)
- a one-year guarantee (*one point*)

2.1 About business Customer service
Discussion and presentation (page 22, Exercise 6)

Group B
Discuss what your chart shows. Find connections with the ideas in the article. Then present your chart to the class.

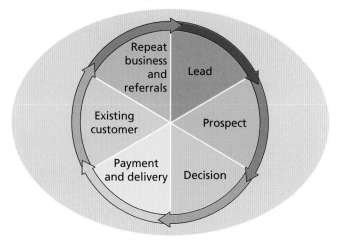

4.3 Grammar Past tenses
Information exchange (page 52, Exercise 4)

Student B
Find the missing information in the text by asking Student A questions. Answer Student A's questions.

What did Sylvester Stallone study?

SYLVESTER STALLONE

Sylvester Stallone was born in 1946 in New York and grew up in Philadelphia. He studied (1) _____ at the University of Miami, but he didn't finish his degree. Because (2) _____, Stallone found other jobs in New York. He even cleaned lions' cages at Central Park Zoo. Life was difficult, and he sold (3) _____ for $25 because (4) _____. Two weeks later, Stallone wrote the screenplay for *Rocky*. A studio offered him (5) $_____, but Stallone didn't take it because they refused to give him the lead role.

Finally, the studio agreed to let Stallone star in the movie and paid him (6) $_____. Stallone immediately tried to get his dog back. At first, the new owner refused to sell it. In the end, he agreed to take (7) _____! The movie won an Oscar and Stallone got his dream job. Thanks to *Rocky* and *Rambo*, he became (8) _____.

7.4 Speaking Negotiating
Roleplay (page 95, Exercise 7)

Student(s) B
You are a travel agent/agency. Your objective is to satisfy your customer and make a reasonable profit. You can negotiate any price between the catalogue price and the cost to you.

All prices are <u>per person</u>.

	Catalogue price	What it costs you
RETURN AIR FARE		
1st class	$1,100	$800
Economy class	$600	$400
RETURN AIRPORT TRANSFER		
Limo	$80	$40
Bus	$4	$4
HOTEL & BREAKFAST, PER NIGHT		
Double room	$75	$60
Single room	$100	$90
TOURS AND SHOWS		
New York Bus Tour	$30	$20
Broadway show	$75	$60
Liberty Harbour Cruise	$20	$12
Empire State Building	$20	$15

7.6 Case study Doug's Mugs
Negotiation (page 99, Exercise 5)

Sellers
Read the message and prepare your strategy for the negotiation.

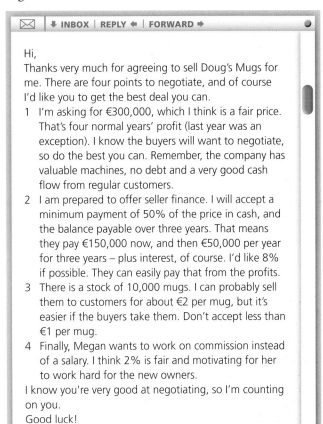

INBOX | REPLY | FORWARD

Hi,

Thanks very much for agreeing to sell Doug's Mugs for me. There are four points to negotiate, and of course I'd like you to get the best deal you can.

1 I'm asking for €300,000, which I think is a fair price. That's four normal years' profit (last year was an exception). I know the buyers will want to negotiate, so do the best you can. Remember, the company has valuable machines, no debt and a very good cash flow from regular customers.

2 I am prepared to offer seller finance. I will accept a minimum payment of 50% of the price in cash, and the balance payable over three years. That means they pay €150,000 now, and then €50,000 per year for three years – plus interest, of course. I'd like 8% if possible. They can easily pay that from the profits.

3 There is a stock of 10,000 mugs. I can probably sell them to customers for about €2 per mug, but it's easier if the buyers take them. Don't accept less than €1 per mug.

4 Finally, Megan wants to work on commission instead of a salary. I think 2% is fair and motivating for her to work hard for the new owners.

I know you're very good at negotiating, so I'm counting on you.
Good luck!
Doug

8.3 Grammar **Present perfect**
Progress report (page 105, Exercise 9)

Student B

With a partner, update the report on a franchise project in Mexico.
Ask and answer questions to complete the report.

2   Have they found premises yet? Have they had any problems with that?

PROGRESS REPORT, 1 JUNE			
	STEP	**DONE?**	**PROBLEMS**
1	sign franchising agreement	yes	but/still/not receive/copy
2	find premises	?	?
3	obtain phone number	no	because/not find/premises
4	obtain bank loan	?	?
5	order stock	yes, but not delivered	because/not rent/office
6	plan advertising campaign	?	?
7	print flyers	no	because/not confirm/address
8	do training	?	?
9	interview administrative staff	yes, recently finished	not sign/contracts
10	arrange opening event	?	?

4.2 Vocabulary **Job interviews**
Roleplay (page 51, Exercise 12)

Student B

You are a careers adviser. Ask the student about:
- their CV: place of birth, school, university, internships, experience, current situation
- their personality
- their strengths and weaknesses
- their professional ambitions

Answer the student's questions about:
- suitable jobs and careers for them
- more details about a job that interests them
- how to get this kind of job

4.6 Case study **Onestop job search**
Survey results (page 58, Exercise 2)

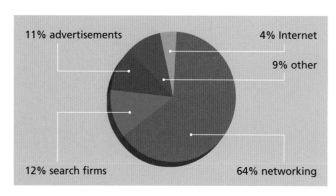

11% advertisements
4% Internet
9% other
12% search firms
64% networking

2.1 About business **Customer service**
Discussion and presentation (page 22, Exercise 6)

Group C

Discuss what your chart shows. Find connections with the ideas in the article. Then present your chart to the class.

Ally: sells the product for you

Advocate: recommends the product

Client: buys the product regularly

Customer: buys the product

Prospect: needs the product

3.4 Speaking Presenting a process
Presentation (page 43, Exercises 8 and 9)

Student Bs
Work together to prepare a presentation about the process of returning goods. Use the flow chart below and the useful expressions on page 42 to help you.

RETURNS PROCESS
order delivered to customer
▼
product damaged or faulty
▼
customer requests product return number online
▼
return number and address provided
▼
customer returns product and delivery note to distribution centre
▼
product and delivery note checked at distribution centre
▼
goods repaired, replaced or returned to manufacturer
▼
repaired or replacement product shipped to customer, or payment refunded

8.2 Vocabulary Franchising and project management
Quiz (page 102, Exercise 1)

If you scored mostly As, you have the profile to become an independent entrepreneur. You like the freedom to try new ideas and solve problems. And you are not afraid to take risks.

If you scored mostly Bs, you have the profile to become a franchiser. You are a leader and you are good at planning ahead. And you are prepared to compromise when necessary.

If you scored mostly Cs, you have the profile to become a franchisee. You prefer to achieve your objectives without taking unnecessary risks. You are practical, and you are prepared to accept help and advice from other people.

1.4 Speaking Meeting people and making conversation
Roleplay (page 17, Exercise 9)

You are going to an international conference. Before you start, complete the questionnaire. Use real information, or invent the details. Then stand up and socialize! Meet as many 'new colleagues' as possible and make conversation.

International Business Conference, New York

Before you arrive at the conference, please tell us more about yourself by completing this form:

Name: _____
Nationality: _____
Company: _____
Position: _____
Home town or city: _____
Hotel: _____
Marital status: _____
Number and age of children: _____
Hobbies and interests: _____
Special food requirements: _____
Other: _____

6.2 Vocabulary Business organization and people
Crossword (page 77, Exercise 8)

Student B
Work with a partner to complete your crossword. Take turns to give definitions for the words you have. Don't say the word itself. Write the missing words.

A: *What's 1 down?*
B: *It's the person who is responsible for running a company in the UK.*

Business fundamentals **CVs and cover letters**
Writing and roleplay (page 9, Exercise 4)

NAME: _____

DATE OF BIRTH: _____

NATIONALITY: _____

ADDRESS: _____

_____

EDUCATION

_____

WORK HISTORY

_____

POSITIONS OF RESPONSIBILITY

_____

SKILLS

_____

7.5 Writing **Asking for payment**
Output (page 97, Exercise 7)

Student(s) B

1 You are the owner(s) of a business that supplies special packaging materials for e-businesses. Student A owns an e-business selling photographic equipment. Student A is one of your regular customers, but is often a slow payer. You are still waiting for payment for an invoice you sent three months ago for $5,075. Their orders are also unclear, which leads to delays and mistakes in deliveries. Delays and mistakes cost you money to correct. Write an email to Student A asking for quick payment.

2 When you receive emails from Student A, write appropriate answers.

3.2 Vocabulary **Supply chain and product life cycle**
Crossword (page 39, Exercise 8)

Student B

Work with a partner to complete your crossword. Take turns to give definitions for the words you have. Don't say the word itself. Write the missing words.

A: What's 2 down?
B: It's when you don't have enough of something.

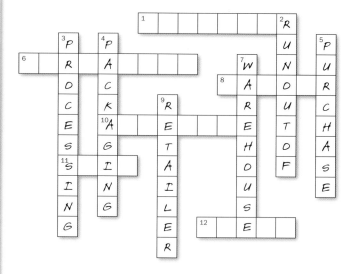

4.3 Grammar **Past tenses**
Information exchange (page 52, Exercise 4)

Student A

Find the missing information in the text by asking Student B questions. Answer Student B's questions.

Where did Sylvester Stallone grow up?

SYLVESTER STALLONE

Sylvester Stallone was born in 1946 in New York and grew up in (1) _____. He studied drama at the University of Miami, but he didn't finish (2) _____. Because it was very difficult to become an actor, Stallone found other jobs in New York. He even cleaned (3) _____ at Central Park Zoo. Life was difficult, and he sold his dog for (4) $_____ because he didn't have enough money to feed it. Two weeks later, Stallone wrote (5) _____. A studio offered him $325,000, but Stallone didn't take it because (6) _____.

Finally, the studio agreed to let Stallone star in the movie and paid him $35,000. Stallone immediately tried to (7) _____. At first, the new owner refused to sell it. In the end, he agreed to take $15,000 and a part in the movie! The movie won (8) _____ and Stallone got his dream job. Thanks to *Rocky* and *Rambo*, he became a multimillionaire.

6.4 Speaking **Meetings**
Roleplay (page 81, Exercise 7)

Student C
Suggest, develop and defend the ideas in the notes.

Bread 'n' butter
AGENDA

Promotional mix

1 Advertising *too expensive; word of mouth is more*
   effective. Just need a neon sign on the shop and an
   interactive website.

2 Personal selling *not appropriate for a*
   sandwich bar

3 Sales promotion *discounts are bad for company*
   image; events, competitions, free samples

4 Public relations *use social media, Twitter,*
   Facebook, blogs, etc.

5 Direct marketing *mobile messaging; give out*
   flyers in the street

2.1 About business **Customer service**
Discussion and presentation (page 22, Exercise 6)

Group A
Discuss what your chart shows. Find connections with the ideas in the article. Then present your chart to the class.

7.6 Case study **Doug's Mugs**
Negotiation (page 99, Exercise 5)

Buyers
Read the message and prepare your strategy for the negotiation.

BIRCH, BIRCH AND LOCKWOOD, SOLICITORS

Dear Client,

I am writing in connection with your search for a small business to buy. Doug's Mugs is for sale. (See attached financial documents.)

1 The owner is asking for €300,000, but this year's results were disappointing. We believe he will accept €250,000.
2 The owner is also prepared to offer seller finance. He will probably accept a 30% cash payment, with the balance payable over five years, plus interest of about 5%.
3 You also need to negotiate a price for the current stock of 10,000 mugs.
4 Megan Smith, who is responsible for sales, wants to be paid commission instead of a salary. We suggest not more than 1% on sales.

All of these points are negotiable. We are confident that you will obtain a good deal.

Yours faithfully,

G. S. Birch

Grammar and practice

Present simple

1 Study the form of the present simple in the box. Then do the exercise below.

> **Present simple**
> Positive
> *I/You/We/They work.*
> *He/She/It works.*
> Negative
> *I/You/We/They don't work.*
> *He/She/It doesn't work.*
> Questions
> *Do I/you/we/they work?*
> *Does he/she/it work?*

> **Present simple: *to be***
> Positive
> *I'm late.*
> *You're/We're/They're late.*
> *He's/She's/It's late.*
> Negative
> *I'm not late.*
> *You/We/They aren't late.*
> Or *You're/We're/They're not late.*
> *He/She/It isn't late.*
> Or *He's/She's/It's not late.*
> Questions
> *Am I late?*
> *Are you/we/they late?*
> *Is he/she/it late?*

> **Contractions**
> The contractions *don't* (*do not*), *you're* (*you are*), etc.
> are the forms we use most often in speech and informal
> writing.

Complete the dialogue. Use contractions where possible.

A: Where (1) _____ you work?
B: I work in Lyon.
A: Lyon? Oh, I thought you worked in Paris.
B: No, I often go there for meetings, but I (2) _____ work there. I work in Lyon.
A: Oh, that must be nice. I hear it's a very lively city. And (3) _____ you married?
B: Yes, I (4) _____. My wife's name is Zsi-Zsi.
A: That's an unusual name. (5) _____ she French?
B: No, she (6) _____ French. She (7) _____ Hungarian.
A: And (8) _____ she have a job?
B: No, she (9) _____ – not at the moment. We have two young children and she stays at home to look after them.
A: Two children! How wonderful! How old (10) _____ they?
B: The girl is six and the boy is two.
A: Two years old! I imagine that you (11) _____ get much sleep!
B: Yes, you (12) _____ right. I must look tired!
A: And what about your daughter? (13) _____ she enjoy school?
B: Yes, she (14) _____.

2 Correct the mistake in each sentence.
1 Do you working for Siemens?
2 I doesn't work for Siemens. I work for Bayer.
3 And your wife, do she work?
4 My wife work as a teacher.
5 She is German?
6 No, she not German. She's Hungarian.

3 Complete the paragraph about cultural stereotypes with the correct present simple form of the verbs in brackets.

(1) _____ (you/believe) in cultural stereotypes? Many people (2) _____ (think) they are not true, and that you should treat each person you (3) _____ (meet) as an individual. But this (4) _____ (not/be) always easy. For example, if an Italian colleague (5) _____ (arrive) late for a meeting, what (6) _____ (everybody/think)? Well, in theory, we know that people (7) _____ (be) late for all sorts of genuine reasons, so maybe it (8) _____ (not/be) their fault. But, in practice, the colleague (9) _____ (not/get) much sympathy because people (10) _____ (have) a stereotype in their head that Italians (11) _____ (be) always late. (12) _____ (the stereotype/be) fair? Probably not, but that (13) _____ (not/help) your Italian colleague!

4 Read the last two lines of the dialogue in Exercise 1. Then complete the replies to the questions below.

A: *Does she enjoy school?*
B: *Yes, she **does**.* (not *Yes, she ~~enjoys~~.*)

1 **A:** Do you enjoy your work?
   B: Yes, I _____.
2 **A:** Do you know this restaurant?
   B: No, I _____.
3 **A:** Does your wife work?
   B: No, she _____.
4 **A:** Does your son go to school?
   B: Yes, he _____.
5 **A:** Are you Czech?
   B: Yes, that's right, I _____.
6 **A:** Are you Czech?
   B: No, I _____. I'm Slovakian.

5 Match examples 1–3 with the uses of the present simple a–c. Choose the best answer for each.

1 Most days I **leave** home around 7.00. ☐
2 The Rhine **flows** through six countries. ☐
3 Our company **offers** a range of investment products. ☐

a) facts
b) routines
c) permanent situations

> The **present simple** is used for:
> • **facts**: things that are always true
> • **routines**: regular activities, habits
> • **permanent situations**: long-term, not temporary

6 Complete the exchanges with the question words in the box. To help you, read the reply first.

> How much   How often   What   When
> Where   Who   Whose   Why

1 **A:** _____ do you normally negotiate with?
  B: I negotiate with our suppliers.
2 **A:** _____ do you travel abroad on business?
  B: Oh, three or four times a year, I suppose.
3 **A:** _____ do you think about the economic situation in Europe?
  B: I think things will slowly get better.
4 **A:** _____ do you want to apply for an internship?
  B: Because I think it's the best way to gain experience.
5 **A:** _____ does your flight leave?
  B: At nine o'clock tomorrow morning.
6 **A:** _____ does the CEO earn?
  B: I don't know exactly, but I guess more than 200,000 euros per year.
7 **A:** _____ is the meeting?
  B: In the conference room on the second floor.
8 **A:** _____ newspaper is this?
  B: It's mine, but you can read it if you want to.

> **Present simple questions**
> To make a *Wh-* or *How* question, put the question word before the auxiliary verb *do* or the verb *be*.
> **Do** you live here?
> **Where do** you live?
> **Is** her name Meifen?
> **What is** her name?

Adverbs of frequency

7 Put the adverbs on the frequency scale.

> always   nearly always   never   not often
> often   rarely   ~~sometimes~~   usually

100%   1 _____
↑   2 _____
       3 _____
       4 _____
       5 *sometimes*
       6 _____
↓   7 _____
0%   8 _____

8 Complete the sentences with the word *often*. Leave one of the gaps empty.

1 He _____ works _____ late.
2 He _____ is _____ at the office until late.
3 I _____ am _____ in Singapore for meetings.
4 I _____ go _____ to Singapore for meetings.

> Adverbs of frequency come *before* the verb.
> But … adverbs of frequency come *after* the verb *to be*.

9 Put the adverb of frequency in the correct place. Use an arrow to show where it goes.

1 a) I use different passwords for different websites. (always)
  b) But I don't remember them! (always)
2 a) We get an end-of-year bonus. (often)
  b) But they don't give us very much. (usually)
3 a) We give a discount greater than 5%. (never)
  b) But we offer 60 days' credit instead of 30. (sometimes)
4 a) People click on the ads on our website. (rarely)
  b) But I think they remember the product names in the ads. (sometimes)

10 Put the words in **bold** in the correct order to make sentences with the present simple.

1 **you Do have always** the sales conference in Atlanta?
  _____
2 **check usually I** my emails as soon as I arrive at work.
  _____
3 **am I often** the first person to arrive at my desk.
  _____
4 **Jake does What time** usually leave the office?
  _____
5 **I get don't often** the chance to travel on business.
  _____
6 **Luigi arrives always** on time.
  _____
7 **forget sometimes I** to back up my work.
  _____
8 **Tim always Is** the salesman with the best results?
  _____

Prepositions of time: *in, on, at*

11 Complete the phrases with *in, on, at,* or *~* (no preposition). If you don't know, say the phrase aloud with different prepositions, to see if it sounds right.

1 _____ 2007
2 _____ ten o'clock
3 _____ yesterday
4 _____ Christmas
5 _____ Christmas Day
6 _____ 28 July
7 _____ today
8 _____ the morning
9 _____ last week
10 _____ winter
11 _____ next April
12 _____ Saturday
13 _____ New Year's Day
14 _____ July
15 _____ the evening
16 _____ night
17 _____ the weekend (UK)
18 _____ the weekend (US)

> **Prepositions of time**
> Use:
> • *in* with parts of the day (*in the morning*), months, quarters, seasons, years
> • *on* with dates, days of the week, special days, the weekend (US)
> • *at* with *night*, festivals, times of the clock, the weekend (UK)
> • **no preposition** for *yesterday, today, tomorrow, last (week), next (year)*
> Note: Speakers of American English use **no preposition** for days of the week (*I'll see you Wednesday*)

Present continuous

1 Study the form of the present continuous. Then do the exercise below.

Present continuous
Positive
I'm working.
You're/We're/They're working.
He's/She's/It's working.
Negative
I'm not working.
You/We/They aren't working.
Or *You're/We're/They're not working.*
He/She/It isn't working.
Or *He's/She's/It's not working.*
Questions
Am I working?
Are you/we/they working?
Is he/she/it working?

Contractions
The contractions *I'm* (*I am*) *you're* (*you are*), etc. are the forms we use most often in speech and informal writing.

Complete the sentences with the present continuous form of the verb in brackets. Use contractions where possible.

1 We _____ (redesign) our website.
2 _____ (you/enjoy) the conference?
3 The photocopier _____ (not/work) at the moment. Try again later.
4 Is that Stephanie on the phone? _____ (she/ call) from Paris?
5 I _____ (read) a great book about solutions to the energy crisis.
6 They _____ (not/stay) at the Novotel this time, they chose the Mercure instead.

2 Match examples 1–3 with the uses of the present continuous a–c. Choose the best answer for each.

1 Let's go for lunch. I want to tell you about my news – **I'm working** on a big project in Turkey. ☐
2 I'll finish the spreadsheet in about half an hour. **I'm working** as fast as I can. ☐
3 Developments in communication technology mean that more people **are working** from home. ☐

a) an action happening right now, at the moment of speaking
b) an action happening around now, but not at the moment of speaking
c) a trend or slow change happening now

The **present continuous** is used for temporary activities in progress now.

Present simple and present continuous

3 Study the differences between the present simple (*I do/She does*) and the present continuous (*I'm doing/ She's doing*). Then do the exercise below.

Present simple	Present continuous
permanent situations	temporary situations
routines and habits	activities in progress now
facts	slow changes and trends

Complete the sentences with the present simple or present continuous form of the verbs in brackets.

1 a) We _____ (sell) our products all over the world.
   b) January sale! For one month only, we _____ (sell) this product at a 20% discount.
2 a) They _____ (change) their advertising agency – they aren't happy with the old one.
   b) Every year we _____ (change) our advertising agency to keep all our advertising fresh.
3 a) She _____ (work) for SAP.
   b) Today she _____ (work) from home.
4 a) Looking at the world economy, we see that inflation _____ (rise) at the moment.
   b) When the euro falls in value, imports cost more and inflation _____ (rise) in the eurozone.

4 We use different time expressions with the present simple and present continuous. Underline the correct time expressions in *italics*.

1 *This year / Every year* we're building a new factory in Indonesia.
2 *This year / Every year* we increase our market share in Indonesia.
3 *At the moment / Most years* we're recruiting a lot of new staff – business is going very well right now.
4 *At the moment / Most years* we service our machines over the summer period.

State verbs

5 Put a tick (✓) if the sentence is correct. Put a cross (✗) if it is incorrect.

1 That Audi belongs to our Marketing Director. ☐
2 That Audi is belonging to our Marketing Director. ☐
3 It all depends on the situation. ☐
4 It's all depending on the situation. ☐
5 I know exactly what you mean. ☐
6 I'm knowing exactly what you're meaning. ☐

State verbs
There are a number of verbs that describe states, not activities. These verbs are not usually used in a continuous form. State verbs include:
agree, know, remember, think, understand
hate, like, need, want, wish
belong to, contain, own
be, exist
cost, depend, mean, measure, owe, weigh

Requests with *can, could* and *would*

6 Read the information in the box. Then do the exercise below.

> **Requests**
> To request that someone else does something, we use
> *can, could* and *would*.
> (informal)   *Can you* pass the salt?
> (neutral)   *Could you* open the window, please?
> (polite)   *Would you* help me move this desk?
> To request something for ourselves (to ask for
> permission), we use *can, could* and *may*.
> (informal)   *Can I* ask a question?
> (neutral)   *Could I* use your phone to make a local call?
> (polite)   *May I* interrupt for a moment?

Underline the best words in *italics* for each situation.

1   You are a receptionist in a large company speaking on the phone to an unknown caller.
   Can I / Could I ask who's calling?
2   You are speaking to your sister.
   Can you / Would you give James a message? Tell him I'll be late for lunch today.
3   You want to enter a room where you left your bag. Some other people are having a meeting there.
   Can I / May I come in? I think I left my bag here.

Saying *yes* and *no* to a request

7 Match requests 1–8 with replies a–h.

1   Can I ask you a few questions about this report? ☐
2   Is this chair free? Could I possibly take it for our table? ☐
3   Could you work late on Tuesday this week? ☐
4   Would you help me move these tables to get the meeting room ready? ☐
5   Could you give us a larger discount if we order 1,000 pieces? ☐
6   Can you supply this item with our company logo printed on it? ☐
7   May I help you with your bags? ☐
8   Can we put the meeting back to next week? ☐

a)   Actually, I'm really busy right now. Ask me again tomorrow. I'll have more time.
b)   That's OK. I can manage, thanks.
c)   Of course. Just let me save this document and I'll be right there.
d)   Sorry, we can't give a bigger discount for 1,000 pieces. But we could help you with the terms of payment – perhaps another 30 days' credit.
e)   I'm afraid I can't; it's my daughter's birthday. Why not ask Mariana? She's probably free that evening.
f)   Sure. Go ahead. We're not expecting anyone else.
g)   Certainly, no problem. But it will add 5% to the cost and we'll need an extra day to set up the machines.
h)   That's fine. In fact, next week is better for me.

> **Saying *yes* and *no* to a request**
> If we say *yes* to a request, we don't just use the word *yes*.
> Instead, we say something like *Of course/Sure/*
> *No problem* and then add a few more words to be friendly.
> If we say *no* to a request, we don't just use the word *no*.
> Instead, we start with *I'm afraid/Actually/Sorry/*
> *I'm sorry, but* and then give a reason.
> Note: the phrase *I'm afraid …* is not used in this way in
> American English: it is only used in sentences like *I'm*
> *afraid of spiders*.

Offers of help and Invitations

8 Tick (✓) the correct sentences. Put a cross (✗) by the incorrect sentences.

1   a)   Shall I send you a copy of the report? ☐
    b)   Would you like me to send you a copy of the report? ☐
    c)   Would you like that I send you a copy of the report? ☐
2   a)   Do you want to join us for lunch? ☐
    b)   Do you like to join us for lunch? ☐
    c)   Would you like to join us for lunch? ☐

> For **offers of help** (a suggestion that you do something):
> *Shall I …?* (informal/neutral)
> *Do you want me to …?* (informal/neutral)
> *Would you like me to …?* (polite)
> For **invitations** (a suggestion that the other person does something):
> *Do you want to …?* (informal/neutral)
> *Would you like to …?* (polite)

9 Complete each sentence with one word.

1   _____ I take a message for her?
2   _____ you want me to take a message for her?
3   _____ you like me to take a message for her?
4   Do you _____ to leave a message for her?
5   Would you _____ to leave a message for her?

> **Would you like …?** and **Do you like …?**
> Compare:
> 1 **Would you like** some tea?
> 2 **Do you like** tea?
> These two uses of *like* are different.
> In 1, *would like = want*
> In 2, *like = enjoy*
> The situations where we use them are different.
> In 1, you say this in one particular situation, for example
> in the reception area of an office:
> A: **Would you like** some tea?
> B: *Yes, please. Milk, no sugar.*
> In 2, we are talking about tea in general:
> A: **Do you like** tea?
> B: *Yes, I do, but in my country it's more usual to drink*
> *coffee.*
> For **offers of help** and **invitations** we use 1, so:
> *Would you like …? = Do you want …?*

Prepositions of place

1 Read the notes in the box. Then do the exercise below.

---

in and on
We use *in* with spaces like boxes, rooms, towns and countries. These have three dimensions.
We use *on* with surfaces like floors, desks, walls and areas of the body (*on your head/arm/skin*). These have two dimensions.
People are *in* clothes (*Who is that in the blue dress?*).
Clothes are *on* people (*That dress looks good on you*).
Here are some expressions with *in* and *on*:

in a book/magazine	on page 36
in a story	on the left/right
in the street	on the screen
in the photo	on the first floor
in the middle	on the plane/bus/train
in the corner	on the platform/pavement
in line/in a queue	on the phone
in a car/taxi	on the computer
in the country	on the Internet

---

at
We use *at* to show where something happens, for example with meeting places (*at the cinema/at the theatre*) or points on a journey (*at the bus stop/at the next corner*).
We also use *at* for things that people do (*at breakfast/lunch*) and for the places where people do things (*at the office/at my house/at a party*).
Here are some expressions with *at*:
at the top/bottom/side
at the front/back
at the beginning/end
at the station/airport
at home/at work (not *at the home, at the work*)
at breakfast/lunch/dinner

---

in or at?
Sometimes *in* and *at* are both possible. We prefer *in* when we are thinking about the place itself, and *at* when we are thinking about the activity we do there.
There are very comfortable seats in the cinema.
I'll meet you at the cinema.
But note that in the above examples *in* and *at* are both possible.

Complete each sentence with *in*, *on* or *at*.

1 Our offices are _____ the second floor.
2 I never have any money left _____ the end of the month.
3 At passport control I had to wait _____ line for ages.
4 I saw an amazing video _____ the Internet.
5 Who is that man over there _____ the grey suit?
6 I'll pick you up _____ the airport – I'll be in Arrivals.
7 I don't think all five of us will fit _____ a taxi.
8 Turn off your phone when you get _____ the plane.
9 I'm working _____ home tomorrow.
10 She told me about her plans _____ lunch.
11 I was talking to him _____ the phone this morning.
12 I met my boss by chance _____ the street.
13 Their website is too complicated – there is too much text _____ the screen.
14 My parents live _____ the country – they retired and moved to a smaller place.
15 Please sign right here – _____ the bottom of the page.
16 Those shoes look fabulous _____ you!
17 I'm leaving _____ the 9.15 train from Zurich.
18 Go down the corridor and you'll see my office _____ the right.
19 Turn left _____ the top of the stairs and you'll see the coffee machine.
20 There's a socket for the projector _____ the corner.

2 Read the notes in the box. Then do the exercise below.

Other prepositions of place
Above and *below* mean 'higher than' and 'lower than'. We use them to talk about positions, amounts and places in a document.
*The accounts department is on the floor **above** this one.*
*Sales this quarter are **below** the figure for the same period last year.*
*Market share is increasing – see the chart **below**.*
These are opposites:
in front of – behind
inside – outside
on top of – under
The preposition *between* means 'with things on each side or each end'. You can sit *between* two people on a bench, or a train can run *between* San Francisco and San Diego.
And study these carefully:
opposite = exactly on the other side of
next to = exactly at the side of
near (to) = close to

Complete the sentences with the words in the box.

---
above   behind   below   between   in front of
next to   on top of   under
---

1 I just have to make a quick call. You start walking to the restaurant and I'll be right _____ you.
2 Winter temperatures in Moscow rarely rise _____ 0°C.
3 Summer temperatures in Delhi rarely fall _____ 30°C.
4 They sat in the meeting according to their position in the company. The CEO was at the head of the table, the Finance Director was _____ her, and then there were all the other managers.
5 The only empty seat at the table was _____ the CEO and the Finance Director, so I was able to read both their notes!
6 My pen rolled _____ the bookcase. Could you help me to get it, please?
7 The plant _____ the bookcase is very high. I need to stand on a chair to water it.
8 Taxis stop right _____ the hotel entrance, so you won't get wet if it's raining.

Prepositions of movement

3 Read the notes in the box. Then do the exercise below.

> **Prepositions of movement**
> These are opposites:
>
> up – down   over – under
> into – out of   towards – away from
>
> You drive *along* (or *up* or *down*) a road and *across* (or *over* or *under*) a bridge.
> You drive *through* a tunnel or *through* a city/town if you are not stopping.
> You drive *past* buildings and things at the side of the road – you pass them.
> You drive *round* in circles if you are lost, and you walk *round* a town if you are shopping.

In each sentence, cross out the one item that is not usual.

1 You can walk into *the bank / the conference hall / the bridge*.
2 You can walk out of *the station / the stairs / the building*.
3 You can climb over *the corner / the wall / the fence*.
4 You can drive towards *the floor / Paris / the sea*.
5 You can walk across *a bridge / a park / the stairs*.
6 You can drive through *a bridge / a tunnel / the city centre*.
7 You can drive past *a cinema / a church / a highway*.
8 You can walk round *the tunnel / the park / the shops*.

Present simple passive

4 Underline the correct verb forms in the text.

Wheat – from field to table
More foods (1) *make / are made* from it than from any other grain. So how does wheat become the bread, rolls, pancakes, cereals and cookies on your table?
The wheat seed (2) *plants / is planted* in the autumn. Growth (3) *happens / is happened* slowly at first, but by the following summer, the grain is ready to harvest. The farmer (4) *uses / is used* a machine called a combine to cut, separate and clean the grain. The combine (5) *unloads / is unloaded* the wheat onto a truck and the truck carries it to a grain elevator where it (6) *stores / is stored*.
The wheat (7) *then takes / is then taken* to a a flour mill. At the mill, the grain is ground* into flour. It (8) *puts / is put* into bags and then transported to bakeries.
At the bakery, machines (9) *mix / are mixed* the flour with water, yeast, salt and fat to make the thick, sticky dough. This (10) *puts / is put* into an oven to bake. When the baking is finished, out comes the hot, crusty bread. Other stages at the bakery include cutting and wrapping.
The final stage is distribution. The bread (11) *takes / is taken* in large quantities to a wholesale distribution centre, where it is divided into smaller batches to deliver to shops. There, it (12) *places / is placed* on the shelves and we (13) *buy / are bought* it to make sandwiches and toast.
* = broken and pressed into powder

> **Present simple passive**
> Compare sentences a) and b):
> a) *My friend Simon **makes** lovely traditional bread.*
> b) *Bread **is made** from flour, water, yeast, salt and fat.*
> Sentence a) is called **active**. We are interested in who does the action.
> Sentence b) is called **passive**. We are interested in the action rather than who does it.
> We form the passive with *be* + the past participle (third column of verb tables)
> Compare:
>
> | Active | Passive |
> |---|---|
> | *He does it.* | *It is done.* |
> | *He doesn't do it.* | *It isn't done./It's not done.* |
> | *Does he do it?* | *Is it done?* |

5 Complete the sentences with the words in brackets in the present simple passive. Use contractions where possible.

1 **A:** Am I doing it right? _____ (it/do) like this?
   B: No, _____ (it/not/do) like that. Here, let me show you.
2 **A:** _____ (hummus and falafel/know) in Europe?
   B: Oh, yes. _____ (they/sell) in every big supermarket.
3 **A:** _____ (any Korean cars/make) in the Czech Republic?
   B: Yes, _____ (Hyundai cars/produce) at Nosovice.
4 **A:** _____ (you/pay) weekly or monthly in your company?
   B: _____ (I/pay) weekly.
5 **A:** _____ (rice/grown) in your country?
   B: Yes, _____ (it/grow) here, even though it's a cold country.
6 **A:** _____ (English/use) as the company language where you work?
   B: Well, _____ (it/speak) by most people, but it isn't the official company language.

6 Match examples 1–3 with the uses of the passive a–c. Choose the best answer if several are possible.

1 The wheat **is taken** to a flour mill. At the mill, the grain **is ground** into flour. Then it **is put** into bags and **transported** to bakeries. ☐
2 More foods **are made** from wheat than from any other grain. ☐
3 **It is put** into bags and then transported to bakeries. ☐

a) subject 'it' refers back to a noun in the previous sentence
b) describing a process
c) the person who does the action is not important or not known

Past simple

1 There are three different pronunciations of the regular past simple -ed ending. First practise saying the six examples in the blue table. Then write the words in the box in the correct columns.

accepted   closed   complained   constructed
developed   discussed   finished   introduced
prepared   realized   started   visited

/d/	/t/	/ɪd/
moved	asked	decided
opened	focused	wanted

-ed endings
There is a rule for these endings, but you have to know a little about pronunciation to understand it. There are 'voiced' and 'unvoiced' sounds.
'Voiced' means that your vocal chords vibrate (go up and down) as you produce the sound. Try tapping your fingers lightly on your throat as you say the 'v' of move and listen for the vibrating sound.
'Unvoiced' means that your vocal chords do not vibrate as you produce the sound. Try tapping your fingers lightly on your throat as you say the 's' of focus – there is no vibrating sound.
Regarding the -ed endings of the past simple:
• If the sound at the end of verb is voiced, like the /v/ in move, then the -ed ending is pronounced /d/.
• If the sound at the end of verb is unvoiced, like the /s/ in focus, then the -ed ending is pronounced /t/.
• Some other verbs, like decide or want, already have the sound /d/ or /t/ at the end. It isn't possible to make the sounds /d/ or /t/ twice. So the -ed ending is pronounced /ɪd/.

2 How many irregular past simple forms do you know? Write them in the table.

infinitive	past simple	infinitive	past simple
become	1 _____	leave	16 _____
begin	2 _____	lose	17 _____
bring	3 _____	make	18 _____
buy	4 _____	meet	19 _____
choose	5 _____	pay	20 _____
cost	6 _____	see	21 _____
fall	7 _____	sell	22 _____
find	8 _____	set	23 _____
forget	9 _____	speak	24 _____
give	10 _____	spend	25 _____
go	11 _____	take	26 _____
grow	12 _____	tell	27 _____
have	13 _____	think	28 _____
keep	14 _____	understand	29 _____
know	15 _____	write	30 _____

3 Complete the dialogue about Google with the correct past simple form of the verbs in brackets. (These include positives, negatives and questions.)

A: What (1) _____ (be) the names of the founders of Google?

B: Their names were Larry Page and Sergey Brin. According to the company myth, they (2) _____ (not/like) each other when they first (3) _____ (meet).

A: Really! So when (4) _____ Larry and Sergey _____ (meet)?

B: They (5) _____ (meet) in 1995 at Stanford University.

A: And where (6) _____ they _____ (start) their business?

B: They (7) _____ (start) it in a garage with a staff of just three – themselves and one other person. This first 'office' (8) _____ (not/be) very luxurious – it also (9) _____ (contain) a washing machine and a dryer for clothes.

A: Wow! So when (10) _____ Google _____ (make) a profit for the first time?

B: It (11) _____ (make) a profit in 2001, although they (12) _____ (not/have) a stock market listing until 2004.

A: And what (13) _____ (be) their source of income?

B: The company (14) _____ (grow) by developing a 'cost per click' model of advertising. Advertisers (15) _____ (pay) to have their names on the search page, and then paid again when users (16) _____ (click) on the link.

A: Why (17) _____ Google _____ (have) so much success compared to other search engines?

B: They (18) _____ (have) a lot of success for two main reasons. First, their search technology (19) _____ (find) better results than the competitors. And second, in the year 2000, they (20) _____ (introduce) an innovative tool called Google Toolbar. This was a browser plug-in that (21) _____ (make) it possible to use Google search without going first to the Google homepage. The Toolbar also (22) _____ (highlight) key words in search results, and (23) _____ (block) annoying advertising pop-ups.

Past simple
Positive
I/You/He/She/It/We/They worked.
Negative
I/You/He/She/It/We/They didn't work.
Questions
Did I/you/he/she/it/we/they work?

Past continuous

4 Study the form of the past continuous in the box. Then do the exercise below.

> **Past continuous**
> Positive
> *I/He/She/It was working.*
> *You/We/They were working.*
> Negative
> *I/He/She/It wasn't working.*
> *You/We/They weren't working.*
> Questions
> *Was I/he/she/it working?*
> *Were you/we/they working?*

Match examples 1 and 2 with the uses of the past continuous a) and b).

1   It was the summer of 2010 and **I was working** at Estée Lauder. One day the phone rang – it was a headhunter! They had a job vacancy with a bigger salary and more responsibility, and they wanted me to apply for it! ☐
2   **I was waiting** in Departures all that time – the flight was delayed by 3 hours. It was terrible. Everyone **was complaining**. What could we do? Some people **were looking** round the shops, others **were trying** to sleep on the chairs, and a few **were working** on their laptops or **browsing** the net on their smartphones. ☐

a)   Telling a story: the past continuous is used first to give the background situation. Then the individual events are in the past simple.
b)   Telling a story: there are several activities happening at the same time, all in the past continuous.

> **Past continuous**
> We use the past continuous for an activity in progress in the past.
> It is often used for telling a story. We use it first to give the background situation (with the individual events in the past simple), or to talk about several activities all happening at the same time.

5 Match sentence beginnings 1–6 with endings a–f. Look for the background situation and the event.

1   I was walking to the station from my office [b] ☐
2   Mary was listening to my presentation ☐
3   While I was working on the project, ☐
4   He was talking to a client, ☐
5   We were rushing to the meeting in a taxi ☐
6   After six months in the company I was thinking about asking for a pay rise, ☐

a)   the team leader became ill and I took his place.
b)   when it suddenly started to rain very heavily.
c)   when the driver crashed into the car in front.
d)   so I didn't want to interrupt him.
e)   but, in the end, I decided to wait until the end of my first year.
f)   and at the end she asked a very good question.

6 Study these four sentences. Then do the exercise below.

1   While *I was eating lunch*, the doorbell **rang**.
2   While *I was eating lunch*, my smartphone **rang** – but it was in my bag and I didn't hear it.
3   While *I was working at my computer*, I **saw** Rita fall to the floor.
4   While *I was working at my computer*, I **saw** Andy in his new suit.

> **Past continuous interrupted**
> Sometimes the activity in the past continuous continues, and sometimes it stops, because the event in the past simple interrupts it.

Look back at sentences 1–4 above. Read the activities in *italics* and underline the most likely situation:

1   a) the activity continued   b) the activity stopped
2   a) the activity continued   b) the activity stopped
3   a) the activity continued   b) the activity stopped
4   a) the activity continued   b) the activity stopped

7 Study the information in the box. Then do the exercise below.

> **when and while**
> In Exercise 6, notice that *while* is often used with the past continuous; *when* can be used with the same meaning. The two parts of the sentence can be in either order:
> *While/When I was walking home, it started to rain.*
> OR *It started to rain while/when I was walking home.*
>
> **so and because**
> If we change the sentence order, we need to change *so* and *because*:
> *He was talking to a client, so I didn't want to interrupt him.*
> OR *I didn't want to interrupt him because he was talking to a client.*

Complete the second sentences with a word from the box.

> because   so   when   while

1   I was giving my presentation when the bulb in the projector exploded.
    OR The bulb in the projector exploded _____ I was giving my presentation.
2   I was waiting in reception for ages because she was still in a meeting.
    OR She was still in a meeting, _____ I was waiting in reception for ages.
3   A headhunter called me while I was working at Estée Lauder.
    OR _____ I was working at Estée Lauder, a headhunter called me.
4   The flight was delayed so I was working on my laptop.
    OR I was working on my laptop _____ my flight was delayed.

Countable and uncountable nouns

1 Read the information in the box. Then do the exercise below.

Countable nouns
- We use countable nouns for separate things we can count. Countable nouns can be either singular or plural: *a house, two houses, some houses; one product, two products, a lot of products*.
- A few countable nouns are irregular and make a plural without using -s: *a man, two men; a person, some people*.

Uncountable nouns
- We use uncountable nouns for things we cannot count. Examples: *air, electricity, happiness, health, money*. Uncountable nouns have no plural form. So these forms are not correct: *airs, electricities, happinesses, healths, monies*.
- Uncountable nouns cannot be used with *a/an*. Instead, we often say *some*: *some money, some air*. So these forms are not correct: *a money, an air*.
- Uncountable nouns take a singular verb, not a plural verb: *Good health is important for a happy life.* So this form is not correct: *Good health are important for a happy life.*
- Beware of these common mistakes: *accommodation ✓ accommodations ✗ advice ✓ advices ✗, information ✓ informations ✗, software ✓ softwares ✗, training ✓ trainings ✗*.
- When we use an uncountable noun in a general way, we do not put *the* in front: *For me, football is like life.* So this form is not correct: *For me, the football is like the life.*
- If we want to count an uncountable noun, we can use a phrase like *a piece of*: *two pieces of information, three bottles of water*.

Put these words into the correct column below:

---

accommodation advice bag chair dollar fact furniture hotel information job litre luggage machine machinery milk money suggestion time week work

---

Countable nouns	Uncountable nouns

some and *any; many/much; a few/a little*

2 Study the information in the box. Then do the exercises below.

In positive sentences we use:
some (countable and uncountable)
*I have **some** euros/money.*
a few (countable)
*I have **a few** euros.*
a little (uncountable)
*I have **a little** money.*
In negative sentences and questions we use:
any (countable and uncountable)
*I don't have **any** euros/money.*
*Do you have **any** euros/money?*
many (countable)
*I don't have **many** euros.*
*Do you have **many** euros?*
much (uncountable)
*I don't have **much** money.*
*Do you have **much** money?*
In informal speech, the phrase *a lot of* is common and can be used in all contexts: countable and uncountable, and in positives, negatives and questions.

Complete the sentences with the most likely word: *some* or *any*.

1 Do you have _____ questions to ask me?
2 Yes, there are _____ questions that I'd like to ask.
3 OK, that's all. I don't have _____ more questions to ask.
4 Sorry, I didn't get _____ paper for the photocopier.
5 Did you get _____ paper for the photocopier?
6 Yes, I got _____ – here it is.

3 Complete each sentence with the most likely word: *many, much, a few* or *a little*.

1 I don't have _____ information to give you.
2 I have some information for you, but only _____.
3 I have some facts about the situation, but not _____.
4 I have some facts, but only _____.
5 Does it cost _____ money?
6 Go on, buy it. It only costs _____ dollars.
7 I need _____ time to think about your proposal.
8 I need _____ weeks to think about your proposal.
9 Sorry, I don't have _____ time. Can I do it tomorrow?
10 My holidays are limited – I don't have _____ days left.

---

some and any: exceptions to the rules
There are some exceptions to the rules in the previous box.
- We can use *some* in a question if it is an offer or a request.
  *Would you like **some** more water?* (offer)
  *Could I have **some** more water?* (request)
- We can use *any* in a positive sentence if it means 'no limit'.
  *I'm free **any** time next week.*
  *We can make this product in **any** colour you want.*

Comparatives

4 Try this exercise to see how much you already know. Underline the correct words in *italics*.

1 My new job is *better / more better* that my last one.
2 Internet speeds are *faster / more fast* with this new model.
3 This perfume is *expensiver / more expensive* than the other one.
4 This year we made a *much biger / much bigger* profit than last year.
5 It's *more expensive / most expensive* to buy an Audi than to buy a Citroën.
6 Please make your desk look a bit *tidier / tidyer* – the CEO is visiting our offices this afternoon.
7 Every year the situation is getting *gooder and gooder / better and better*.
8 Every year the situation is getting *badder and badder / worse and worse*.

Before you check your answers, read the information in the box. Then try Exercise 4 again.

Comparatives
- We use the comparative form of an adjective to compare two things.
- With short adjectives, we add -er: **small – smaller**
  In spelling, we double the consonant when the word ends in one vowel + one consonant: **hot – hotter**
  We change -y at the end to -i: **heavy – heavier**
- With long adjectives, we use *more*: **convenient – more convenient**
- Note these irregular forms:
  good – better   bad – worse   far – further
- Notice the use of *than*.
  This is a **newer** model **than** the one you're currently using.

Superlatives

5 Try this exercise to see how much you already know. Underline the correct words in *italics*.

1 This smartphone is *best / the best* on the market.
2 Of all the perfumes in this shop, this one is *the expensivest / the most expensive*.
3 That type of engine has *the highest / the most high* fuel consumption.
4 *Our furthest / Our most far* market is Turkey.
5 Their head office is one of *the most beautiful / the most beautifulest* buildings in the city.
6 This is *the more powerful / the most powerful* engine we've ever produced.
7 The design is terrible – it's one of *the worst / the worse* I've ever seen.
8 The design is great – it's one of *the best / the better* I've ever seen.

Before you check your answers, read the information in the box. Then try Exercise 5 again.

Superlatives
- We use the superlative form of an adjective to compare one thing in a group with all the others.
- With short adjectives, we add -est: **small – the smallest**
  In spelling, we double the consonant when the word ends in one vowel + one consonant: **hot – the hottest**
  We change -y at the end to -i: **heavy – the heaviest**
- With long adjectives, we use *the most*: **convenient – the most convenient**
- Note these irregular forms:
  good – the best   bad – the worst
  far – the furthest
- Notice the use of *the*.
  This is **the** newest model on the market.

6 Study the information in the box. Then do the exercise below.

Comparatives and superlatives: key points
- A few short (one syllable) adjectives can make comparatives and superlatives in both ways. Examples:
  clear, fair, free, proud, safe, sure, true
  The new system is a lot **safer**. ✓
  The new system is a lot **more safe**. ✓
- Two-syllable adjectives usually have *more/the most* like long adjectives. Examples: **correct, famous, frequent, modern, normal, recent**
  Flights to Beijing are **more frequent** these days.
  This model is **the most recent** one in our range.
- But a few two-syllable adjectives can make comparatives and superlatives in both ways. Examples:
  clever, common, handsome, likely, narrow, polite, quiet, secure, simple, stupid, tired
  In Japan, it's **politer** to give your business card with two hands. ✓
  In Japan, it's **more polite** to give your business card with two hands. ✓
  Android is **the commonest** operating system. ✓
  Android is **the most common** operating system. ✓
- We can use *less* and *the least* with long adjectives.
  Citroën is **less expensive than** Audi.
  Of all the cars on sale here, Kia is **the least expensive**.
  We rarely use *less/the least* with short adjectives.

Tick (✓) the sentence if the form in *italics* is correct. Put a cross (✗) if it is incorrect.

1 The new instruction manual is *bigger*. ☐
2 The new instruction manual is *more big*. ☐
3 The new instruction manual is *clearer*. ☐
4 The new instruction manual is *more clear*. ☐
5 The buildings in this part of town are *moderner*. ☐
6 The buildings in this part of town are *more modern*. ☐
7 This museum is *the famousest* in the city. ☐
8 This museum is *the most famous* in the city. ☐
9 The new instruction manual is *simpler*. ☐
10 The new instruction manual is *more simple*. ☐
11 Zander is *the commonest* fish on the menu in Central Europe. ☐
12 Zander is *the most common* fish on the menu in Central Europe. ☐

Modal verbs

1 Study the information in the box. Then do the exercise below.

Modal verbs: form

- Here is a list of modal verbs: *can, could, will, would, must, may, might, shall* and *should*.
- Modal verbs do not have a 'meaning' like other verbs. Instead, they show things like ability, obligation and probability.
  I can do it. = I am able to do it.
  I must do it. = I believe it is necessary for me to do it.
  I might do it. = There is a 50/50 chance I will do it.
- Modal verbs are followed by a main verb in the base form (without *to*).
  You must do it. ✓   *You must to do it.* ✗
- We cannot put two modal verbs together, one after the other.
  You will be able to do it. ✓   *You will can do it.* ✗
  You will have to do it. ✓   *You will must do it.* ✗
- To make a question we change the word order.
  I can work.   **Can** *I work?*
  I must work.   **Must** *I work?*
  I should work.   **Should** *I work?*
- To make a negative we use *not*, often contracted to *n't* in speech: *cannot (can't), could not (couldn't), will not (won't), would not (wouldn't), must not (mustn't), may not* (not usually contracted), *might not* (not usually contracted), *should not (shouldn't)*

<u>Underline</u> the correct words in *italics*.

1 You *must call them / must to call them* right now.
2 You *don't must / mustn't* turn off this computer.
3 *Do you can / Can you* speak Spanish?
4 Why *I should / should I* work late on Friday?
5 I *will can / will be able to* help you when I have time.
6 You *shouldn't / don't should* speak like that to a client.
7 *Must you / Do you must* go so soon?
8 When *we can / can we* have our meeting this week?

Obligation, permission, advice

2 Study the information in the box. Then do the exercise below. Note that *have to, need to* and *be allowed to* are not modal verbs but we use them to express the same ideas.

Modal verbs: meaning

meaning	verb
it's possible; it's permitted	*can, be allowed to*
it's forbidden; it's not allowed	*can't, mustn't, not be allowed to*
it's necessary; it's obligatory	*must, have to, need to*
it's not necessary	*don't have to, don't need to*
it's a good idea; it's the right thing to do	*should*
it's a bad idea; it's the wrong thing to do	*shouldn't*

What do the verbs in *italics* mean? Match sentences 1–6 with the meanings a–f below.

1 At the end of every work day you *should* tidy your desk. It feels like you're making a fresh start when you arrive the next morning. ☐
2 When you meet your colleagues socially after work, you *shouldn't* gossip about other people in the office. ☐
3 You *have to* wear a suit and tie if you are meeting a client. ☐
4 You *don't have to* wear a suit and tie if you work in the marketing department – only our more senior managers wear formal clothes. ☐
5 At the age of 16, you *can* leave school, apply for a passport and join the armed forces. ☐
6 At the age of 16, you *can't* get married, go to prison or get a tattoo (unless your parents agree). ☐

a) possible or permitted
b) forbidden or not allowed
c) necessary or obligatory
d) not necessary (you have a choice)
e) good idea, or the right thing to do
f) bad idea, or the wrong thing to do

3 Put the words in the correct order to make questions.

1 I / later today / Can / call you back
   A: <u>*Can I call you back later today?*</u>
   B: Of course. Any time after three.
2 we / Should / our phones / switch off / in the meeting
   A: _____?
   B: Yes, please put them on silent mode and go outside if you get an urgent call.
3 I / have to / the report today / Do / finish
   A: _____?
   B: No, you don't. Friday will be fine.
4 allowed / to give / we / Are / a small gift at the end of the visit
   A: _____?
   B: Yes, you can take a book with some photographs of our country, but don't give anything expensive.
5 organize / we / a leaving party for her / Shouldn't
   A: _____?
   B: Yes, that's a nice idea. She's retiring after working here for twenty years.

4 <u>Underline</u> the most likely words in *italics*.

1 You *mustn't / don't have to* criticize your previous employer in a job interview.
2 You *need to / shouldn't* have personal phone conversations in the office while everyone around you is working.
3 We *don't need to / shouldn't* come to work on Christmas Eve – the boss said we could take the day off if there was nothing urgent to do.
4 You *have to / are allowed to* turn off your phone when the plane is taking off.
5 Sorry, I *should / must* go now – I'm going to miss my flight!
6 We *must / don't have to* use all the money on just one training course – I think it's a good idea to save some money for other courses.

7 On a normal flight you *must / are allowed to* take 20kg in your baggage, but no more.

8 I know I *should / must* go to the sports club every week, but it's difficult to find the time.

9 You *don't need to / shouldn't* arrive late for a meeting in any country – not just in Switzerland and Germany.

10 In a job interview in the US and UK, your employer *is not allowed to / doesn't need to* ask you about your age, marital status, race or religion.

5 Complete the sentences with the most likely words from the box. Think carefully about the situation.

can	can't	don't have to	have to	should	shouldn't

1 You _____ park there – it's against the law and you'll get a fine.

2 You _____ park there – it's not against the rules, but everyone knows it's where the boss usually parks.

3 You _____ park over there. It's absolutely fine. It's where everyone parks.

4 When you arrive, you _____ park where it says 'Visitors'. There's nowhere else. All the other spaces are reserved for employees of the company.

5 You _____ park over there – you can park right here instead. It's more convenient.

6 I think you _____ try to park as close to the entrance as possible because it's going to rain later.

Verb patterns

6 Study the information in the box. Then do the exercise below.

> **say, tell, and ask**
> We **say** something.
> We **say** to someone. (not ~~say someone~~)
> We **tell** someone something. (not ~~tell to someone~~)
> We **ask** someone (about) something.
> *He asked me what I thought.* (not ~~asked to me~~)

Complete the sentences with *said*, *told* or *asked*.

1 She _____ me she was leaving the company.

2 She _____ that she was leaving the company.

3 She _____ me if I was happy working here, and I _____ 'yes'.

4 She _____ to Michael that she was leaving the company.

5 She _____ Michael that she was leaving the company.

6 She _____ Michael what he thought about the company, and he _____ her that he was happy here.

7 Study the information in the box. Then do the exercise below.

> **say, tell, talk, speak** and *discuss*
> These words have different meanings and patterns.
> **say** (= express in words)
> *say something*
> *say something to someone*
> **tell** (= give information)
> *tell someone*
> *tell someone (about) something*
> *tell someone (not) to do something*
> **talk/speak** (= say things as part of a conversation)
> *talk/speak to/with someone*
> *talk/speak about something*
> *talk/speak to/with someone about something*
> **discuss** (= talk in a serious, detailed way)
> *discuss something*
> *discuss something with someone*

Complete the sentences. If a word is needed in a gap, write it in. If no word is needed, leave it blank.

1 I spoke _____ my boss _____ the delays on the project.

2 I talked _____ the arrangements for the conference _____ the Events Organizer.

3 I discussed _____ the arrangements for the conference _____ the Events Organizer.

4 I told _____ Joelle _____ be careful what she said.

5 I told _____ Joelle _____ to say anything that is personal and confidential.

6 I said _____ Joelle that she should be careful.

7 It was a useful meeting – we discussed _____ everything.

8 It was a useful meeting – we talked _____ everything.

9 In the meeting I said _____ Joelle that it was a good idea.

10 He asked _____ me what I thought, and I told _____ him.

> **Reporting verbs**
> *Say*, *tell* and *ask* are called 'reporting verbs'. They report the words that someone said. There are many other reporting verbs like *explain*, *promise*, *remind*, *propose*, etc. It is important to know the verb patterns:
>
> | | |
> |---|---|
> | *Vitaly said (**that**) we did it.* | verb + (*that*) + subject-verb-object |
> | *Vitaly explained **it to us**.* | verb + object + *to* + object |
> | *Vitaly promised **to do** it.* | verb + *to* + infinitive |
> | *Vitaly reminded **us to do** it.* | verb + object + *to* + infinitive |
> | *Vitaly proposed **doing** it.* | verb + -*ing* |
>
> Verbs sometimes have more than one pattern. The verb *suggest* has three of the five patterns above:
> *Vitaly suggested (that) we did it.* ✓
> *Vitaly suggested it to us.* ✓
> *Vitaly ~~suggested to do it.~~* ✗
> *Vitaly ~~suggested us to do it.~~* ✗
> *Vitaly suggested doing it.* ✓

will and *won't*

1 Read the information in the box. Then do the exercise below.

> *will* and *won't* are used in four main ways:
> 1 to talk about facts in the future
> 2 to make predictions
> 3 to make decisions
> 4 to make promises
> • Facts are definite. We know what will happen.
>   *The company **will** celebrate its twentieth anniversary next year.*
>   *Prices **will definitely** increase next year.*
>   ***I'm sure that** we **will** reach an agreement, but it might take time.*
> • Predictions are not definite. We think we know what will happen, but we accept that we might be wrong.
>   ***I think** they **will** agree to our proposal, but I'm not sure.*
>   *Prices **will probably** increase next year.*
>   ***My guess is** that we **will** reach an agreement, but I could be wrong.*
> • Decisions are choices that we make.
>   *It's raining. **I'll** take an umbrella.*
>   *She **won't** speak to me.* (decision not to do something)
> • Promises are when we say we will definitely do something.
>   ***I'll** call you back this afternoon.*
>   *Don't worry, I **won't** tell anyone.* (promise not to do something)
> • Note that *will* is often used for instant decisions and promises we make at the moment of speaking.

Match examples 1–4 with the uses of *will* a–d.

1 It's hot in here. **I'll** open the window. ☐
2 She**'ll** be in Toulouse all next week, so there's no point calling her at the Hamburg office. ☐
3 Don't worry, **I'll** speak to my boss about it this afternoon. ☐
4 I think sales **will** probably improve next quarter. ☐

a) future fact   c) instant decision
b) prediction   d) promise

> ### *will* and *won't*: key points
> • *will* is often shortened to *'ll* in speech, particularly after pronouns (*I'll, he'll,* etc.).
> • The negative of *will* is **won't**. We use the full form *will not* in formal writing and when our feelings are strong.
> • To make a question, change the word order.
>   ***They will** arrive tomorrow.*
>   ***Will they** arrive tomorrow?*
>   *When **will they** arrive?*
> • We put *probably* <u>after</u> *will*, but <u>before</u> *won't*.
>   *They**'ll probably** sign the contract this week.*
>   *They **probably won't** sign the contract today.*
> • We usually say *I don't think … will* rather than *I think … won't*.
>   ***I don't think** this product **will** sell in Asia.* ✓
>   *~~I think~~ this product **won't** sell in Asia.* ✗

2 Correct each sentence by changing or adding a form of *will*.

1 I'm sure tomorrow is a beautiful day.
2 Your phone's ringing – don't worry, I answer it.
3 I send you an email this afternoon to confirm the details.
4 Sorry, but I not be able to come to the meeting next week.
5 It's difficult to negotiate with them – they not tell us what they want.
6 Don't worry, I'm sure you get better.
7 I won't probably join you in the restaurant tonight – I have an early flight.
8 I think we won't make a profit next year.

3 Put the words in **bold** in the correct order to make predictions.

1 **'ll they I think probably** give the job to Anita, not Miguel.

_____

2 **They won't probably** give the job to Marcus.

_____

3 **I 'll think don't they** give the job to Carla.

_____

be going to

4 Read the information in the box. Then do the exercise below.

> ***be going to*** is used in two main ways:
> 1 to make predictions
> 2 to talk about plans made in advance (the plan can be definite, or it can be just an intention)
> • Examples:
>   *Have you seen the news? I think the factory **is going to** close.* (prediction)
>   *I think this new product **is going to** sell very well.* (prediction)
>   *We**'re going to** launch the product in October.* (plan)
>   *I**'m going to** start my own business when I get enough money.* (intention)
> • Contractions (*We're, I'm*) are used in speech and informal writing.
> • Negatives and questions are shown below.
>   *I**'m not going to** start my own business – it's too risky.*
>   ***Are** we **going to** launch the product in October?*
> • In informal speech (and songs) we often say *gonna* for *be going to*.

Match examples 1–3 with the uses of *be going to* a–c.

1 We**'re going to** move to a new office in January. We signed the rental agreement last month. ☐
2 Travel around the world? **I'm going to** do that when I retire. I'm focused on my career right now. ☐
3 I think we**'re going to** get complaints from our customers when we put up our prices. ☐

a) prediction
b) definite plan
c) intention

5 Correct each sentence by changing or adding a form of *be going to*.

1 I think the Social Democrats going to win the election.
2 Unemployment is going increase if the recession continues.
3 I received some money when my aunt died – I going to invest it.
4 We not going to redesign this model until next year.
5 Do you going to spend Christmas with your parents?

6 Read the information in the box. Then do the exercise below.

> **will and be going to**
> Predictions
> *will* and *be going to* are both used to make predictions. In most cases there is very little difference and you could use either one.
> However, if there is strong evidence in the present situation, then *be going to* is more likely.
> *Look at those clouds. I think it's going to rain.* (I can see grey clouds right now.)
> Decisions
> *will* is used for an instant decision made at the moment of speaking.
> *be going to* is used for a plan or intention. The decision is made before the moment of speaking.

Complete each sentence with a form of *will* or *be going to* and the verb in brackets. In every case both are possible, but decide which form is the most likely.

Predictions
1 Look at the time! We _____ (be) late.
2 I think it _____ (probably/rain) at the weekend.

Decisions
3 Yes, we _____ (give) you a 2% discount. But you have to place a large order – 1,000 pieces or more.
4 I was talking to my wife about this last week. We _____ (buy) a small apartment for our daughter to live in while she's at university.

First conditional

7 Read the information in the box. Then do the exercise.

> • A sentence beginning with *If* … is called a conditional. There are different types of conditional. The most common type is the first conditional. It is used when a future event is likely to happen (it's probable).
> *If they **like** our business plan, they'll invest.*
> *If I **decide** to buy shares, I'll have to accept some risk.*
> • A conditional has two parts, a condition with *If* and a result. Notice the form of the verbs in the two examples above:
> **If + present simple, … will …**
> Do NOT use *will* in the *If* … part.
> *If they will like our business plan, …*
> *If we will decide to buy shares, …*

> • The *If* … part can come at the end.
> *They'll invest **if they like our business plan**.*
> *We'll have to accept some risk **if we buy shares**.*
> • We can use negatives in any part of the sentence.
> *If they like our business plan, we **won't** have to worry about finance.*
> *If they **don't like** our business plan, we'll have to rethink everything.*
> *If they **don't like** our business plan, we **won't** get the money.*
> • There are other types of conditional called second and third conditionals. They are covered in later levels of *The Business 2.0*.

Find and correct two mistakes in each of these sentences.

1 If you will pay cash, I give you a discount.
2 If I don't will hear from them soon, I will to send them an email.
3 Don't worry, I don't will say anything about your new job if your colleagues will ask anything.
4 If the company will be successful, they probably hire more staff.
5 If I not hear anything from them by the end of the week, I call them and remind them.
6 The sales director not keep his job if sales not improve.

8 Complete these first conditional sentences with the correct form of the verbs in brackets. Use contractions where possible.

1 If you _____ (sign) today, I _____ (give) you the items at the lower price.
2 If you _____ (take) our extended warranty, you _____ (not/have to) worry about service and spare parts for four years.
3 We _____ (miss) the deadline if we _____ (not/get) more resources for this project.
4 I _____ (ask) for directions if we _____ (not/find) their offices soon.
5 If I _____ (not/get) promoted to a more senior position in the next few years, I _____ (not/stay) with the company.

9 Read the information in the box. Then do the exercise.

> **Time expressions + present simple**
> Use a present tense, NOT *will*, after these time expressions: ***when, until, as soon as, before, after***
> *I'll give her your message **when I see her**.* ✓
> NOT *I'll give her your message **when I will see her**.* ✗
> Notice how *will* appears in the other part of the sentence (*I'll give her …*).

Correct the mistake in each sentence.

1 I'll call you as soon as I will get the information.
2 I should know if we have finance for the project after I will meet the bank manager.
3 When she will arrive, we can start the meeting.
4 I won't do anything until I will hear from you.

1 Complete the table below. The third column is needed to make irregular forms of the present perfect.

infinitive	past simple	past participle
become	became	1 _____
begin	began	2 _____
bring	brought	brought
buy	bought	bought
choose	chose	3 _____
cost	cost	cost
fall	fell	4 _____
find	found	found
forget	forgot	5 _____
give	gave	6 _____
go	went	7 _____
grow	grew	8 _____
have	had	had
keep	kept	kept
know	knew	9 _____
leave	left	left
lose	lost	lost
make	made	10 _____
meet	met	met
pay	paid	paid
see	saw	11 _____
sell	sold	sold
set	set	set
speak	spoke	12 _____
spend	spent	spent
take	took	13 _____
tell	told	told
think	thought	14 _____
understand	understood	understood
write	wrote	15 _____

Check your answers. Then cover the third column with a piece of paper and test yourself. Repeat until you have learned all the forms!

Present perfect

2 Match examples 1–3 with the uses of the present perfect a–c below.

1 We**'ve** just **opened** a new office in Prague. Our operations in central Europe will be much more efficient now. ☐
2 The Prague office **has been** open for three months. ☐
3 I**'ve never been** to our office in Prague. ☐

a) a recent action with a result in the present
b) life experience up to now
c) an unfinished state

Present perfect: form and meaning

- The form of the present perfect is *has/have* + past participle (third column of verb tables). Contractions are common in speech.
  Positive
  *I **have (I've) seen** the new designs.*
  *He **has (He's) seen** the new designs.*
  Negative
  *I **have not (I haven't) talked** to my colleagues about it.*
  *He **has not (He hasn't) talked** to his colleagues about it.*
  Questions
  ***Have** I **done** everything?*
  ***Has** he **done** everything?*
- The present perfect connects the present with the past. It 'looks back' from the present. This is true of all three uses below.
  <u>A recent action with a result in the present</u>
  *I've **finished** the report.* (You can read it now)
  *Your taxi **has** just **arrived**.* (It's waiting for you now)
  Giving news:
  *I've **bought** a new car.* (I want to tell you about it now)
  *We've **improved** the functionality of our website.* (I want to tell you now about the new things you can do)
  The important thing is not when the action happened, but the result of the action right now.
  In this type of sentence the words *just*, *already* and *yet* are very common.
  <u>Life experience up to now</u>
  *I've **been** to Morocco several times.* (in my life)
  ***Have** you ever **seen** a whale?* (in your life)
  *I've never **heard** anything so ridiculous.* (in my life)
  Here we are talking about our whole life experience until now.
  In these sentences the words *ever* in a question and *never* in an answer are very common.
  <u>An unfinished state</u>
  *She's **worked** here for three years.* (and she still works here)
  *I've **known** her since university.* (and I still know her)
  Here we are talking about states or actions that began in the past and are still continuing now.
  In these sentences, the words *for* with a period of time and *since* with a point in time are very common.
- In American English, the present perfect is used, but less frequently. In American English you often use the past simple with *just/yet/already* to talk about life experience up to now.

3 Complete the sentences with the correct present perfect form of the verb in brackets. Use contractions where possible.

1 _____ (we/make) the right decision?
2 I had a headache but I _____ (take) an aspirin and I'm going to feel better soon.
3 Do you know where Marta is? I _____ (not/see) her since lunchtime.
4 The meeting _____ (not/begin) yet, so we

still have time to check these figures.

5   We need to see Peter's market report. _____ (he/write) it yet?

6   _____ (anyone/lose) their keys? I found these by the water cooler.

7   Are we reaching every type of customer with our advertising? We _____ (spend) half the marketing budget just on Internet banner ads.

8   Yes, I know I need to enter all the sales data into the spreadsheet. I _____ (not/forget).

ever and never

4 In each exchange, correct the mistake in the form of the present perfect.

1   **A:** Have you ever work abroad?
    B: No, never.
2   **A:** What's it like in Turkey?
    B: I don't know. I never be there.
3   **A:** You ever forget a client's name?
    B: Yes, I have. It was really embarrassing.
4   **A:** Chris never tell me about his family.
    B: No, he likes to keep his work and his private life separate.

just, already and yet

5 Read the information in the box. Then do the exercise below.

- We often use the present perfect with *just*. It means 'a short time ago'.
  *I've **just** read your report. We need to have a meeting as soon as possible.*
- We often use the present perfect with *already*. It means 'before now'.
  *I've **already** spoken to the supplier. The goods will arrive by courier tomorrow.*
- We often use the present perfect with *yet*. It means 'up to now'. It is used in questions and negatives and comes at the end of the sentence.
  *Has your sister found a job **yet**?*
  *The goods haven't arrived in our warehouse **yet**.*

Write sentences in the present perfect using the words in brackets.

1   **A:** When will the new machine be ready?
    B: Soon. _____ (We/already/test/ the prototype)
2   **A:** Can we start work on the project?
    B: No. _____ (We/not/sign/the contract/yet)
3   **A:** Has the technician fixed the photocopier?
    B: Yes. _____ (He/just/do/it)
4   **A:** They're working very slowly. Should we contact another firm?
    B: It's too late. _____ (We/ already/pay/them)
5   **A:** _____? (you/install/the software/yet)
    B: No. It's better if someone from IT does it.

since and for

6 Read the information in the box. Then do the exercise below.

We often want to know *How long …?* If we ask the question, the verb is in the present perfect.
*How long **has** she **worked** here?*
*How long **have** you **known** her?*
When we answer, we can use *for* + length of time or *since* + point in time.
*How long **has** she **worked** here?*
***For** three years./**Since** 2012.*
*How long **have** you **known** her?*
***For** ages./**Since** university.*

Complete B's answer with *for* or *since*.

1   **A:** How long have you been married?
    B: _____ a long time! Twenty-two years.
2   **A:** How long has he supported Manchester United?
    B: _____ he was a boy.
3   **A:** How long has Chen had his own business?
    B: _____ three years – he started making a profit this year.
4   **A:** How long has this product been on the market?
    B: _____ the beginning of the year. It's selling very well.

Present perfect vs past simple

7 Read the information in the box then do the exercise below.

Past simple
- We use the past simple for finished actions.
  *I **worked** there after I left university.* (I don't work there any more)
- Time expressions: *yesterday, on Tuesday, last week, in 2002, a few months ago, when I was young,* etc.

Present perfect
- We use the present perfect for unfinished actions, and for the present result of a past action.
  *I've **worked** here for three years.* (unfinished 'work')
  *Have you ever **been** to Morocco?* (unfinished 'life')
  *We've recently **improved** our website.* (result more important than action)
  *He's **fixed** the photocopier.* (result more important than action)
- Time expressions: *for two years, since January, recently, until now, ever, never, just, already, yet*

Complete the sentences with either the past simple or the present perfect form of the verbs in brackets.

1   a) My PC _____ (get) a virus last week so I'm using my tablet.
    b) Oh, no! My PC _____ (get) a virus! What am I going to do now?
2   a) Have you heard the news? There _____ (be) an earthquake in San Francisco.
    b) There _____ (be) a small earthquake just outside San Francisco while we were there on holiday.

Recordings

Business fundamentals

Business activities

 1:01

… So, we can divide all business activities into three sectors. In the primary sector, we find activities that extract raw materials from the earth or from the oceans. These are businesses like agriculture, mining, and oil and gas. The secondary sector covers activities like manufacturing, construction and civil engineering – building roads and bridges, for example. Finally, in the tertiary sector, we have commercial services such as advertising, health care, software and transport. Now, let's go to …

Business organization

 1:02–1:05

Speaker 1: Hi, I'm Michael. I'm a product engineer. I love working in R&D. I test new products and find solutions to technical problems. It's my dream job!

Speaker 2: Hello. My name's Jessie. My job is hard. There's a lot of stress. I work in purchasing – it's part of supply chain. I'm responsible for buying the materials we need for production.

Speaker 3: Hi! I'm Pete. I work in accounts, and it's my job to check that customers pay their bills. I receive payments and I enter the information on the computer. If customers don't pay, I call them. They're usually very friendly so, yes, it's a good job.

Speaker 4: Sorry, I don't have much time to talk. I'm always busy! I'm Kim and I work in sales. It's my job to call customers and sell our products. I'd really like to work in marketing, but the money's better in sales!

CVs and cover letters

 1:06

Ms Finlay: Now, Ben, you say you'd like to work for Rose Inc. to gain experience.

Ben: That's right. I hope to work as an intern before finding a permanent job.

F: Mm. And you already have some experience in our industry?

B: Yes, with L'Oréal in Paris. I was responsible for conducting an online market survey.

F: Uh-huh. Do you have any experience of managing people?

B: Well, I managed a team of volunteers when I was President of the Salsa Society. We organized dances and competitions.

F: Right. Any other work experience?

B: Yes. I worked as a repair technician in the Czech Republic in the summer holidays.

F: Ah, yes. So, do you have a working knowledge of the language?

B: Yes. My Dad's from Prague.

F: I see. That's interesting. We have a factory there. Do you drive?

B: Yes, I hold a clean driving licence.

F: Good. So, Ben, can I contact you in Coventry?

B: Yes. My address, email and telephone numbers are all in my CV, um, in my résumé.

F: All in your résumé. That's perfect. Thank you, Ben.

1 Gaining experience

1.1 About business Internships abroad

 1:07

Lena: I really want to work in the film industry, but with just a degree, it's impossible to get a job. So my parents paid an agency nearly ten thousand dollars to arrange this internship in a film studio. Yes, ten thousand dollars! So, here I am in Hollywood, and do you know how I demonstrate my ability to adapt to a different culture? I make coffee and cook burgers for the film crew! Well, I suppose it's good for team spirit, but I'm not learning about managing uncertainty or how to build relationships! I live in a terrible, cheap hotel and I don't even get paid! I call the agency every week, but they say it's the only job available in the film industry. Making coffee and cooking burgers is show business? I don't think so!

 1:08

Jamie: I have a degree in economics. To get a good job, I need to acquire some professional experience, so I found this internship here in Brazil with an agency. It was expensive – about five thousand dollars – but they organized everything for me: my visa, my flight, an apartment near the beach, language lessons … I work for an international firm of consultants. Cultural values are different here, so I'm learning a lot about intercultural sensitivity. For example, it's very important to adjust my communication to the local style – Brazilians are informal and direct. The company pays me a small salary, and maybe I can get a permanent job at the end of my internship. So, yes, I'm very satisfied. Like they say at the agency, it's an investment in my future.

1.2 Vocabulary Personal details

1:09

ninety-nine
one hundred and one
one thousand
one thousand five hundred *or* fifteen hundred
seven thousand seven hundred and seventy-seven
eighty-eight thousand eight hundred and eighty-eight
one hundred thousand
nine hundred thousand nine hundred and ninety-nine

one million
three point five million
two point five billion
two point five seven five
a hundred and ten dollars
fifteen euros ninety-nine

 1:10

A: OK, I'll go first. So, I have to think of a secret number between one and one million. Is that right?

B and C: Yes, that's right.

A: OK, I'm ready.

B: All right, I guess one hundred thousand.

A: Too high.

C: Er, one thousand?

A: Too high.

C: Oh!

B: Five hundred.

A: Too low.

C: Aha! Eight hundred and fifty.

A: Too low.

B: Hm. Nine hundred?

A: Too high.

C: Eight hundred and eighty-five.

A: Too low.

B: Eight hundred and ninety-six.

A: Too low.

C: Eight hundred and ninety-nine?

A: Yes, well done.

C: Yeah!

1:11

/eɪ/ A, H, J, K
/iː/ B, C, D, E, G, P, T, V
/e/ F, L, M, N, S, X, Z
/aɪ/ I, Y
/əʊ/ O
/uː/ Q, U, W
/ɑː/ R

1:12

Receptionist: Hello.

Mo: Hi.

Jen: Hello. We'd like to register, please.

R: Certainly. Can I have your names, please?

J: Yes, I'm Jennifer Oxenbury and this is Mo Qureshi. Sorry, I mean Mohammad Qureshi!

R: Can you spell those, please?

J: Yes, of course. J-E-double N-I-F-E-R, O-X-E-N-B-U-R-Y.

R: Thank you, and it's …?

M: Mohammad, that's M-O-H-A-double M-A-D.

R: Sorry, was that M-E-D or M-A-D at the end?

M: Double M-A-D.

R: OK?

M: Qureshi. Q-U-R-E-S-H-I.

R: Thank you. Now, I just need your dates of birth and passport numbers, please.

J: Really? OK, mine's the fifteenth of April 1994.

M: And mine's the twenty-eighth of December 1993.

R: Thank you. And your passport number, Mr Qureshi?

M: Just a second. Ah, here it is. 08-JG…

R: That's J for Juliet and G for Golf, right?

M: Right. 08-JG-double 4-double 6-69.

J: And mine is 07-EI-98-45-02.

R: Thanks. Sorry about that. New security regulations! So, here are your keys. Miss Oxenbury, you're in A309. That's on the third floor.

J: Thank you.

R: And Mr Qureshi, you're in E214, that's in the new building over there, on the second floor.

M: Thanks.

R: Your course reference numbers are on your badges. Miss Oxenbury, you're doing the Assertiveness course, aren't you? That's ASS67/GL. And Mr Qureshi, Leadership Skills, that's LEA43/JH. Your course starts tomorrow, Mr Qureshi – that's June 30th – and it's at 8.45 with Dr Higgs.

M: OK, June 30th, quarter to nine, with Dr …?

R: Higgs. H-I-double G-S. She's very nice!

M: Thanks.

J: And I start the day after tomorrow … at the same time?

R: Um, Assertiveness … Yes, July 1st. Oh, you start at 6.30.

J: 6.30am?

R: No, half past six in the evening. It's a late class, 6.30 to 10.30pm.

J: Oh.

R: Yes. But you're lucky. You're with Professor Lockhart. He's great!

J: Oh, good. Is that L-O-C-K-H-A-R-T?

R: Yes!

J: Great!

R: All right, then. So, for you Mr Qureshi, that's $455, and for Miss Oxenbury, it's $545. How would you like to pay?

1.3 Grammar **Present simple**

 1:13

Part 1

Presenter: So, how often do we Europeans travel abroad?

Journalist: Well, it depends. A lot of us often go abroad. On average, 27% of Europeans visit another country once a year, mostly in the summer.

P: But not everybody, right?

J: No. In Bulgaria, only 5% of people go abroad.

P: Only 5% of Bulgarians go abroad? Wow! And which country travels most?

J: Oh, the Netherlands. 65% of Dutch people leave Holland. They travel once or twice a year.

 1:14

Part 2

Presenter: What about watching TV in a foreign language? How often do we watch a foreign film?

Journalist: Well, nearly always in Denmark! 74% of Danes watch foreign language TV or films.

P: Wow! Well done, Denmark! 74%! And when do they do that?

J: All the time! At the weekend, on weekdays, in the evening …

P: OK, and on average?

J: On average, 19% of Europeans watch foreign TV.

P: And which countries don't?

J: Well, Italy. Only 3% of Italians watch films in another language.

P: Only 3%? Oh, really?

 1:15

Part 3

Journalist: Finally, reading a newspaper in a foreign language. On average, 9% of Europeans read a foreign newspaper.

Presenter: Hm. 9% … that's not much.

J: Well, I'm afraid only 3% of Italians read a foreign newspaper.

P: Probably the same ones who watch foreign films!

J: Perhaps!

P: Come on, Italy, you can do better! Just once every six months, or once a quarter?

J: But in Luxembourg, 71% of people read a foreign newspaper.

P: Excellent! 71%! Way to go, Luxembourg!

1.4 Speaking **Meeting people and making conversation**

 1:16

Greg: Excuse me. Is this seat free?

Silke: Yes, of course.

G: Thanks. The weather's terrible, isn't it?

S: Yes, it's really cold for May!

G: Mm. Are you here for the conference?

S: Yes. You too?

G: Yes. My name's Greg. Greg Baird. I'm with Sanofi.

S: Silke Werner, with GSK.

G: Pleased to meet you, Silke.

S: Pleased to meet you, too.

1:17

Greg: Hi. I'm Greg Baird, with Sanofi.

Receptionist: Welcome to the conference, Mr Baird. Here's your badge.

G: Thanks.

Alan: Hi, Greg!

G: Alan, great to see you!

A: Good to see you, too, Greg. How are you doing?

G: I'm good, thanks. And you? Still with Merck, I see?

A: Yes, for the moment anyway. Listen, talking of jobs, do you have time for a cup of coffee? I want to ask you a favour …

1:18

Greg: Mm, it's good coffee! OK, Alan. I'll do my best. Oh, hi, Silke. Alan, do you know Silke Werner?

Alan: No, I don't think so.

G: Silke, this is Alan Banks, an old friend from Merck.

Silke: Nice to meet you.

A: Nice to meet you, too. Do you work with Greg?

S: No, we met on the shuttle bus. I'm with GSK in London.

A: London? Really?

S: Yes. I work in R&D.

A: Go on. Do tell me more!

G: Silke, Alan, do excuse me. I really must take my bags up to my room.

A: OK. See you later.

1:19

Alan: More bread?

Silke: No, thanks. I'm fine.

A: So, now I'm in France, in Lyon.

S: Uh-huh?

A: Yes. Nice town … good rugby team … but it's quite far from home.

S: I see.

A: That's why I'd really like to move to London. But, enough about me. Let's talk about you. Is this your first visit to Serbia?

S: Yes, it is, actually.

A: Me too. I love visiting new countries and meeting new people, don't you?

S: Yes, it's always good to see new places.

A: By the way, there's a tour of the old town this evening. Are you interested in coming?

S: Sorry, no. I have a meeting this evening. Anyway, Alan, I really must make some phone calls, so …

A: Oh, OK. Well, it was nice talking to you.

S: Yes. See you later.

1.6 Case study **The Intern Shop**

1:20–1:22

1

Interviewer: Tai, can I just check how you spell your name? Is it S-H-I-N-A-W-O-T-R-A?

Tai: That's nearly right – but it's W-A-T-R-A, not W-O.

I: OK, and you were born on September 8th, 1990?

T: No, August 9th, 1990.

I: Oh, yes. Sorry about that.

T: That's all right.

I: And you're from Thailand, but you studied in California. Is that right?

T: Right. At the Leavey School of Business, in Santa Clara.

I: L-E-A-V-E-Y?

T: Yes.

I: So, Tai, what's your professional objective?

T: Well, I don't know. Right now, I just want to see the world and get some experience, I guess.

2

Interviewer: Karen, I'm sorry, I don't have your date of birth here …

Karen: It's the fifth of May, 1991.

I: Thank you. Now, you're Irish, aren't you?

K: I'm from Northern Ireland. From Belfast.

I: And you studied languages at Bradford University. Which languages?

K: Hungarian and Japanese.

I: An interesting choice!

K: Yes. I love exotic languages, don't you?

I: So, would you like to learn Chinese or Portuguese?

K: Oh, yes, absolutely!

I: What about your intercultural skills? Can you adapt to a different culture?

K: I'm sure I can. Bradford is an international university. I have friends from all over the world. And I love travelling and meeting people. That's my hobby!

3

Interviewer: Where are you from, Julio?

Julio: My parents are from Mexico City. But we live in Barbados. I studied at the University of the West Indies at Cave Hill.

I: Can you spell Cave Hill for me, please?

J: Sure. C-A-V-E new word H-I-double L.

I: Thanks. So you're a Mexican national?

J: Yes. But I don't know Mexico very well!

I: But you speak Spanish. Any other languages?

J: No, I'm afraid not. Just Spanish and English.

I: Now, you studied physics, but you want to work in business. Why is that?

J: Actually, my real interest is computers and software. I'd really like to be a software developer.

🎵 1:23–1:25

1

Interviewer: Just one last question, Tai. These days, a lot of internships are unpaid. Is that a problem for you?

Tai: Um, yes, that's a little difficult. I don't need a lot of money – just enough to live on and to pay for my ticket home.

2

Interviewer: Just one last question, Karen. These days, a lot of internships are unpaid. Is that a problem for you?

Karen: Not really. I hope to earn a good salary in a few years. I see this internship as an investment for the future.

3

Interviewer: Just one last question, Julio. These days, a lot of internships are unpaid. Is that a problem for you?

Julio: Well, I know I won't get rich. That's not a problem. But I need to pay for food and accommodation. My parents can't pay for everything.

2 Customer satisfaction

2.1 About business Customer service

🎵 1:26–1:27

Speaker 1: I always buy my fruit and vegetables from a specialist shop. There's a market near my home, and a supermarket too. They're both cheaper, but I prefer my fruit and vegetable shop. I'm happy to pay a little more, because everything is always fresh, but mainly because of the service. The assistants all know my name and they know what I like. They're very friendly. They always seem pleased to see you and make conversation. They help you with your bags and they always give you something free – some herbs, or a nice red apple … I suppose they just make you feel special!

Speaker 2: I'm not the sort of person who complains. If the service isn't good in a restaurant, for example, I don't say anything. I just don't give a tip and I don't go back. Or if an Internet service provider doesn't have good technical support, I change to another company. There's so much competition these days, I'm surprised that there's still so much bad service. Consumers always have a choice, so bad service just doesn't make sense. I really don't understand it!

2.2 Vocabulary Contacting customers

🎵 1:28–1:30

1

Customer service: Customer service, good morning. How can I help you?

Customer 1: Hello. I'm calling about my Internet box. I'm having installation problems.

CS: I'm sorry to hear that. But if you contact the helpline, they can provide technical support. The number to call is 0800 …

2

Customer service: Customer service, good afternoon. Can I help you?

Customer 2: Yes, good afternoon. It's about the TV I ordered from you. It doesn't work. But you have a money-back guarantee, is that right?

CS: That's absolutely right, sir. I'm sorry your TV doesn't work. But if you return the faulty product, we'll give you a full refund.

3

Customer service: Customer service. Good evening.

Customer 3: Good evening. I'm calling to complain about the ski jacket I ordered. You shipped the wrong product. It's too small, and it's a really horrible colour.

CS: I'm sorry to hear that. If you …

C3: And it's not the first time. It's really not good enough!

CS: I do apologize, madam. We'll be happy to exchange the product.

🎵 1:31–1:36

1 I'm just finishing a call on my mobile. Ask her to wait for a minute or two, please.

2 OK, that's my checklist done. Now, where's the number? Here it is, 0371 629404.

3 I'm sorry; I'm out of the office today. Please record your details after the beep, and I'll get back to you as soon as possible.

4 Hello, hello? Can you hear me? Hello?

5 Hi, it's Philip. I know you're busy, but I need the sales results as soon as you can. Thanks.

6 Hello. Could I speak to Julia Martin, please?

2.4 Speaking Telephoning

🎵 1:37

Receptionist: Marchman Video. Good morning. Can I help you?

Mike: Good morning. Could I speak to Sue Downing, please?

R: Could I have your name, please?

M: Yes, this is Mike Woods, from Pixxel Inc.

R: Just a moment, please.

…

R: I'm sorry, Mr Woods. She isn't answering. Would you like to speak to her assistant?

M: Yes, please.

R: I'll put you through.

M: Thank you.

Paula: Paula Rice.

M: Hello, Paula. It's Mike, from Pixxel. How are you?

P: Oh, hi, Mike. I'm fine thanks, and you?

M: Good, thanks. Is Sue there, please?

P: I'm sorry, she isn't available this morning. She's in a meeting. Can I take a message?

M: Yes, please. I'm calling about her next order. Could you ask her to call me back?

P: Sure. Is lunchtime OK for you?

M: Yes, that's fine.

P: I'll ask her to get back to you as soon as the meeting is finished.

M: Great. Thanks for your help, Paula.

P: You're welcome.

M: Goodbye.

P: Bye!

🎵 1:38

Mike: Hello?

Sue: Is that Mike?

M: Yes, speaking.

S: It's Sue Downing here, returning your call. Is this a bad time?

M: Sue, hi! No, I'm just finishing my sandwich, but it's fine. Thanks for getting back to me.

S: No problem. What can I do for you?

M: Well, it's about your next order. As you know, we have a new product, and …

2.6 Case study Rock tour

🎵 1:39

Hi, this is Scott Nelson, President of the Illinois Einstein fan club. Listen, the concert in Burlington on Thursday was awesome. But a lot of our members are very unhappy because it's so difficult to get tickets. The band is famous now. We don't understand why you don't play bigger venues. I mean, the Burlington Plaza only has two thousand seats – that's far too small for a great band like Einstein! You can easily sell five thousand tickets in Burlington. The other problem in a theatre is there's no space to dance! There are too many seats! Anyway, please call me back or email me – S dot Nelson, that's N-E-L-S-O-N at A-O-L dot com. Thank you!

3 Product and process

3.1 About business Supply chain management

 1:40

Jake: We need to talk about supply chain problems. First, there's packaging costs. The boxes we buy from Packobox are more and more expensive.

Luke: That's why you ordered 400,000 boxes? To get a better price?

J: Yes, Luke. But I understand we don't have enough storage.

L: Exactly.

Brendan: What about foreign suppliers? I'm sure we can get better prices in Asia or India.

L: That's true. But people at Packobox could lose their jobs!

J: Yes, that's a difficult decision … OK, the second problem is raw materials.

B: What's the problem? Polyplasto supply the right product, at the right price. If you remember to order, of course …

J: Yes, all right, Brendan. The problem is we only have one supplier. We put all our eggs in one basket! That's a big risk. If they can't deliver, or if they decide to increase their price, we're in trouble.

L: And if we work with two suppliers, it's more expensive?

J: Right. For smaller quantities, the price is always higher … There's also a third problem: deliveries to the shops. Luke?

L: Yes. Smalltruck are unhappy because sometimes we need three trucks a week, sometimes only one, and sometimes none at all. It's very difficult for them to manage.

J: I can understand that. They never know how many trucks and how many drivers they need.

B: Perhaps we can give them more information about our orders and production?

J: But it's risky, Brendan. We don't want our competitors to have that sort of information … Look, these are all difficult decisions. I think we need to have another meeting.

3.2 Vocabulary Supply chain and product life cycle

 1:41

Lecturer: Today, I'm going to talk about eight stages in the product life cycle. The cycle begins when raw materials like iron ore, trees or oil are extracted from the ground or from the sea. This is called extraction.

In the next stage, which is called processing, raw materials are processed to make materials like steel, wood or plastic.

Before the product can be manufactured, it is designed to be easy to produce and use.

This design stage is followed by manufacture: the product is manufactured in large quantities to reduce costs.

Next, the product is distributed to customers by ship, train, truck or plane. This is the distribution stage.

Then, the product is used by consumers. After the use stage, we have repair: if it breaks, the product is repaired by the manufacturer.

Finally, in the recycling stage, the product is recycled at the end of its useful life.

 1:42–1:47

Speaker 1: Nowadays, 85% of the materials used to make a car can be recovered and used again.

Speaker 2: If you order before 3pm, we can deliver anywhere in the country the next day.

Speaker 3: We use 3D models on computers, so we know exactly what the product will look like, and how we can manufacture it.

Speaker 4: We use a lot of powerful machinery, but it's still a dirty job: dirty, hard work and dangerous.

Speaker 5: More and more processes are controlled by computers. In fact, most of the time, there are only three or four people on a line that makes hundreds of pieces per day.

Speaker 6: It's quicker and cheaper to just change the PCB, the printed circuit board. It takes too long to look for individual components that aren't working.

3.3 Grammar Prepositions and present simple passive

1:48

Factory manager: Hi, everybody, and welcome to the cookie factory! Now, first of all, the flour, butter, eggs and sugar are mixed in large containers and then the chocolate chips are added. Please don't touch anything. You can taste some cookies at the end of the visit! Next, the cookie mix is poured into silicon moulds. We use moulds so that every cookie is exactly the same size and weight. After that, the cookies are baked in the ovens for eleven minutes. As you can see, everything is done by machines.

Visitor: Excuse me, but are the machines operated by people?

FM: No, they aren't. They're controlled by computer. Now, just behind the ovens you can see the cooling area. When they come out of the ovens, the cookies are very hot. They are cooled for fifteen minutes. After that, they are packed. Finally, the cookies are shipped to customers worldwide. Now, who would like to taste some cookies?

3.4 Speaking Presenting a process

1:49

Good morning, and thank you for inviting me here today. I'm here to tell you how a distribution centre works. I'd like to start by explaining what a distribution centre is. When you order two or three different items from an online store like Amazon or eBay™, it's the distribution centre that sends your products just a day or two later, all in one box. So, how do we do it?

Well, first of all, the distribution centre has millions of products in stock, all in one place. The goods are delivered by truck from manufacturers all over the world. When the goods arrive, they are checked by a receiver and identified with an electronic tag. If we don't record every item in the database, we don't know what we have in stock and where everything is. Next, the goods are put on racks or, if they are large products in boxes, like TVs, they are stored on pallets.

Are there any questions so far? No? All right.

Moving on to the next stage; when you place your order with the store, a picking list is sent to the distribution centre. This is a list of products to be picked – or collected – from the racks. Then, we pack your goods carefully in a box; an invoice or a delivery note is also included. After that, a shipping label with your name and address is printed and stuck on the box. Finally, your order is shipped and an email is sent to confirm the shipment date. I'd like to finish by pointing out that, very often, your goods are shipped only a few hours after your order, so you can receive them in less than 48 hours!

Now, if you have any questions, I'll be happy to answer them. Yes?

3.6 Case study Digidisc Ltd

1:50

Noah: So, the first thing you see when you arrive in front of the building is the loading bay, on the left. This is where all the parts are delivered, and where the finished products are loaded onto trucks.

Lily: Oh, all in the same place?

N: Yes. But the logistics department is just behind the loading bay, and it's divided into two sections, IN on the left, and OUT on the right. OK, let's go inside. Now, as we come through the main entrance, the packaging department is straight in front of you and logistics is on your left, just round the corner.

L: Oh, yes, I see.

N: When the parts arrive from the loading bay, first they're checked in logistics and then we put them in the store, which is here on the right, between the entrance and the warehouse. Before they're assembled, some of the parts are painted. The painting department is next to packaging, on the left. After painting, the parts go to assembly, on your right, opposite the warehouse. Some of the Digidiscs are tested. The testing department is over there in the opposite corner, next to painting.

After that, all the finished products are packaged and then stored in the warehouse. Any questions so far?

L: No, I don't think so.

N: OK, so there are just two more important places. The first is order processing, which is the open-plan office between logistics on one side and testing and painting on the other. That's where you're working. And, last but not least, we have the coffee machine, which is over there in front of the warehouse. Are you ready for a cup of coffee?

L: Oh, yes, please!

1:51

Noah: Hello, everybody. Thanks for coming. I want to talk about the way the factory is organized. I know some of you are having problems. Can we start with logistics? Saeed?

Saeed: Well, first of all, the store is too far from the loading bay. All the boxes and pallets go through order processing every time we move something!

N: Yes. But the store needs to be close to assembly and packaging.

S: Well, yes, but a lot of parts don't go directly from the store to assembly. They go to painting first.

N: That's true, I suppose. Is that a problem for you in order processing, Katie?

Katie: Oh, yes, it's really difficult to work. We're interrupted all the time. And what's more, there's the terrible smell from painting, and the noise from testing!

N: Yes, I can see that. What about packaging? Tina?

Tina: Well, the main problem is that we need more space. The packaging department is just too small!

N: Well, there's empty space in the warehouse …

T: Yes, the warehouse is too big. The finished products don't stay there very long anyway.

N: Right. What else? Lily?

Lily: Well, there's the coffee machine.

N: What's wrong with the coffee machine? I think the coffee's quite good!

L: Yes, but it's in a really dangerous place. There's always a lot of traffic between assembly, the warehouse and the store. I'm surprised we don't have more accidents!

N: Well, yes, I suppose you're right. But do you have a better idea?

L: Hm. Can we move the walls?

N: The walls? Yes. They're all moveable. We can change everything except the loading bay.

L: All right. Well, I think we need to …

4 Job interviews and career

4.1 About business Getting a job

1:52

Amy: My name's Amy. I did a four-year Bachelor of Commerce course. When I graduated, I wanted a job with an international hotel chain. Unfortunately, nobody was hiring, especially a new graduate like me with no experience. Eventually, I saw an ad in the newspaper for an entry-level job with a small hotel in my home town. The money wasn't very good, but I took the job. I worked hard to make a good impression and I was extremely flexible. After six months, I was a supervisor. In less than a year, I was promoted to a management position. About a year later, my experience and skills got me my dream job with Marriott International.

1:53

Rob: My name's Rob. I found my dream job on Twitter – seriously! I was working in a software company and I wanted a more creative – and less boring – job with a cool company, so I made a list of everything I wanted to find with my next employer. Unfortunately, my ideal company didn't exist. At the same time, I was learning a new programming language. I started talking to other people about it on Twitter. One day, one of my Twitter friends was talking about the company he worked for. I visited the website and found everything that was on my ideal employer list! I sent them my CV and my Twitter friend gave me a personal recommendation. After three interviews, I got the job!

1:54

Denise: My name's Denise. In my last year before graduating from engineering school, I was desperate to find an internship. I had lots of interviews, but no luck. One day I was flying home from an interview when I started a conversation with the man sitting next to me. He was an engineer and he suggested some companies to contact. When I got home, I sent my résumé to all of them. A few weeks later, I was an intern at Honeywell! Everything went really well and, at the end of the internship, my supervisor asked me to apply for a full-time position. So I did, and I was the first person in my class to get a job!

4.2 Vocabulary Job interviews

1:55

Man: How do you feel about the future? Are you optimistic or pessimistic?

Woman: Oh, I'm always very optimistic. For example, I never carry an umbrella!

M: Oh, right! What about your career? Are you an ambitious person?

W: Well, not really. But I'm not unambitious. I certainly don't want to be a President or a CEO, for example, but I do want to have a satisfying career with variety and challenge.

M: OK. So are you hard-working?

W: Yes, I think so. Of course, I can be lazy sometimes – I think everybody's the same. But when there's something important to do, I think I'm quite hard-working.

M: Right. So you're also very organized, I suppose?

W: No, actually, I'm terribly disorganized. You have no idea! But I'm working on my time management skills!

1:56

Speaker 1: I'm responsible for taking orders, presenting new products and taking care of customers. I do a lot of travelling.

1:57

Speaker 2: I'm in charge of the company's image: I organize events and I deal with journalists. So the job requires excellent spoken and written communication skills.

1:58

Speaker 3: I manage a team of business analysts. We provide key data on revenues, profitability and cash flow to the management team.

1:59

Speaker 4: I assist the General Director. I handle letters, email and phone calls and I run the Director's office on a day-to-day basis.

1:60

Speaker 5: I look after the development needs of all departments. I deal with external course providers and I also coach individuals when necessary.

4.3 Grammar Past tenses

1:61

1 looked – I looked around a job fair.
2 dreamed – I dreamed of working for an airline.
3 talked – I talked to someone called Sally.
4 asked – Sally asked for my CV.
5 emailed – I emailed Michael.
6 posted – I posted a comment on his blog.
7 replied – I was delighted when Michael replied.
8 wanted – I really wanted to impress Michael.
9 seemed – He seemed satisfied.
10 offered – They offered me the job.

4.4 Speaking Interviews

 1:62

Part 1

Interviewer: This is just a short, first contact so that we can get to know you a little better. OK, so tell me, Jessica, why did you apply for this job?

Jessica: Well, I really do think social media can make the world a better place, and I want to be part of that.

I: Some people say that Facebook is already finished.

J: I'm sorry, I can't agree with that. Of course, the world is always changing, so Facebook needs to change too. I'd like to help the company to develop.

I: OK. How do you feel about working abroad?

J: No problem. I'm ready to go anywhere in the world.

I: Anywhere? That sounds very ambitious. Some places are very difficult for a young woman.

J: I agree with you up to a point, but I'm a very flexible and tolerant person.

I: Uh-huh. How do you see your future in, say, five years' time?

J: I hope to gain business experience and develop my management skills. In five years' time, I intend to be in my first management position.

I: Five years is not very long to become a manager.

J: Well, perhaps you're right, but, as I said, I'm ambitious, but I'm also very loyal and very hard-working.

 1:63

Part 2

I: Jessica, what are your strengths and weaknesses?

J: That's always a difficult question! I'm quite good at managing my work. My friends say I'm never stressed. I think that's just because I'm a very organized person. I don't enjoy doing things at the last minute!

I: And do you have any weaknesses you'd like to work on?

J: Well, I'm usually calm and easygoing, but I know I'm sometimes impatient when things aren't going well. But I'm working on it!

I: And how good are your communication skills?

J: I really enjoy working with people, and people say I'm very good on the telephone. Um, I don't enjoy presentations, because I'm not very good at public speaking. But I took a presentations course last month, and I'm improving!

I: Good. So, Jessica, do you have any questions you would like to ask?

4.5 Writing CVs

 1:64

Consultant: What do you include in your CV? Well, for almost everything, my answer is 'It depends'. It depends on

the country, on the culture, on the company, on the job … There are so many variables. It's important to think about those variables and write your CV accordingly. So, for example, if you want to work in a country where religion is important, then, of course, mention your religion. But in most countries, religion is a personal matter, so it's not relevant or appropriate in a CV. If an attractive photo gives you an advantage, include it. If you're applying for a job as a pet shop manager, include your pets in your CV. I think the main thing is to ask yourself, does this information make my CV more attractive to the employer? If the answer is 'yes', then include it. If the answer is 'no', then don't.

5 Marketing and selling

5.1 About business Sales versus marketing

 2:01

Interviewer: Clare, you're in sales. What is it about sales and marketing? Why is it so hard to live together?

Clare: I think it's a cultural problem. Marketing generally have degrees. Sales usually don't. They don't teach sales at business school, so marketing don't really know what it's like. They think it's easy!

I: Is there a solution?

C: Yes. Make them work in sales for a year before they start in marketing.

I: It's certainly an interesting idea. What else?

C: In company organization charts, sales usually report to marketing. To me, that's crazy. Marketing are supposed to support sales, not the other way round.

I: So you think marketing should report to sales?

C: Yes. You could save money that way, too. Marketing waste a lot of money on things that are of no help to sales.

I: What sort of things?

C: Advertising, brochures, trade shows …

I: I see. Is there anything else?

C: The other big cultural difference is pay. In sales, we're paid commission. If our results are good, we get paid more. If our results are not good, we get less. But marketing are paid fixed salaries, so they don't feel concerned. If sales are good, they take the credit. If sales are not good, it's our fault, not theirs.

I: So you think you'll get better support if marketing's pay depends on sales results?

C: Exactly.

I: Well, thank you, Clare. That's an, er, interesting point of view.

5.2 Vocabulary Marketing, sales and advertising

 2:02

Hi, I'm Gareth. I'm a salesman. I sell professional software, and I love my job!

The selling process starts with an enquiry from a potential customer, in other words, a 'prospect'. Sometimes we get a name and address from marketing. I send out some information and a few days later I call the prospect and arrange a sales visit. I usually give a product demonstration first. We've got a great product with a really good USP. It has features and benefits that no similar product has. My customers are usually friendly, and they always love to get their hands on the software! Then I analyze the company's needs, the number of users, and so on. I answer questions and deal with any objections they have. When I get back to the office, I write a proposal and send a quotation. We don't usually need to offer discounts because our product is good value for money. Most of my customers place an order immediately. That means my job is done, and I get my commission!

5.3 Grammar Comparatives and superlatives

 2:03

1 With a record 429 kilometres per hour, the Bugatti Veyron Super Sport is the fastest production car on the market. It costs … $2.4 million.

2 Russian Railways' Moscow to Vladivostok is the longest regular service in the world, covering 9,259 kilometres.

3 23% of UK car buyers take home silver cars. The least popular colour is pink, with 0%.

4 Passengers on the M50 from 1st Avenue to 12th Avenue in Manhattan say it's the slowest bus in the world. It's quicker to walk.

5 Qatar Airways' economy seats are considered to be the most comfortable in the world, with more generous legroom than other airlines.

6 According to *USA Today*, this cruise is probably the least luxurious in the world. Some of the bathrooms had no water and some of the passengers slept on mattresses on the floor.

5.4 Speaking Persuading

2:04

David: You wanted to talk about childcare?

Rosie: Yes. A lot of staff have childcare problems, which means that the company loses hundreds of hours of work every year. We really need a day care centre, here on site.

D: Well, maybe you're right, Rosie, but there are two main problems. It's a big investment and it needs specialist staff that we don't have.

R: I see your point, David. But can we take those two issues one by one?

D: OK …

R: Good. I agree that a day care centre is a big investment. However, in reality, it can save you money. Keep in mind that most of the cost is paid by the employees. The cost is taken off their salaries. As a result, the company pays less tax.

D: OK, but what about the problem of specialist staff?

R: Well, it's certainly true that we need specialist staff. But we plan to work with a service company like Happiday Ltd. They provide the staff. What's more, they provide all the toys, equipment, and so on. That allows us to focus on our business and Happiday to take care of the children.

D: Hm. I'll need some figures. It's never easy to persuade the board to try new ideas.

R: I know what you mean. On the other hand, there are several women on the board. I'm sure they'll see the advantages. A day care centre will help us to hire and keep the best young women. And don't forget that it's really good for morale because parents can see their kids during the lunch break. Does that make sense?

D: Yes, I suppose so.

R: The figures are all here, in this report. Is there anything else you want to ask about?

D: No, I don't think so.

R: All right. The next step is for Happiday to present their proposal to management. I'm going to call them now to fix a date. Is that all right with you?

D: OK, yes, that's fine, Rosie. Thanks …

5.6 Case study **Dallivan Cars**

 2:05

Duncan: Hi, Aileen.

Aileen: Oh, hi. How was the meeting?

D: Well, there's good news and bad news. Which do you want first?

A: Oh, give me the bad news first. Good news is too big a surprise around here!

D: Hm. You saw the sales figures, I suppose?

A: Yes. They're down again. That's no surprise.

D: No. And inventory is up.

A: Again.

D: Yes. We *really* need to sell the Compact more quickly now.

A: It's not easy, Duncan. It's just so boring! It's an average car that gives the average customer, well, average value for money! Did you see the customer satisfaction survey? Boring, I'm afraid.

D: I know it's not your fault. The old marketing manager didn't do a very good job.

A: I don't know what he was thinking! Just make an average car, and then try to sell it to everyone?! That's not the way to do it. You have to think about who your customers are and what they want. Are they students, or singles, or families, or retired people? Do they want a city car, a sports car, a luxury model, a four-wheel drive?

D: I know, I know. Just do the best you can, all right?

A: OK. I will do. You said there was some good news?

D: Yes. The board agreed to develop a new car. It's your big chance to give us a really good product, a fantastic marketing strategy and some new ideas for the advertising campaign.

A: That's brilliant news!

D: Yes, they want you to present your team's ideas as soon as possible. As I said, it's your big chance. But it's also our last chance. If the new model isn't a success, it's the end of the road for Dallivan Cars!

6 Entrepreneurship

6.1 About business **Entrepreneurs**

 2:06

Hello and welcome to *The Back Office*. Today, we look at the careers of three inspirational entrepreneurs.

Michael Dell's first job – at the age of 12 – was washing dishes in a Chinese restaurant. When he went to the University of Texas to study medicine, he started making and selling personalized PCs. At the end of his first year, he had revenues of $80,000 per month. He left university at 19 and borrowed money from his family to expand Dell Computer. He was named Entrepreneur of the Year at the age of 24. He is now worth over 15 billion dollars.

 2:07

Cher Wang was born in Taipei, the daughter of the second richest man in Taiwan. She graduated from high school in California and went to Berkeley to study music, but soon changed to economics. She got a Master's degree and went to work in her sister's company, First International Computer. When she founded HTC in 1997, the company made computers. A few years later, Wang persuaded her partners to change to making cell phones. HTC now makes one in every six smartphones that are sold in the United States. Wang's photo is rarely in the newspapers. She prefers a simple life at home with her family or playing basketball with business partners.

 2:08

Sir Richard Branson left school at 16 to start a newspaper for students. He started advertising records at discount prices in the newspaper, and his record sales quickly became more profitable than the newspaper. Virgin Records started in a small office above an old shoe shop. Branson launched a record label in 1972, Virgin Atlantic Airways in 1984 and Virgin Mobile in 1999. He is now the fourth richest citizen of the United Kingdom and owns a Caribbean island in the British Virgin Islands.

6.2 Vocabulary **Business organization and people**

 2:09–2:12

Speaker 1: The big advantage for me is that everybody already knows our name and our product. It's less risky than starting a completely new business. Of course, the disadvantage is that I have to pay a percentage of all revenues in order to use the name.

Speaker 2: My great-grandfather founded the company nearly a hundred years ago. The advantage of being a well-known name on the stock exchange is that it's easier to get finance for new projects. Unfortunately, the family lost control of the business twenty years ago. We only own about 12% now.

Speaker 3: I didn't start the organization to get rich; I wanted to help people. That's the big advantage: all the profit we make is used for the good of the public. On the other hand, although I'm the founder, I'm not really in control. The business doesn't belong to me, and I can lose my job if I disagree with the board.

Speaker 4: If we lose money, my partner and I are personally responsible for all debts. That's the big risk in our business. But then, of course, we do share all the profits.

6.3 Grammar **Modal verbs**

2:13–2:17

Petra: It's a bad idea to sign a franchise agreement alone. It's better to ask a lawyer to explain the details.

Malcolm: A strategy plan isn't really necessary. The franchiser tells you exactly what to do.

Birgit: In this slide, you can see some typical franchises and their fees. Most franchises ask for 20 to 50 thousand dollars. There's no choice – every franchisee pays to get in.

Bernd: It's not possible to choose the cheapest suppliers. The contract forces you to buy from the official suppliers. You don't have a choice.

Miguel: Now, I want to say a few words about royalty payments. You can choose to pay once a quarter, but it's best to pay regularly every month. The payments are usually between five and ten per cent of sales. And remember they're obligatory, not optional!

6.4 Speaking **Meetings**

2:18

Emily: … Good, so we all agree that the business district is the best place for Bread 'n' butter.

Tim and Sheryl: Oh, yes.

E: Next, we need some new ideas for sandwiches that are different and exciting. Tim?

T: OK. I suggest brainstorming some interesting combinations. How about ham and banana, or apple and cheese …

S: I'm sorry to interrupt, Tim, but I really don't think that's the best way.

T: Are you saying you don't like unusual combinations?

S: No, I love your ideas. Apple and cheese is delicious! What I mean is, we don't have to define the recipes now, but we must decide on a strategy.

E: Sheryl, may I interrupt? I see what you mean, but let's brainstorm everything for the moment, and see what ideas we have.

S: OK, if you want. But, as I was saying, we need a strategy. What about having a different menu of sandwiches each day, so customers always have new choices?

E: I agree with you up to a point, but it makes things complicated.

T: Why not change the menu every week then?

E: Do you mean, some weeks you can't get apple and cheese? Some customers like to eat the same thing every week.

S: Hm. Perhaps you're right. But we need something different. Why don't we have different types of bread each week?

T: Yes, I like it. And lots of unusual fillings: fruit, salad, vegetables …

E: How about inviting customers to choose their own combinations?

S: Yes, mix and match! You choose your bread, your fillings, your dressing … that's excellent!

T: Wait a minute, do you mean we have to make every sandwich to order? It will take too long!

E: It's a good point. But I suggest having two different sections – one for standard sandwiches, and another for mix and match.

S: Yes, and different prices too!

T: OK, that makes sense.

6.5 Writing **Agendas and minutes**

 2:19

Chris: Helen, could you write the agenda for our next meeting?

Helen: Sure. That's on the 18ᵗʰ, right? At the usual time?

C: Yes.

H: OK. Will everyone be there?

C: I hope so. We have two important decisions to make. First, the new offer. APL say they want €350,000 and 50% cash. So we have to decide how to react.

H: OK. What else?

C: The other item for decision is about Mr Jarvis, the Managing Director. He tells me he wants to stay in his job for another year.

H: Jarvis. Is that J-A-R-V-I-S?

C: Yes.

H: OK. That's a difficult problem.

C: Yes. We probably need half an hour for that point, and 45 minutes to discuss the offer.

H: Do *you* want to present those two points?

C: Yes, I think that's a good idea. And there's also Simon's update on inventory. That's just for information, so

we only need ten minutes for that. And that's all, I think.

H: Can I also have 15 minutes to talk about a problem with the website?

C: Of course. That will still leave about twenty minutes for any other business. Is the website something we need a decision on?

H: Not immediately – it's just for discussion. What about the order of the items?

C: Let's talk about the big issues first: the offer, then Mr Jarvis. Then we'll have Simon's update on inventory, and your item on the website last.

H: OK.

C: Thanks, Helen.

 2:20–2:23

1

Chris: OK, everyone. We need a decision here. Do we all agree to offer €310,000 and 40% cash?

Helen, Simon and Val: Yes, that's OK. Yes, agreed.

C: All right. I'll call them this afternoon with the new offer.

2

Simon: I don't think we can work with Mr Jarvis in the office. It will be really difficult to change things.

Helen: I like Val's idea. Let's offer him a role as a consultant. But he can't have his old job in the office.

Chris: I think that's a good compromise. Val, can you talk to Mr Jarvis and ask him what he thinks of the idea?

Val: Yes, I will.

C: Great. Let us know as soon as possible how he reacts.

V: OK.

3

Simon: So basically, that's the inventory situation.

Chris: OK, thanks, Simon, I think we're all happy with that. No action required. Now, what's next? Helen, your website problem, I think.

4

Helen: … So, what I'm saying is we can't use APL dot com or APL dot co dot UK.

Simon: What about dot biz or dot org?

H: Well, I think dot org is for non-profit organizations, isn't it?

Chris: How about dot EU or dot net?

H: Well, I'm not sure, actually …

C: OK, can you check and get back to us next time?

H: All right. That's for the 25ᵗʰ then, next week.

6.6 Case study **Solar Mobile**

 2:24

Tara: Hi, Henry. I just read a really interesting article about mobile phones.

Henry: Oh, right. What was that about, then?

T: Well, apparently, there are 500 million people in the world who have a phone, but no electricity.

H: Really?

T: Yes. Sometimes they have to travel miles and then pay someone to charge their phone.

H: Wow!

T: In many parts of the world, they don't have a regular or stable power supply. For example, in most of Africa, only 25% of the population have electricity, and that's in towns. In rural parts of Africa, only 10% of people have a regular and stable electricity supply!

H: Only 10%? Really?

T: Well, don't you see what that means?

H: No, I don't. What?

T: It means there's an enormous market for solar battery chargers like yours, especially if you can ship them really cheaply to sunny countries!

H: Oh, yes. I see what you mean!

7 Business costs

7.1 About business **Cutting costs**

 2:25–2:26

1

Maria: My company had to reduce its prices because of competition from Asia. The first thing they cut was the travel budget. Instead of travelling to meetings, we do everything by conference call now. It isn't always easy, but it's a lot cheaper. They also stopped our annual bonus, so we had to make cuts in the family budget. We wanted to go to the USA for our holidays, but we decided it was too expensive. Fortunately, nobody lost their jobs. So I think I'm quite lucky, actually.

2

Steven: My company was taken over by an American group. They wanted to cut costs to improve their margins. Several people lost their jobs. I was one of them. I was unemployed for six months, which was hard. I had to sell my car and I spent most of my savings. But, in the end, I found a new job with a start-up company. It's more interesting than my old job and the money's better. So, I suppose I was lucky really!

7.2 Vocabulary **Profit, loss and payment**

 2:27

1 If you look on the back of your invoice, Mr Jones, everything is explained in black and white.

2 No, I'm sorry. We can't give credit for export orders. We need payment before we ship the goods.

3 Yes, that's OK, madam. You can give the delivery man cash or a cheque.

4 Yes, regular customers can pay one month after we send the invoice …

5 … but you can deduct 2% from the total if you pay in less than ten days.

6 Because it's a special order, we'll need 20% now, Mrs Black.

7 Thank you, Mrs Black. You can pay the rest when you come to pick it up.

8 Annabel, do you remember I lent you £10 last month?

7.3 Grammar Future forms and first conditional

 2:28

Buyer: How long will it take?
Seller: Well, we'll send you a quotation when we receive your specifications.
B: Can't you quote me a price now?
S: Well, we won't know the exact cost until you give us all the details.
B: OK.
S: And then as soon as you confirm your order, we'll start work. We usually need about two weeks.
B: I see. And I'll pay you after I receive the machine. Is that right?
S: No. You'll receive an invoice 48 hours after you confirm the order. You'll need to pay it before we ship the machine.
B: Oh. So, it'll take about *three* weeks, then?
S: Yes. You'll receive the machine two or three days after we ship it.

7.4 Speaking Negotiating

 2:29

Kayla: The programme is looking good, but Brandon and I feel it's expensive. Could you bring the price down a little?
Travel agent: I'm sorry, but it's just not possible … unless we cut some of the activities.
Brandon: No, the activities are perfect. We can't cut anything.
K: What about the train tickets? We're bringing you a lot of business. Can you give us a discount?
TA: Well, I'd like to help you … OK. If you can guarantee thirty participants, we can give you five per cent on the train tickets.
B: Only five per cent? I'm afraid we can't accept that. We're students, remember. It's a lot of money for a weekend. Can we agree on 10%?
K: Yes, if you give us a 10% discount, we'll guarantee … thirty-five participants.
TA: I'm afraid we can't give you 10% unless you can find fifty participants.
B: I don't think we'll get that many. What about 8% for forty participants?
TA: That's acceptable, as long as everything is paid two weeks before the trip.
K: OK, it's a deal.
B: Just a minute, Kayla. We agree, providing you organize a free drink when we arrive at the hotel.
TA: All right. We can live with that.

7.6 Case study Doug's Mugs

 2:30

Doug: Last year, sales were very good, but this year we didn't do so well. Megan was ill. I was, um, very busy, and we lost one of our biggest customers. We made a net loss, but that was only because of depreciation on the machines. We didn't have to borrow any money. But we're confident about next year. Our administrative costs are under control, and they won't change. But we're going to put our price up by 50 cents. Production cost per mug will be the same as this year, so we'll increase our margins. Perhaps we'll lose one or two customers, but our price will still be very reasonable. And, after all, our customers come to us for our designs, not our prices. We think we'll sell 50% more than this year.

8 Global trade

8.1 About business International franchising

 2:31–2:33

Speaker 1: I visited India recently, and some Indian friends took me out for lunch. There was a lot of vegetarian food, and no beef or pork, of course. In India, it's a very sensitive issue and a real problem for restaurants: vegetarians want to be sure their food is never in contact with meat. So, in the kitchen, they had a very clever solution: the cooks had different-coloured uniforms – green for vegetarian and red for those who cooked meat. I had some very spicy chicken. It was delicious! It was a very popular restaurant – I'm sure you know it. It's called McDonald's®!

Speaker 2: Our management training franchise recently opened ten new outlets in Brazil. We were concerned about the language problem: we were especially worried about the cost of translating all our contracts and manuals into Portuguese. The good news is, the Brazilians already have a solution. The law allows you to use English for all the paperwork if the franchisees agree. So that solved the problem. The bad news is that recruiting instructors took a lot more time than we planned, so we opened behind schedule and over budget.

Speaker 3: A Russian friend of mine opened an American coffee shop franchise in Kazan. Well, the first problem was, the customers were happy with coffee and doughnuts in the morning, but in the evening they wanted traditional meat patties and vodka. So my friend gave them what they wanted, and the business did very well. However, the real problem was with the American franchiser. They said my friend had to follow the manual: no more meat patties and no more vodka. My friend refused. And do you know what the franchiser did? They stopped the contract and closed the coffee shop!

8.2 Vocabulary Franchising and project management

 2:34–2:36

1 Our objective is to raise enough capital to start a battery shop franchise. So far, we've raised about half of the $200,000 we need. We're a little behind schedule, but we're on budget. The next step is to get a bank loan for another $100,000. However, there is a problem. There's a delay at the bank because we need our parents to sign guarantees. Some of them live abroad, so it's a little complicated. To save time, we've scanned the documents and sent them by email. I think it's a good solution. We have to pay the franchise fee by the end of next month, but we're optimistic. We think we can get the money in time to meet the deadline.

2 We're trying to recruit new franchisees for our ice-cream shops in India. Currently, we're on schedule, but our big problem is staying within the budget. The thing is, India is such a big country … we're spending too much on plane tickets. So now, to save money, we're going to organize all our interviews in one place. The next step is to start training franchisees and their staff. We're confident we can meet the deadline and open the ice-cream shops on time. Because we've exceeded the budget, we really need those franchise fees as soon as possible!

3 Our objective is to find cheaper products and equipment for our cleaning services. Our first task was to source a new supplier. At the moment, things aren't looking good. We've already missed the deadline and we've also exceeded our budget. And we still haven't found a new supplier. The big problem is stock. We can get better prices if we order large quantities, but we have nowhere to put a lot of stock. The solution is … well, we don't know what the solution is. We're working on it, but we're not optimistic. We think we'll probably be several weeks behind schedule, and maybe 20% over budget.

8.3 Grammar Present perfect

 2:37

Have you ever needed help with a difficult project?
Have you ever wanted to develop your people skills?
Business Coach is here to help in exactly those situations. We provide personal coaching and support for business people. Since 2004, we've helped thousands of people to become great managers and supervisors, and we've coached hundreds of people who were starting their own business.
We've done business in the US and the UK for nearly ten years, and we've already opened franchises in five countries in Europe. We've just opened three new

offices in South America, too. Now *you* can open your own *Business Coach* franchise. We're looking for new franchisees to develop our business in Asia. If you enjoy helping people to become better managers, and if you would like to start a profitable and satisfying business, contact *Business Coach* today.

8.4 Speaking **Giving updates and handling questions**

🔊 2:38

Charlie: It's now Week 9. As you can see on the chart, we are behind schedule because the paperwork was delayed for two weeks. As a result, we couldn't buy the kitchen equipment on schedule. However, we have just installed the kitchens and we have already started decorating the restaurants. We expect to finish by the end of this week. We bought the furniture ahead of schedule in Week 5 because there was a special offer.

Unfortunately, we haven't started hiring staff yet, so we are four weeks behind schedule. Consequently, we have decided to use an agency to save time. They are going to start hiring next week, and we intend to begin training immediately. We are confident that we can still be ready on time. The two restaurants will open on schedule in Week 14.

🔊 2:39

Charlie: So, are there any questions?

Questioner 1: Why didn't you finish the kitchens sooner?

C: Sorry, I didn't catch that.

Q1: Why did you finish the kitchens in Week 8?

C: Ah, that's a very good question. We wanted to finish in Week 5, but as I mentioned earlier, in Week 5, we bought the furniture. We didn't have time to finish the kitchens until last week because we were decorating. Does that answer your question?

Q1: Yes, I see.

Questioner 2: What are you doing this week?

C: We are currently painting the walls. It's a big job, but we hope to start hiring staff next week.

Q1: You didn't mention stock.

C: Right. I'm glad you asked me that. We originally planned to buy stock in Week 6, but because we are still painting the restaurant, we have to wait another week.

Questioner 2: What about advertising? You haven't planned an advertising campaign!

C: Actually, we've planned a very exciting campaign. But can I come to that in a moment? I'd like to finish talking about set-up first.

Q1: And what about money?

C: I'm sorry, I don't quite follow you.

Q1: My question is about money! Are you over budget?

C: Well, I'm afraid I can't go into detail right now, but actually we are just under budget at the moment ...

8.6 Case study **An international opportunity**

🔊 2:40–2:42

Speaker 1: Fair do's hairdos? Well, they're nice people, and the two weeks' training in South Africa was great. However, it's a really competitive market, and I don't think it was a very good choice. Maybe it works in South Africa, but here in Europe, people want something more sophisticated. My partner and I opened a salon in Warsaw last year; we also planned to have salons in other cities, like Krakow and Poznan, but I'm not sure about that now. We're trying different ideas – fortunately, the franchiser is flexible – and we're starting to make a profit, but it's not enough. So, for the moment, it's hard work and it's not very well paid.

Speaker 2: I opened a Mountie Sandwich Shop six months ago in Belgrade. It's a good business, but it's extremely hard work with early mornings and late nights – and I haven't taken a day off since I started! Profitability is good; I'll probably be in a position to open a second shop soon. But I'm sure I could make more profit by selling other products. The problem is, the Mountie's rules are very strict. I'm not allowed to do anything that isn't in their manual. So I'm feeling very tired, and a little frustrated.

Speaker 3: I'll be honest: I thought Tween 'n' Dream was a crazy choice! But my wife wanted to do it, so I said OK, let's try it. The franchiser in Los Angeles said, 'If you follow the manual, you'll make money.' So we did and it's been fantastic! First of all, Tween 'n' Dream only opens in the afternoons, so we have a good quality of life. And secondly, there really is a market for this product! We opened our first store in the centre of Rio, and now we have two more. I thought it was a big investment, but we're making a *lot* of money! And you know, all those little girls? They look so happy! I think it's great!

Glossary

The definitions for the words in this glossary are from the *Macmillan Dictionary*. The red words are high-frequency words, that is to say that they are among the 7,500 which native speakers use for 90% of what they speak or write. See http://www.macmillandictionary.com for more information.

Business fundamentals

page 6 Business activities

extract /ɪkˈstrækt/ verb [transitive] to remove a substance from another substance: *The pulp was crushed to extract the juice.*

mining /ˈmaɪnɪŋ/ noun [uncount] the process of getting coal or metal from under the ground: *Mining is one of the country's main industries.*

monopoly /məˈnɒpəli/ noun [count] ECONOMICS a company that has complete control of the product or service it provides because it is the only company that provides it: *It is the government's intention to break up all monopolies.*

profit /ˈprɒfɪt/ noun [count] BUSINESS money that you make by selling something or from your business, especially the money that remains after you have paid all your business costs. Your total profit before you pay tax is called gross profit, and the amount that remains after you have paid tax on this is called net profit: *Profits rose 31% to £144 million.*

raw materials /ˌrɔː məˈtɪəriəlz/ noun [plural] substances such as coal or iron that are in their natural state before being changed by chemical processes

supplier /səˈplaɪə(r)/ noun [count] a company, organization or country that supplies or sells a product or a service: *Colombia is our main supplier of coffee beans.*

USP /ˌjuː es ˈpiː/ noun [count] BUSINESS unique selling proposition, or unique selling point: the thing that makes a product or service special or different from the others

value /ˈvæljuː/ noun [count/uncount] the amount that something is worth, measured especially in money; [uncount] the degree to which someone or something is important or useful: *educational/nutritional value*

page 7 Business organization

entrepreneur /ˌɒntrəprəˈnɜː(r)/ noun [count] someone who uses money to start businesses and make business deals

hire /ˈhaɪə(r)/ verb [transitive/intransitive] to pay someone to work for you, especially for a short time: *I hired someone to paint the house.*

human resources /ˌhjuːmən rɪˈzɔː(r)sɪz/ noun [uncount] BUSINESS the department within a company that is responsible for employing and training people, and for looking after workers who have problems

joint venture /ˌdʒɔɪnt ˈventʃə(r)/ noun [count] BUSINESS an agreement between two companies to work together on a particular job, usually in order to share any risk involved

logistics /ləˈdʒɪstɪks/ noun [plural] BUSINESS the activity of transporting goods to customers or to places where they are bought or sold

share /ʃeə(r)/ noun [count] BUSINESS one of the equal parts of a company that you can buy as a way of investing money: *The scheme allows employees to buy shares in the company.*

shareholder /ˈʃeə(r)ˌhəʊldə(r)/ noun [count] BUSINESS BRITISH someone who owns shares in a company

strategy /ˈstrætədʒi/ noun [count] a plan or method for achieving something, especially over a long period of time: *The countries hope to devise a common strategy to provide aid.*

supply chain /səˈplaɪ ˌtʃeɪn/ noun [count] BUSINESS a series of processes involved in supplying a product to someone

page 8 Profit and loss

break even /ˌbreɪk ˈiːv(ə)n/ verb [intransitive] if a person or business breaks even, they neither make a profit nor lose money

cost of goods sold (COGS) /ˌkɒst əv ɡʊdz ˈsəʊld/ noun [uncount] BUSINESS the cost of making a product, which includes materials, manufacturing and labour

day job /ˈdeɪ ˌdʒɒb/ noun [count] the main job of someone who is also trying to succeed in some other career

fixed cost /ˌfɪkst ˈkɒst/ noun [count] [usually plural] BUSINESS a cost such as rent that a company has to pay that does not depend on how much it produces

improve /ɪmˈpruːv/ verb [transitive] to make something better: *Our main objective is to improve educational standards.*

margin /ˈmɑː(r)dʒɪn/ noun [count] BUSINESS **profit margin**: the difference between how much money you get when you sell something and how much it costs you to buy or make it

overheads /ˈəʊvə(r)ˌhedz/ noun [plural] BUSINESS money that you pay regularly as the costs of operating a business or organization

revenue /ˈrevənjuː/ noun [count/uncount] income from business activities or taxes: *The magazine had been losing advertising revenue for months.*

stock /stɒk/ noun [uncount] the goods that are available to buy in a shop: *We're having some new stock delivered this afternoon.*

variable cost /ˌveəriəb(ə)l ˈkɒst/ noun [count] BUSINESS a cost that changes according to how much of a product is made

page 9 CVs and cover letters

apply /əˈplaɪ/ verb [intransitive] to make an official request for a job or a place in a college or university, or for permission to do or have something: *We advertised three jobs, and over 50 people applied.*

cosmetics /kɒzˈmetɪks/ noun [plural] substances that you use on your skin to make yourself look more attractive

counsellor /ˈkaʊns(ə)lə(r)/ noun [count] someone whose job is to give advice and help to people with problems

gain /ɡeɪn/ verb [transitive/intransitive] to get more of something, usually as a result of a gradual process: *She hopes to gain experience by working abroad for a year.*

intern /ˈɪntɜː(r)n/ noun [count] AMERICAN a student, or someone who has recently obtained a degree, who works in a job in order to get experience

internship /ˈɪntɜː(r)nˌʃɪp/ noun [count] AMERICAN a job that a student or someone who has recently obtained a degree takes in order to get experience

survey /ˈsɜː(r)veɪ/ noun [count] a set of questions that you ask a large number of people or organizations: *This survey shows the percentage of single-parent households in each area.*

trainee /ˌtreɪˈniː/ noun [count] someone who is training for a particular profession or job: *Trainees will learn a skill that is valued in many countries.*

1 Gaining experience

1.1 About business
Internships abroad

acquire /əˈkwaɪə(r)/ verb [transitive] to get new knowledge or a new skill by learning it: *the way children acquire language*

crew /kruː/ noun [count] a group of people with a particular skill who work together: can be followed by a singular or plural verb: *a film crew*

fierce /fɪə(r)s/ adjective involving a lot of force or energy **fierce competition/opposition**: *We face fierce competition from overseas competitors.*

impress /ɪmˈpres/ verb [intransitive/transitive] if someone or something impresses you, you admire them: *Experience in voluntary work will often impress a potential employer.*

reference /ˈref(ə)rəns/ noun [count] a statement from someone who knows you or has worked with you that gives information about you. You often need to provide a reference when you apply for a new job: *I don't think I've got the job – they haven't taken up my references.*

skill /skɪl/ noun [count] a particular ability that involves special training and experience: *The course helps people gain the skills they need to run a successful business.*

team spirit /ˌtiːm ˈspɪrɪt/ noun [count] an enthusiastic attitude towards working or playing together with other people as a team

1.2 Vocabulary
Personal details

analogue /ˈænəˌlɒg/ adjective or **analog** an analogue watch or clock shows the time using hands (= long parts that move round) that point to numbers, instead of numbers that change every second

badge /bædʒ/ noun [count] BRITISH a small round object that fastens onto your clothes with a pin and usually has a picture or writing on it. The American word is button.

digital /ˈdɪdʒɪt(ə)l/ adjective a digital clock or instrument shows information as a row of numbers

register /ˈredʒɪstə(r)/ verb [intransitive] to put your name and other information on an official list in order to be allowed to vote, study, stay in a hotel, etc.: *Where do we go to register?*

1.3 Grammar
Present simple

abroad /əˈbrɔːd/ adjective in or to a foreign country: *We try to go abroad at least once a year.*

communicator /kəˈmjuːnɪˌkeɪtə(r)/ noun [count] someone who expresses thoughts, feelings or information to another person, for example by speaking or writing: *an effective/natural communicator*

example /ɪgˈzɑːmp(ə)l/ noun [singular] a person or way of behaving that is considered as a model for other people to copy **set an example**: *You should be setting an example for your little brother.*

foreign /ˈfɒrɪn/ adjective from another country, or in another country: *Working in a foreign country takes some getting used to.*

problem-solver /ˈprɒbləm ˌsɒlv ə(r)/ noun [count] a person who is good at finding solutions to problems

quarter /ˈkwɔː(r)tə(r)/ noun [count] one of four periods of 15 minutes that an hour is divided into when you are telling the time: *They arrived at a quarter past three.*; one of four periods of three months that the year is divided into, especially when you are talking about financial accounts: *The company's profits fell in the third quarter.*

share /ʃeə(r)/ verb [transitive] to give a part of something to someone else: *The money will be shared between 30 different environmental organizations.*

team player /ˈtiːm ˈpleɪə(r)/ noun [count] INFORMAL someone who works well with other people as part of a group

workaholic /ˌwɜː(r)kəˈhɒlɪk/ noun [count] someone who spends most of their time working and has little interest in other things

1.4 Speaking
Meeting people and making conversation

anyway /ˈeniˌweɪ/ adverb SPOKEN used for ending a conversation, or for showing that you have come to the end of what you are telling someone: *Anyway, in the end we decided to stay at home.*

favour /ˈfeɪvə(r)/ noun [count] something that you do for someone in order to help them: *Could you do me a favour?*

shuttle /ˈʃʌt(ə)l/ noun [count] a bus, train or plane that makes frequent short journeys between two places: *A shuttle service operates between the hotel and the beach.*

tip /tɪp/ noun [count] a useful suggestion: *The booklet gives some good tips on getting the most out of your software.*

well-paid /welˈpeɪd/ adjective a well-paid job pays a lot of money: *well-paid work/employment*

1.5 Writing
Informal emails

instead /ɪnˈsted/ adverb used for saying that one person, thing or action replaces another: *The committee has rejected our proposal. Instead, they have brought forward an alternative plan.*

pick up /pɪk ˈʌp/ phrasal verb [transitive] to go and meet someone or something that you have arranged to take somewhere in a vehicle: *I'll pick up my luggage in the morning.*

training /ˈtreɪnɪŋ/ noun [uncount] the process of teaching people or of being taught for a profession or activity: *Employees are given training in business ethics.*

1.6 Case study
The Intern Shop

accommodation /əˌkɒməˈdeɪʃ(ə)n/ noun [uncount] a place for someone to stay, live or work in. The usual American word is accommodations: *The hotel provides accommodation for up to 100 people.*

allowance /ə'laʊəns/ noun [count] an amount of money that someone receives regularly, in order to pay for the things they need: *She receives a monthly allowance of £500.*

arrange /ə'reɪndʒ/ verb [intransitive/transitive] to provide what someone needs, by doing what is necessary: *The bank can arrange travel insurance for you.*

intercultural /ˌɪntə(r)'kʌltʃ(ə)rəl/ adjective involving or relating to different cultures

overtime /'əʊvə(r)ˌtaɪm/ noun [uncount] extra hours that someone works at their job: *I've been working a lot of overtime lately.*

TOEIC /'təʊɪk/ trademark a registered trademark for a test of English used for international communication. The TOEIC® test shows employers how well speakers of other languages read and understand English.

visa /'viːzə/ noun [count] an official document or mark in your passport that allows you to enter or leave a country for a specific purpose or period of time: *an entry/exit/tourist visa*

warehouse /'weə(r)ˌhaʊs/ noun [count] a big building where large amounts of goods are stored

2 Customer satisfaction

2.1 About business
Customer service

advocate /'ædvəkət/ noun [count] someone who strongly and publicly supports someone or something: *a tireless advocate of political reform*

ally /'ælaɪ/ noun [count] someone who is ready to help you, especially against someone else who is causing problems for you: *If you're going to succeed in this job you will need allies.*

consumer /kən'sjuːmə(r)/ noun [count] ECONOMICS someone who buys and uses goods and services. The expression *the consumer* is often used for referring to consumers as a group: *more choice for the consumer*

lead /liːd/ noun [count] a potential sales contact; a piece of information that may result in a sale

loyalty /'lɔɪəlti/ noun [uncount] continued use of the products or services of a particular business: *a high level of brand loyalty*

prospect /'prɒspekt/ noun [count] BUSINESS a possible or likely customer: *She's been on the phone all day calling various new prospects.*

referral /rɪ'fɜːrəl/ noun [count/uncount] the process of sending someone to another person or place for help, information or advice: *My doctor gave me a referral to a heart specialist.*

upgrade /'ʌpˌgreɪd/ noun [count] a piece of equipment or software designed to make a computer more powerful: *hardware upgrades*

2.2 Vocabulary
Contacting customers

apologize /ə'pɒlədʒaɪz/ verb [intransitive] to tell someone that you are sorry for doing something wrong or for causing a problem: *I apologize for taking so long to reply.*

complain /kəm'pleɪn/ verb [intransitive/transitive] to say that you are not satisfied with something: *She complained that she never had any time to herself.*

faulty /'fɔːlti/ adjective not working correctly or made correctly: *You are only entitled to a refund if the goods are faulty.*

greet /griːt/ verb [transitive] to behave in a polite or friendly way towards someone when you meet them: *The Prime Minister greeted him at the airport.*

refund /'riːfʌnd/ noun [count] money that was yours that you get again, especially because you have paid too much for something or have decided you do not want it: *You will receive a full refund if you cancel the holiday.*

schedule /'ʃedjuːl/ noun [count] a plan of activities or events and when they will happen: *What's on your schedule today?*

voicemail /'vɔɪsmeɪl/ noun [uncount] an electronic system that records and stores spoken messages from people

2.3 Grammar
Present continuous

decrease /diː'kriːs/ verb [intransitive] to become less: *Prices are expected to decrease by less than 1% this year.*

drop /drɒp/ verb [intransitive] to fall to a lower amount or value: *European sales have dropped by over 30%.*

fall /fɔːl/ verb [intransitive] to become lower in level, amount or value: *The temperature has been falling steadily all day.*

improve /ɪm'pruːv/ verb [intransitive] to become better: *Your English will improve with practice.*

increase /ɪn'kriːs/ verb [intransitive] to become larger in amount or number: *Our costs increased dramatically over the last decade.*

rise /raɪz/ verb [intransitive] to increase in size, amount, quality or strength: *Salaries will continue to rise in line with inflation.*

2.4 Speaking
Telephoning

free-to-air /ˌfriː tʊ 'eə(r)/ adjective BRITISH free-to-air television programmes can be watched without having to pay anything extra

hang on /ˌhæŋ 'ɒn/ phrase SPOKEN used for asking someone to wait for a short period of time, especially someone who you are talking to on the telephone

hold (the line) /ˌhəʊld ðə 'laɪn/ verb [intransitive/transitive] to wait in order to speak to someone on the telephone: *Could you hold the line, please?*

premium /'priːmiəm/ adjective more expensive or of higher quality than other similar things: *premium-rate phone calls*

subscription /səb'skrɪpʃ(ə)n/ noun [count] an agreement to pay an amount of money so that you will receive something such as a magazine or a service. You take out a subscription, usually for a year, and renew it if you want to continue the arrangement for another year.

2.5 Writing
Formal letters and emails

apology /ə'pɒlədʒi/ noun [count] a statement that tells someone that you are sorry for doing something wrong or for causing a problem: *He made a public apology for his remarks.*

database /'deɪtə,beɪs/ noun [count] COMPUTING a large amount of information stored in a computer in an organized way that allows individual pieces of information to be found quickly

discount /'dɪs,kaʊnt/ noun [count] a reduction in the price of something: *Customers can get huge discounts by booking in advance.*

inconvenience /,ɪnkən'viːniəns/ noun [count/uncount] an annoying problem or situation, especially one that forces you to make an extra effort to do something: *We apologize for the inconvenience caused to passengers.*

lift /lɪft/ noun [count] BRITISH a machine that carries people up or down between different levels of a tall building. The American word is elevator: *Do you want to take the lift or use the stairs?*

make up for /meɪk 'ʌp fɔː(r)/ phrasal verb [transitive] to provide something good, so that something bad seems less important: *The good weather made up for the bad organization.*

workshop /'wɜː(r)k,ʃɒp/ noun [count] a room or building where things are made using tools and machines

2.6 Case study
Rock tour

awesome /'ɔːs(ə)m/ adjective INFORMAL extremely good. This word is used mainly by young people.

behavior the American spelling of **behaviour** /bɪ'heɪvjə(r)/ noun [uncount] the way that someone behaves: *violent/aggressive/disruptive behaviour*

deadline /'ded,laɪn/ noun [count] a specific time or date by which you have to do something: *They've given us a five o'clock deadline.*

fire /'faɪə(r)/ verb [transitive] to make someone leave their job, sometimes as a punishment: *She was fired for refusing to comply with safety regulations.*

gross revenues /grəʊs 'revənjuːz/ noun [count/uncount] income from business activities before taxes or costs have been taken out

invoice /'ɪnvɔɪs/ noun [count] a document giving details of goods or services that someone has bought and must pay for: *We submit our invoices on a monthly basis.*

roadie /'rəʊdi/ noun [count] someone whose job is to travel with musicians and move their equipment

venue /'venjuː/ noun [count] the place where an activity or event happens: *a popular venue for wedding receptions*

3 Product and process

3.1 About business
Supply chain management

cash /kæʃ/ noun [uncount] money in the form of notes and coins: *Do you want to pay in cash or by credit card?*; money in any form, especially money that is available for you to use when you need it: *The government has cash reserves of about £500 billion.*

cash flow /'kæʃ ,fləʊ/ noun [uncount] BUSINESS the rate at which a business takes in money through sales and pays it out for the things it needs to continue operating: *Getting the money upfront will improve our cash flow significantly.*

credit /'kredɪt/ noun [uncount] an arrangement to receive goods from a shop or money from a bank and pay for it later: *Some suppliers will not give credit to their customers.*

labour /'leɪbə(r)/ noun [uncount] ECONOMICS the workers in a particular country, industry or company considered as a group: *a plentiful supply of cheap labour*

pellet /'pelɪt/ noun [count] a small round piece of a substance: *fish food pellets*

process /'prəʊses/ noun [count] a series of actions that have a particular result: *Learning a language is a slow process.*

purchasing /'pɜː(r)tʃəsɪŋ/ noun [uncount] buying
purchasing department: the section of a company that deals with buying stock, raw materials, equipment, etc.

put all your eggs in one basket phrase to depend completely on just one idea, plan or person so that you have no other possibilities if things go wrong: *The basic advice with investment is don't put all your eggs in one basket.*

stock /stɒk/ noun [uncount] the goods that are available to buy in a shop: *We're having some new stock delivered this afternoon.* **out of stock** phrase not available now: *I'm afraid that size is out of stock.*

storage /'stɔːrɪdʒ/ noun [uncount] space where things can be stored: *The area underneath provides useful storage.*

3.2 Vocabulary
Supply chain and product life cycle

ground /graʊnd/ noun [singular] the layer of soil and rock that forms the Earth's surface: *the destruction caused by getting coal out of the ground*

handle /'hænd(ə)l/ verb [transitive] to touch or hold someone or something: *All chemicals must be handled with care.*

iron /'aɪə(r)n/ noun [uncount] a hard heavy metal that is a common element. It is used for making steel and is also used in many types of machine and building structures.

oil /ɔɪl/ noun [uncount] a thick dark smooth liquid from under the ground, used for making petrol and other fuels: *The Middle Eastern countries produce most of the world's oil.*

ore /ɔː(r)/ noun [count/uncount] CHEMISTRY rock or earth from which metal can be obtained: *a company that mines and smelts iron ore*

site /saɪt/ noun [count] an area of land where something is being built or could be built: *a construction site*

slave /sleɪv/ noun [count] someone who belongs by law to another person as their property and has to obey them and work for them

steel /stiːl/ noun [uncount] a strong metal made from a mixture of iron and carbon: *The works produced a million tons of steel a year.*

3.3 Grammar
Prepositions and present simple passive

bake /beɪk/ verb [intransitive/transitive] to make bread, cakes, etc. using an oven: *I'm baking a cake for Tom's birthday.*

container /kən'teɪnə(r)/ noun [count] something used for storing or holding things, for example a box, bottle or bowl

forklift truck /,fɔː(r)klɪft 'trʌk/ noun [count] a vehicle that uses two long metal bars at the front for lifting and moving heavy objects

mould /məʊld/ noun [count] a shaped container into which you pour a liquid that then becomes solid in the shape of the container

pour /pɔː(r)/ verb [transitive] to make a liquid or substance flow out of a container that you are holding: *Pour the mixture into a dish, and bake for 45 minutes.*

rack /ræk/ noun [count] an object used for storing things that consists of a row of small shelves, spaces or hooks

roundabout /'raʊndə,baʊt/ noun [count] BRITISH a circular area where three or more roads meet that you have to drive around in one direction in order to get onto another road. The American word is traffic circle or rotary.

weight /weɪt/ noun [uncount] a measurement of how heavy a person or thing is: *It was about 12 pounds in weight.*

3.4 Speaking
Presenting a process

crash /kræʃ/ verb [intransitive] COMPUTING if a computer or computer program crashes, it suddenly stops working

pack /pæk/ verb [transitive] [often passive] to put goods into containers so that they can be sent somewhere and sold: *This is where the fruit is packed.*

pallet /'pælət/ noun [count] a flat wooden or metal surface used for moving or storing heavy goods

pick /pɪk/ verb [transitive] to choose someone or something from a group

picking list /'pɪkɪŋ ,lɪst/ noun [count] a paper or electronic list of things to be collected from a warehouse for packing and distribution to customers

strike /straɪk/ noun [count] a period of time during which people refuse to work, as a protest about pay or conditions of work: *Pilots were striking for a 6% salary increase.*

tag /tæg/ noun [count] a small piece of paper or other material that is fixed to something to give information about it, or is fixed to someone to show who they are: *I can't find the price tag for this coat.*

3.5 Writing
Instructions and directions

accessory /ək'sesəri/ noun [count] [usually plural] additional objects, equipment, etc.: *car/kitchen/computer accessories*

damaged /'dæmɪdʒd/ adjective broken, spoiled or injured: *Many buildings and cars had been damaged in the blast.*

delivery note /dɪ'lɪv(ə)ri 'nəʊt/ noun [count] a short official document that accompanies goods that are brought to a place

frame /freɪm/ noun [count] a structure that forms a border for a picture or mirror and holds it in place: *a silver photograph frame*

industrial estate /ɪn'dʌstriəl ɪ'steɪt/ noun [count] BRITISH an area of land where industrial companies have their buildings

pickup point /'pɪkʌp ,pɔɪnt/ noun [count] a place where goods can be collected from

policy /'pɒləsi/ noun [count/uncount] a set of plans or actions agreed on by a government, political party, business or other group: *It is not the hospital's policy to disclose the names of patients.*

RMA /,ɑːr em 'eɪ/ noun [count] return merchandise authorisation: a number that is required to send goods back to where they were bought

3.6 Case study
Digidisc Ltd

loading bay /'ləʊdɪŋ ,beɪ/ noun [count] an area from which goods can be loaded on and off trucks, trains, etc.

open-plan /,əʊpən 'plæn/ adjective an open-plan office, house, flat, etc. has few walls and a lot of open space

traffic /'træfɪk/ noun [uncount] the movement of goods or passengers

workflow /'wɜː(r)k,fləʊ/ noun [uncount] the sequence of jobs which results in a final product or service

4 Job interviews and career

4.1 About business
Getting a job

boring /'bɔːrɪŋ/ adjective not at all interesting, and making you feel impatient or dissatisfied: *a boring badly-paid job*

creative /kri'eɪtɪv/ adjective involving a lot of imagination and new ideas: *Painting is a creative process.*

entry-level /'entri ,lev(ə)l/ adjective an entry-level job is at the lowest level in a company or organization

exhausted /ɪg'zɔːstɪd/ adjective extremely tired and without enough energy to do anything else: *Trying to find a solution to the problem had left the sisters mentally exhausted.*

job fair /'dʒɒb ,feə(r)/ noun [count] an event where employers or recruiters meet job seekers, and vice versa

passionate /'pæʃ(ə)nət/ adjective showing or expressing strong beliefs, interest or enthusiasm: *He has a passionate interest in music.*

short list /'ʃɔː(r)t ,lɪst/ noun [count] or **shortlist** a list of the people or things that you think could be suitable for a job, prize, team, etc. chosen from a larger number of people or things: *Who is on the short list of candidates for the job?*

4.2 Vocabulary
Job interviews

coach /kəʊtʃ/ verb [transitive] to teach someone a special skill: *a stage school where they coach children in singing and dancing*

demanding /dɪ'mɑːndɪŋ/ adjective a demanding person needs a lot of attention and is not easily pleased or satisfied: *Young children can be very demanding.*

dress /dres/ verb [intransitive] to put on clothes. This verb is common in writing, but when you are speaking it is more usual to say that you get dressed: *It only took her ten minutes to shower and dress.*

require /rɪ'kwaɪə(r)/ verb [transitive] to need someone or something: *The cause of the accident is still unclear and requires further investigation.*

smart /smɑː(r)t/ adjective clean and neat in appearance and dressed in nice fashionable clothes, especially in a slightly formal way: *Sandy's looking very smart today.*

strength /streŋθ/ noun [count] something that someone does very well: *Ron's main strength is his ability to motivate players.*

weakness /'wiːknəs/ noun [count] a fault or problem that makes something or someone less effective or attractive: *They listed the strengths and weaknesses of their product.*

4.3 Grammar
Past tenses

fencing /ˈfensɪŋ/ noun [uncount] the sport of fighting with a light thin sword

IPO /ˌaɪ piː ˈəʊ/ noun [count] BUSINESS initial public offering: an occasion when shares in a company are first sold to the public

philanthropist /fɪˈlænθrəpɪst/ noun [count] someone who believes in helping people, especially by giving money to those who need it

raise /reɪz/ verb [transitive] to collect money for a particular purpose: *We managed to raise over £4,000 through sponsored events.*

4.4 Speaking
Interviews

devil's advocate /ˌdev(ə)lz ˈædvəkət/ phrase **play/be devil's advocate** to pretend to disagree with someone in order to start an argument or interesting discussion

easygoing /ˌiːziˈgəʊɪŋ/ adjective relaxed, calm and not getting easily upset about things

NGO /ˌen dʒiː ˈəʊ/ noun [count] non-governmental organization: an organization that is not owned by the government, but may work with government departments

partially /ˈpɑː(r)ʃəli/ adverb not completely: *The airline is partially owned by British Airways.*

4.5 Writing
CVs

bartender /ˈbɑː(r)ˌtendə(r)/ noun [count] MAINLY AMERICAN someone whose job is to serve drinks in a bar

marital status /ˌmærɪt(ə)l ˈsteɪtəs/ noun [uncount] the legal position of a person, relating to whether they are single, married, separated, divorced or widowed

pet /pet/ noun [count] an animal or bird that you keep in your home and look after

pickup or **pickup truck** /ˈpɪkʌp ˈtrʌk/ noun [count] a truck with an open back and low sides

regatta /rɪˈgætə/ noun [count] a series of boat races

sailing /ˈseɪlɪŋ/ noun [uncount] the sport or activity of travelling across water in a sailing boat: *She's really keen on sailing.*

stand /stænd/ noun [count] a large table at an exhibition where an organization offers information, goods or services: *the Porsche™ stand at the recent Paris show*

variable /ˈveəriəb(ə)l/ noun [count] something that can change and affect the result of a situation: *All these variables can affect a student's performance.*

4.6 Case study
Onestop job search

health care /ˈhelθ ˌkeə(r)/ noun [uncount] the services that look after people's health: *Homeless people need better access to health care.*

in the field /ˌɪn ðə ˈfiːld/ phrase in conditions that you find in the real world, not in a laboratory or classroom: *The new drugs have not yet been tested in the field.*

networking /ˈnetˌwɜː(r)kɪŋ/ noun [uncount] the activity of meeting and talking to people to exchange information and advice about work or interests

orthopaedic /ˌɔː(r)θəˈpiːdɪk/ adjective [only before noun] MEDICAL relating to the medical treatment of injuries and diseases affecting bones, muscles, joints and ligaments: *an orthopaedic surgeon*

rewarding /rɪˈwɔː(r)dɪŋ/ adjective giving you satisfaction, pleasure or profit: *Do you find your work rewarding?*

5 Marketing and selling

5.1 About business
Sales versus marketing

agenda /əˈdʒendə/ noun [count] all the things that need to be done or that need to be thought about or solved: *Cutting the number of workers is not on the agenda.*; a plan or aim that is kept secret: *The Minister seems to have her own agenda.*

awareness /əˈweə(r)nəs/ noun [singular/uncount] knowledge or understanding of a subject, issue or situation: *There was a general lack of awareness about safety issues.*

benefit /ˈbenɪfɪt/ noun [count] the way a product or service improves a consumer's life

blame /bleɪm/ verb [transitive] to say or think that someone or something is responsible for an accident, problem or bad situation: *Crime is a complex issue – we can't simply blame poverty and unemployment.*

ceasefire /ˈsiːsˌfaɪə(r)/ noun [count] an agreement to stop fighting for a period of time, especially in order to discuss permanent peace: *He believed the ceasefire would hold.*

commission /kəˈmɪʃ(ə)n/ noun [count/uncount] an extra amount of money that you earn in your job every time you sell a product or get a new customer

feature /ˈfiːtʃə(r)/ noun [count] an important part or aspect of a product or service

incompetent /ɪnˈkɒmpɪt(ə)nt/ adjective lacking the ability or skills to do something: *the worst and most incompetent government in living memory*

5.2 Vocabulary
Marketing, sales and advertising

billboard /ˈbɪlˌbɔː(r)d/ noun [count] a large board for advertisements in an outside public place

competitive /kəmˈpetətɪv/ adjective competitive prices are cheaper than many others: *We offer a wide range of goods at very competitive prices.*

launch /lɔːntʃ/ verb [transitive] to put a new product on the market, which usually involves spending money on advertising it: *The company announced it will launch a new version of its software in January.*

monitor /ˈmɒnɪtə(r)/ verb [transitive] to regularly check something or watch someone in order to find out what is happening: *He will monitor and review company policy.*

trend /trend/ noun [count] a gradual change or development that produces a particular result: *the latest trends in popular music*

value for money /ˌvæljuː fə(r) ˈmʌni/ noun [uncount] the amount that something is worth compared to the money that it costs: *Most customers are looking for value for their money rather than cutting-edge fashion.*

via /ˈvaɪə/ preposition using a particular method or person to send or deliver something: *It's easy to check your bank account via the Internet.*

5.3 Grammar
Comparatives and superlatives

accessory /əkˈsesəri/ noun [count] [usually plural]
additional objects, equipment, decorations, etc. that make
something more useful or attractive: *car/kitchen/computer
accessories*

carbon footprint /ˌkɑː(r)bən ˈfʊtprɪnt/ noun [count]
the amount of carbon dioxide a person, organization,
building, etc. produces, used as a measure of their effect
on the environment

energy /ˈenə(r)dʒi/ noun [uncount] SCIENCE a form of power
such as electricity, heat or light that is used for making
things work: *Environmentally friendly energy sources
include water and wind power.*

harmful /ˈhɑː(r)mf(ə)l/ adjective causing harm: *harmful
effects/consequences*

hybrid /ˈhaɪbrɪd/ noun [count] **hybrid vehicle** or **hybrid
electric vehicle** a vehicle that uses two or more kinds of
power, for example a car that can run using either petrol
or electricity: *Energy giant Exxon Mobil predicts major
growth for hybrids.*

legroom /ˈleɡˌruːm/ noun [uncount] the amount of space in
front of your seat in which you can stretch your legs

luxurious /lʌɡˈzjʊəriəs/ adjective very expensive and
comfortable: *a luxurious hotel/home/bedroom*

satnav /ˈsætˌnæv/ noun [uncount] satellite navigation:
a system for finding the best way to a place using
information from satellites. It is often found in cars.

5.4 Speaking
Persuading

acknowledge /əkˈnɒlɪdʒ/ verb [transitive] to accept or
admit that something exists, is true, or is real: *He never
acknowledges his mistakes (= admits that he has made
them).*

day care /ˈdeɪ ˌkeə(r)/ noun [uncount] MAINLY AMERICAN
childcare /ˈtʃaɪldˌkeə(r)/ noun [uncount] the job of looking
after children, especially while their parents are working:
*The lack of adequate childcare is making it difficult for
women to return to work.*

morale /məˈrɑːl/ noun [uncount] the amount of enthusiasm
that a person or group of people feel about their situation
at a particular time: *Morale is low, and many people are
disillusioned.*

objection /əbˈdʒekʃ(ə)n/ noun [count/uncount] a statement
that shows that you disagree with a plan, or a reason for
your disagreement: *I would like to put forward several
objections to this proposal.*

paperwork /ˈpeɪpə(r)ˌwɜː(r)k/ noun [uncount] the part of a
job that involves producing reports, keeping records and
writing letters: *The new system is designed to reduce the
amount of paperwork we have to do.*

5.5 Writing
'Selling' changes

compliant /kəmˈplaɪənt/ adjective designed to follow a
particular law, system or set of instructions

feedback /ˈfiːdbæk/ noun [uncount] comments about how
well or how badly someone is doing something, which
are intended to help them do it better: *Feedback was
generally positive.*

owing to /ˈəʊɪŋ ˌtuː/ preposition because of something:
*Owing to the rising cost of fuel, more people are using
public transport.*

proud /praʊd/ adjective feeling happy about your
achievements, your possessions or people who you are
connected with **proud of**: *We're so proud of her for
telling the truth.*

sitting /ˈsɪtɪŋ/ noun [count] a period of time during which a
meal is served: *There are two sittings for lunch.*

split /splɪt/ verb [transitive/intransitive] to divide into
smaller groups, or to divide people into smaller groups:
Let's split into groups and work separately.

5.6 Case study
Dallivan Cars

brand /brænd/ noun [count] a product or group of products
that has its own name and is made by one particular
company. The word for a machine or vehicle made by
one particular company is a **make.**: *We stock all leading
brands.*

inventory /ˈɪnvəntəri/ noun [uncount] a list giving details
of all the things in a place: *When the police eventually
arrived, we made an inventory of the missing items.*

segment /ˈseɡmənt/ noun [count] a section of a market
defined by certain criteria

6 Entrepreneurship
6.1 About business
Entrepreneurs

borrow /ˈbɒrəʊ/ verb [transitive/intransitive] to receive
and use something that belongs to someone else, and
promise to give it back to them later: *Can I borrow your
calculator?*

failure /ˈfeɪljə(r)/ noun [count/uncount] a lack of success in
doing something; a situation in which a business cannot
continue operating: *Business failures soared by more than
a third in the second half of this year.*

frustrating /ˈfrʌˌstreɪtɪŋ/ adjective making you feel
annoyed and impatient because you are prevented from
achieving something: *It's frustrating to wait all day for a
repairman who doesn't show up.*

funding /ˈfʌndɪŋ/ noun [uncount] money that a government
or organization provides for a specific purpose: *The
government is still failing to provide adequate funding for
research.*

interest /ˈɪntrəst/ noun [uncount] BUSINESS money that
a person or institution such as a bank charges you for
lending you money: *an increase in the interest charged on
personal loans*

seller financing /ˌselə(r) ˈfaɪnænsɪŋ/ noun [uncount] a loan
from the seller of a business to the buyer

talent /ˈtælənt/ noun [count/uncount] a natural ability for
being good at a particular activity: *She had an obvious
talent for music.*

worth /wɜː(r)θ/ adjective used for saying how rich someone
is: *She is now worth 20 million dollars.*

6.2 Vocabulary
Business organization and people

charity /'tʃærəti/ noun [count] an organization to which you give money so that it can give money and help to people who are poor or ill, or who need advice and support: *The Children's Society is a registered charity.*

cooperative /kəʊ'ɒp(ə)rətɪv/ noun [count] BUSINESS a business or other organization owned by the people who work in it who also share the profits: *agricultural/fishing cooperatives*

full-time /fʊl 'taɪm/ adjective [usually before noun] done for the number of hours that people normally work in a complete week. Part-time work or study is done during just some of these hours: *It is hard to combine study with a full-time job.*

know-how /'nəʊ,haʊ/ noun [uncount] INFORMAL knowledge that is needed to do something, usually something practical

physiotherapist /,fɪziəʊ'θerəpɪst/ noun [count] someone whose job is to treat injuries using special physical exercises

youth /juːθ/ noun [uncount] young people in general: *youth culture/unemployment/training*

6.3 Grammar
Modal verbs

elevator /'eləveɪtə(r)/ noun [count] AMERICAN a lift in a building **lift** /lɪft/ noun [count] BRITISH a machine that carries people up or down between different levels of a tall building: *Do you want to take the lift or use the stairs?*

fee /fiː/ noun [count] [usually plural] money that you pay to a professional person or institution for their work: *Tuition fees at Stanford have now reached $40,000 a year.*

franchise fee /'fræntʃaɪz ,fiː/ noun [count] BUSINESS the initial sum of money that the franchisee pays to the franchiser for the right to join the franchise

franchiser or **franchisor** /'fræntʃaɪzə(r)/ noun [count] BUSINESS a person who licences a franchise; a business that sells franchises

lawyer /'lɔːjə(r)/ noun [count] someone whose profession is to provide people with legal advice and services

obligatory /ə'blɪgət(ə)ri/ adjective FORMAL something that is obligatory must be done in order to obey a law or rule: *It is obligatory for members to be insured.*

royalty /'rɔɪəlti/ noun [count] a payment that someone such as a writer or musician gets each time their work is sold or performed; a payment from a franchisee to the franchiser, usually a percentage of gross sales

6.4 Speaking
Meetings

background music /'bækgraʊnd ,mjuːzɪk/ noun [count] quiet music that plays in a public place

chair /tʃeə(r)/ verb [transitive] to be the person in charge of a meeting, committee or company: *She subsequently chaired the executive board of the UN Children's Fund.*

direct marketing /dɪ'rekt 'mɑː(r)kɪtɪŋ/ noun [uncount] the sale of products to people by post or telephone instead of in shops

flyer /'flaɪə(r)/ noun [count] an announcement or advertisement that is printed on a sheet of paper and given to people: *Someone was handing out flyers advertising the local sales.*

package /'pækɪdʒ/ verb [transitive] to put things into boxes or wrap them so that they can be sold: *a company that manufactures and packages medicines*

personal selling /'pɜː(r)s(ə)nəl 'selɪŋ/ noun [uncount] the job or skill of meeting people face to face (or speaking to people on the telephone) and persuading them to buy things

promotional mix /prə'məʊʃ(ə)nəl 'mɪks/ noun [uncount] the combination of all the elements that make up a company's promotion, for example, TV advertising, direct marketing, etc.

voucher /'vaʊtʃə(r)/ noun [count] an official piece of paper that you can use instead of money to buy a particular product or service: *a gift voucher*

6.5 Writing
Agendas and minutes

acquisition /,ækwɪ'zɪʃ(ə)n/ noun [count] BRITISH a company that is bought by another company: *The industry's wave of mergers and acquisitions continues.*

AOB /,eɪ əʊ 'biː/ abbreviation BRITISH any other business: things that are discussed at the end of a meeting

apologies /ə'pɒlədʒiz/ noun [plural] BRITISH a statement from someone saying that they are sorry that they cannot go to a meeting

chain /tʃeɪn/ noun [count] a group of businesses such as shops, hotels, or restaurants that all belong to the same person or company: *Japan's leading hotel chain*

forecast /'fɔː(r)kɑːst/ noun [count] a statement about what is likely to happen, based on available information and usually relating to the weather, business or the economy: *The Treasury's forecast assumes that inflation will remain below 3%.*

waste of time /'weɪst əv 'taɪm/ noun [singular] a situation in which time, money or energy is used without bringing any useful result

6.6 Case study
Solar Mobile

component /kəm'pəʊnənt/ noun [count] one of the different parts that a machine or piece of equipment consists of: *car components*

device /dɪ'vaɪs/ noun [count] a machine or piece of equipment that does a particular thing: *Secure your bike with this simple locking device.*

gadget /'gædʒɪt/ noun [count] a small tool or piece of equipment that does something useful or impressive: *kitchen gadgets*

high street /'haɪ ,striːt/ noun [count] BRITISH the main street in a town or city, with a lot of businesses along it: *high street shops/banks/prices*

plug in /plʌg 'ɪn/ phrasal verb [transitive] to connect a piece of equipment to an electricity supply or to another piece of equipment: *Then I realized I hadn't plugged the TV in.*

source /sɔː(r)s/ verb [transitive] [often passive] to get a product or basic material from somewhere: *All our timber is sourced from sustainable forests.*

7 Business costs

7.1 About business
Cutting costs

account /ə'kaʊnt/ noun [count] an arrangement in which a bank looks after your money. You can deposit (= put in) or withdraw (= take out) money when you need to: *There was only £50 in his bank account.*; a record showing how much you owe a shop or other business for goods or services that you have received: *I'll settle my account (= pay the money that I owe) in the morning.*

asset /'æset/ noun [count] [usually plural] something such as money or property that a person or company owns: *The business has assets totalling £5.1 million.*

bankrupt /'bæŋkrʌpt/ adjective a person or business that is bankrupt has officially admitted that they have no money and cannot pay what they owe: *Many of the companies that they had invested in went bankrupt.*

freeze /fri:z/ verb [transitive] to stop something from being available to someone: *The courts have frozen her bank account.*

heating /'hi:tɪŋ/ noun [uncount] BRITISH equipment that produces the heat used for heating a building: *the installation of an improved heating system*

homeless /'həʊmləs/ adjective without a place to live: *The floods have killed hundreds and made thousands homeless.*

overtime /'əʊvə(r)ˌtaɪm/ noun [count] extra hours that someone works at their job: *I've been working a lot of overtime lately.*

reserve /rɪ'zɜ:(r)v/ noun [count] [usually plural] a supply of something that a country or an organization can use when they need to: *The company has steadily drained its cash reserves.*

7.2 Vocabulary
Profit, loss and payment

cheque /tʃek/ noun [count] a piece of printed paper that you can use instead of money. The American word is check.: *Can I pay by cheque?*

lend /lend/ verb [intransitive/transitive] to give someone money that you expect them to pay back later: *Can you lend me £10?*

mug /mʌg/ noun [count] a cup with straight sides and no saucer, used mainly for hot drinks: *a coffee mug*

souvenir /ˌsu:və'nɪə(r)/ noun [count] something that you buy during a holiday or at a special event to remind you later of being there: *She kept the tickets as a souvenir of the evening.*

standing order /ˌstændɪŋ 'ɔ:(r)də(r)/ noun [count/uncount] BRITISH an instruction that you give a bank to take a particular amount of money out of your account on a particular day, usually each month, to pay a person or organization for you. A direct debit is a similar arrangement, except that the amount can change and is decided by the person who you are paying.

7.3 Grammar
Future forms and first conditional

bed and breakfast /ˌbed ən 'brekfəst/ noun [uncount] TOURISM the service of providing a room for the night and a meal the next morning: *The price is £30 for bed and breakfast.*

contingency plan /kən'tɪndʒ(ə)nsi 'plæn/ noun [count] a set of plans or actions that help you to prepare for possible bad events

entertainment /ˌentə(r)'teɪnmənt/ noun [count/uncount] performances that people enjoy: *There will be entertainment and a buffet luncheon for a cost of £30.*

quote /kwəʊt/ verb [transitive] to tell someone what price you would charge them to do a particular piece of work: *How much did they quote for the job?*

specification /ˌspesɪfɪ'keɪʃ(ə)n/ noun [count] an exact measurement or detailed plan about how something is to be made: *Specifications require ceilings to be 15 feet high.*

wind farm /'wɪnd ˌfɑ:(r)m/ noun [count] a place where wind turbines are used for producing electricity from the power of the wind

7.4 Speaking
Negotiating

concession /kən'seʃ(ə)n/ noun [count] something you give or allow to someone in order to reach an agreement: *The company has already made several concessions on pay.*

downtown /ˌdaʊn'taʊn/ adjective, adverb MAINLY AMERICAN in or near the centre of a town or city, especially the business or shopping areas: *Let's go downtown.*

limo /'lɪməʊ/ noun [count] INFORMAL **a limousine** /ˌlɪmə'zi:n/ a large expensive comfortable car in which a screen separates the driver from the passengers: *a chauffeur-driven limousine*

pay rise /'peɪ ˌraɪz/ noun [count] BRITISH an increase in your salary. The American word is pay raise: *Nurses have been awarded a 3% pay rise.*

7.5 Writing
Asking for payment

outstanding /aʊt'stændɪŋ/ adjective an amount of money that is outstanding has not yet been paid: *All your outstanding debts must be settled now.*

overdue /ˌəʊvə(r)'dju:/ adjective a payment that is overdue should have been paid before now

promise /'prɒmɪs/ noun [count] a statement in which you say that something will definitely happen, or you will definitely do something: *the party's election promises*

reminder /rɪ'maɪndə(r)/ noun [count] [usually singular] a letter or note that reminds you of something that you need to do or need to remember: *If an instalment is not paid, a reminder is issued.*

suspend /sə'spend/ verb [transitive] [often passive] to officially stop something for a short time: *Operations at the plant have been suspended because of safety concerns.*

threat /θret/ noun [count] a situation or an activity that could cause harm or danger: *Officials were confident there had been no threat to public health.*

7.6 Case study
Doug's Mugs

depreciation /dɪˌpriːʃiˈeɪʃ(ə)n/ noun [uncount] the process of becoming less valuable

emigrate /ˈemɪɡreɪt/ verb [intransitive] to leave your country in order to live in another country: *We're thinking of emigrating to New Zealand.*

Kiwi /ˈkiːwiː/ noun [count] INFORMAL someone from New Zealand

solicitor /səˈlɪsɪtə(r)/ noun [count] in the UK, a lawyer who gives legal advice, writes legal contracts and represents people in the lower courts of law

8 Global trade

8.1 About business
International franchising

BRIC /brɪk/ noun [count] an acronym for Brazil, Russia, India and China, often used to refer to the rapidly growing economies of these countries: *BRIC economy/country/market*

diversity /daɪˈvɜː(r)səti/ noun [singular/uncount] the fact that very different people or things exist within a group or place: *We value the rich ethnic and cultural diversity of the group.*

emerging market /ɪˈmɜː(r)dʒɪŋ ˈmɑː(r)kɪt/ noun [count] a country that is in the process of rapid growth and industrialization

GDP /ˌdʒiː diː ˈpiː/ noun [count] ECONOMICS gross domestic product: the total value of the goods and services that a country produces in a year, not including income received from money invested in other countries

outlet /ˈaʊtˌlet/ noun [count] a shop or place where a particular product is sold: *Most of their sales are through traditional retail outlets.*

penetrate /ˈpenəˌtreɪt/ verb [intransitive/transitive] to reach or affect something such as a part of society: *one of the last cultures in the world that television has not penetrated*

player /ˈpleɪə(r)/ noun [count] a person or organization that influences a situation, especially in business or politics: *Germany is seen as a key player within the European Union.*

reward /rɪˈwɔː(r)d/ noun [count/uncount] money that you receive for working: *Financial rewards and promotion will be linked to performance.*

8.2 Vocabulary
Franchising and project management

completion /kəmˈpliːʃ(ə)n/ noun [uncount] the time when an activity or job is finished: *The completion date for the tunnel is December 2014.*

profile /ˈprəʊfaɪl/ noun [count] a description of a person, group or organization that contains all the details that someone needs: *a detailed profile of the construction industry*

recruit /rɪˈkruːt/ verb [intransitive/transitive] to get someone to work in a company or join an organization: *We won't be recruiting again until next year.*

status /ˈsteɪtəs/ noun [uncount] the level of importance or progress in a particular situation or discussion: *Officials are now discussing the current status of the health reform laws.*

8.3 Grammar
Present perfect

frogs' legs /ˈfrɒɡz ˌleɡz/ noun [plural] a typical French dish, often prepared by frying the frogs' legs in garlic

people skills /ˈpiːp(ə)l ˌskɪlz/ noun [plural] the ability to communicate effectively with people in a friendly way, especially in business

premises /ˈpremɪsɪz/ noun [plural] the buildings and land that a business or organization uses: *The charity is hoping to move to new premises next year.*

snail /sneɪl/ noun [count] a small animal that has a soft body, no legs, and a hard shell on its back. Snails move very slowly.

8.4 Speaking
Giving updates and handling questions

attitude /ˈætɪˌtjuːd/ noun [count] someone's opinions or feelings about something, especially as shown by their behaviour: *an unhealthy social environment that encourages negative attitudes*

Gantt chart /ˈɡænt ˌtʃɑː(r)t/ noun [count] BUSINESS a tool used in planning a project, which shows pieces of work and the time periods within which they should be done

update /ˈʌpdeɪt/ noun [count] a report or broadcast containing all the latest news or information: *The president gets regular updates from the National Security Council.*

8.5 Writing
Progress reports

backup /ˈbækʌp/ noun [count/uncount] people or equipment that can be used when extra help is needed: *a backup generator/crew*

hardwood /ˈhɑː(r)dˌwʊd/ noun [count/uncount] hard strong wood from trees such as oak or mahogany

sustainable /səˈsteɪnəb(ə)l/ adjective using methods that do not harm the environment: *sustainable agriculture*

unsuitable /ʌnˈsuːtəb(ə)l/ adjective not suitable for a particular situation, purpose or person: *an unsuitable candidate*

8.6 Case study
An international opportunity

Mountie /ˈmaʊnti/ noun [count] a member of the Royal Canadian Mounted Police, a special group of the Canadian police who ride horses

pre-teen /ˌpriː ˈtiːn/ adjective and noun [count] relating to children between 9 and 12 years old: *pre-teen tastes/fashions*

ROI /ˌɑː(r) əʊ ˈaɪ/ abbreviation BUSINESS return on investment /rɪˌtɜː(r)n ɒn ɪnˈves(t)mənt/: the profit from a business activity in a financial year compared with the amount invested in it

tween /twiːn/ noun [count] a young person between about 9 and 14 years old

Macmillan Education
The Macmillan Building
4 Crinan Street, London, N1 9XW
Companies and representatives throughout the world

ISBN 978-0-230-43780-7

Text © John Allison and Paul Emmerson 2014
Design and illustration © Macmillan Publishers Limited 2014
The authors have asserted their rights to be identified as the authors of
this work in accordance with the Copyright, Designs and Patents Act
1988.

This edition published 2014
First edition published 2008

Original design by Keith Shaw, Threefold Design Limited
Page make-up by Keith Shaw, Threefold Design Limited
Illustrated by Peter Harper, Boy Fitz Hammond and Ben Hasler
Cover design by Keith Shaw, Threefold Design Limited
Cover photography by Getty Images/RunPhoto
Picture research by Susannah Jayes

Author's acknowledgements
I would like to thank everybody at Macmillan Education; Lidia Zielińska
and the English teachers at Cracow University of Economics; my
colleagues at Infolangues; and, last but not least, Brigitte and my family.

The publishers would like to thank the following people for piloting and
commenting on material for this coursebook:
Paul Bellchambers, Business and Technical Languages, Paris, France;
Bunmi Rolland, Pôle Universitaire Léonard de Vinci, Paris, France; Prof.
Vanessa Leonardi, Faculty of Economics, University of Ferrara, Italy;
Prof. Paola De La Pierre, Faculty of Economics, University of Turin,
Italy; Elżbieta Typek, Cracow University of Economics, Poland; Marlena
Nowak, Cracow University of Economics, Poland; Lucyna Wilinkiewicz-
Górniak, Cracow University of Economics, Poland; Jolanta Regucka-
Pawlina, Cracow University of Economics, Poland; Sebastian Florek-
Paszkowski, Cracow University of Economics, Poland; Bożena Bielak,
Cracow University of Economics, Poland; Małgorzata Held, Cracow
University of Economics, Poland; Anna Wróblewska-Marzec, Cracow
University of Economics, Poland; Lidia Zielińska, Cracow University of
Economics, Poland; Olga Druszkiewicz, Cracow University of Economics,
Poland; Maciej Krzanowski, Cracow University of Economics, Poland;
Lubov Kulik, Moscow Lomonosov State University, Russia; Irina
Ekareva, The Russian Plekhanov University of Economics, Russia; Larisa
Tarkhova, The Russian Plekhanov University of Economics, Russia;
Irina Schemeleva, Higher School of Economics, Russia; Irina Matveeva,
The Academy of Social and Labour Relations, Russia; Galina Makarova,
Denis' School, Russia; Liam James Tyler, IPT, Russia; Tatiana Efremtseva,
The Russian International Academy of Tourism, Russia; Tatiana Sedova,
The University of Finance, Russia; Tony Watson and Kim Draper,
MLS Bournemouth, Bournemouth, UK; Louise Raven, Marcus Evans
Linguarama, Stratford-upon-Avon, UK.

The publishers would like to thank the following people for piloting
and commenting on material for the original edition of this coursebook:
Annette Nolan, Folkuniversitetet, Sweden; Elena Ivanova Angelova,
Pharos School of Languages and Computing, Bulgaria; Sabine Schumann,
Berufsakademie (University of Co-operative Education), Germany;
Vladimir Krasnopolsky, East Ukrainian National University, Ukraine.

The author and publishers would like to thank the following for
permission to reproduce their photographs:
Alamy/Yuri Arcurs p58, Alamy/Aurora Photos p14(tmr), Alamy/
Peter Bowater p69, Alamy/CandyBox Images p70, Alamy/Corbis Super
RF pp31,51,102(tm), Alamy/culture-images GmbH p67(br), Alamy/
Universal Images Group/DeAgostini p62, Alamy/jeremy sutton-hibbert
p21(b), Alamy/Iatham & holmes p12(bl), Alamy/Wayne Hutchinson
p85, Alamy/Image Source p54, Alamy/Images & Stories p109, Alamy/
kmt_rf p18, Alamy/Emmanuel LATTES p108, Alamy/Iain Masterton
p14(tl), Alamy/Matthew Oldfield Editorial Photography p26(tmll),
Alamy/Ian Patrick p105, Alamy/Tim Scrivener p7(c), Alamy/Alex
Segre p101(cr), Alamy/Ed Simons p14(tml), Alamy/Stuwdamdorp
p7(b), Alamy/Jane Tregelles p90, Alamy/Aleksandr Ugorenkov p8,
Alamy/Justin Kase ztwoz p7(e); **Apple**/Courtesy of Apple Computers
p6(4); **Corbis**/Peter Beck p45, Corbis/Lava/beyond p9, Corbis/
Mike Kemp/Blend Images p52, Corbis/Blue Images p79, Corbis/
Fabio Cardoso p104(tm), Corbis/Michael DeYoung p84, Corbis/NIC
BOTHMA/epa p16, Corbis/Ragnar Schmuck/fstop p14(tr), Corbis/
Jon Hicks p19, Corbis/Ronnie Kaufman p73, Corbis/Tom & Dee Ann
McCarthy p26(tmr), Corbis/Mika p7(a), Corbis/ROB & SAS p24,
Corbis/Topic Photo Agency p6(10), Corbis/Kimberly White p49(cr);
Corbis/Michael DeYoung p84, **DIGITAL VISION** p6(6); **Getty** p6(5),
Getty Images p74(a), Getty Images/Peter Adams p93, Getty Images/
AFP pp41,67(bcr),74(b),92(tc),104(tr), Getty Images/Paul Grover/AFP
p98, Getty Images/Asia Images Group p20, Getty Images/Thomas
Barwick p104(tcr), Getty Images/Michael Blann p21(tcr), Getty Images/
Bloomberg via Getty Images pp38,46,97(bl),101(t), Getty Images/Geoff
Brightling p6(1), Getty Images/Joselito Briones p23, Getty Images/
Peter Cade p75, Getty Images/Chabruken p21(cr), Getty Images/
Richard Clark p6(2), Getty Images/DIGITAL VISION pp6(8),83,104(tml),
Getty Images/Hermann Erber p77, Getty Images/Martin Smith/FLPA
p6(9), Getty Images/Jeff Foott p94, Getty Images/Gamma-Rapho via
Getty Images p13, Getty Images/Blend Images/Hill Street Studios/
Gifford Sun p96, Getty Images/Monalyn Gracia p21(tr), Getty Images/
Tim Graham p65, Getty Images/Ray Hems p26(tr), Getty Images/Scott
Hortop p68, Getty Images/Jasper James p11(b), Getty Images/Michael
Krasowitz p89, Getty Images/Frans Lemmens p99, Getty Images/Darryl
Leniuk p102(tr), Getty Images/Rita Mass p110(bcml), Getty Images/
Maximilian Stock Ltd. p6(3), Getty Images/Buero Monaco p107, Getty
Images/Eric Nathan p6(7), Getty Images/Shalom Ormsby p110(cml),
Getty Images/Doug Pearson p95, Getty Images/Isabelle Plasschaert
p80, Getty Images/Monty Rakusen p104(tcm), Getty Images/Antonio
M. Rosario p28, Getty Images/Andersen Ross p110(bm), Getty Images/
Chris Ryan p104(tcml), Getty Images/David Sacks p7(d), Getty Images/
Ellen Skye p42(t), Getty Images/Bill Varie p106(tl), Getty Images/James
Warwick p97(c), Getty Images/Yellow Dog Productions pp30,78(tr);
Glow Images/Juice Images p26(cmll), Glow Images/Ian Lishman p42(cl),
Glow Images/Monty Rakusen p47; **ImageSource** p12(bcl); **Photoshot**
p21(bcr), Photoshot/Photos Horticultural p39, Photoshot/UPPA p43,
Photoshot/Xinhua pp11(tr),106(tr); **Press Association Images**/Jae C.
Hong/AP p92(tr), Press Association Images/Julie Jacobsen/AP p53; **Rex
Features**/Agencia Feriaque p33, Rex Features/Anders Granberg p49(t),
Rex Features/KeystoneUSA-ZUMA p32, Rex Features/Juha Sorri p74(c),
Rex Features/Snap Stills p37; **Stockbyte**/Punchstock p63; **Superstock**/
Flirt p25, Superstock/Michael Steiner/image/imagebroker.net p78(tm);
Thinkstock/Image Source p91.

The authors and publishers are grateful for permission to reprint the
following material:
Statistics from the report 'Cultural statistics in the spotlight' published by
Eurostat 14 April 2011, reprinted with approval.

Printed and bound in Thailand

2018   2017   2016   2015   2014
10 9 8 7 6 5 4 3 2 1